MW00769735

WALKING
WITH GOD

ANDREW MURRAY
TRILOGY ON SANCTIFICATION

Bridge-Logos
Alachua, FL 32615 USA

Bridge-Logos
Alachua, FL 32615 USA

Walking with God
The Andrew Murray Trilogy on Sanctification
by Andrew Murray

Edited by Gene Fedele

Printed in Canada.

Library of Congress Catalog Card Number: 2008931025
International Standard Book Number: 978-0-88270-474-6

Scripture quotations are from the *King James Version* of the Bible.

G532.316.N.m806.35250

CONTENTS

PREFACE

Waiting On God, Working For God, Be Perfect. Here we have a precious and practical unfolding of holy sanctification in the heart and life of each believer in Jesus Christ. I've taken these three classics, written over one hundred years ago by Andrew Murray, and brought them together in one Pure Gold Classic edition. They are truly inseparable, and together, they represent a "trilogy" of blessed truth that will guide Christians into a deeper, more intimate, and more fulfilling relationship with the Lord. Each book is comprised of thirty-one chapters, or lessons, designed to be daily readings for each day of the month.

In this edition, each book builds upon the previous one in order to guide the reader to first *wait upon God*, in patient humility, for His will to be revealed in our lives; then to *work for God*, habitually, in His strength alone; and then to *be perfect* in heart and Christian maturity before God, "seeking to be perfect as their Father in heaven is perfect." Murray beautifully unveils Biblical truths to show the believers in Christ that before they can seek to "be perfect" they must first surrender the will in complete dependence upon God's working, and become "co-laborers" with the Lord amidst the trials and tribulations of this world that the cause of His Kingdom and the glory of His name might be proclaimed.

Rev. Murray so aptly defines the essence of the whole book with these words: "If God's purpose with the perfection of the individual believer, with the appointment of His Church as the body of Christ to carry on His work of winning back a rebellious world to His allegiance and love is to be carried out, waiting and working for God must have much greater prominence given to it as the true glory of our Christian calling. Every believer must be taught that, as work is the only perfect manifestation, and therefore the perfection of life in God and throughout the world, so our work is to be our highest glory. Is it so in our lives?"

It is important to not misunderstand what is spoken about in this book in regards to the concept of perfection. When the author speaks about being perfect, he is not in any way suggesting the possibility of our attaining a state of sinlessness or absence of error in word and deed on this side of eternity. He is talking about our whole-hearted trust in the One who is perfect in every way. As Murray states, "A wholehearted consecration to His will and fellowship, a life that takes as its motto, 'Wholly for God,' has in all ages, even where the Spirit had not yet been given to dwell in the heart, been accepted by Him as the mark of the perfect man."

Patience is indeed one of the most challenging graces that we are able to regularly cultivate in our lives. Whether it's amidst the trials or triumphs of our circumstances, we so often seek our own way and will towards an end to our situation. Yet, God's way is quite the opposite. "In your patience possess ye your souls" (Luke 21:9). "You have need of patience, that, after ye have done the will of God, ye might receive the promise" (Hebrews 10:36). "Let patience have its perfect work, that ye may be perfect and entire, wanting nothing" (James 1:4). Such words of the Holy Spirit show us what an important element in the Christian life and character patience is. And nowhere is there a better place for cultivating or displaying it than in waiting on God. There we discover how impatient we are, and what our impatience means. Murray says, "Patience becomes our highest blessedness and our highest grace. It honors God, and gives Him time to have His way with us. It is the highest expression of our faith in His goodness and faithfulness. It brings the soul perfect rest in the assurance that God is carrying on His work. It is the token of our full consent that God should deal with us in such a way and time as He thinks best. True patience is the losing of our self-will in His perfect will."

"We confess at times that we are impatient with men and circumstances that hinder us, or with our slow progress in the Christian life. If we truly set ourselves to wait upon God, we shall find that it is with Him we are impatient, because He does not at once, or as soon as we wish, do our bidding. It is in waiting upon God that our eyes are opened to believe in His wise and sovereign will, and to see that the sooner and the more completely we yield absolutely to it, the more surely His blessings will come to us."

Rev. Murray defines waiting on God as the "absolute, unceasing, moment-by-moment dependence upon God." He leaves no place for the belief that waiting means doing nothing. He rejects a fatalistic approach to the Christian life that says if God wills then this or that will happen. Certainly that is true from a theological standpoint, but that's God's business. Ours is to exercise faith, wait and work. "Seest thou how faith wrought with works, and by works was faith made perfect? Ye see then how that by works a man is justified, and not by faith only. For as the body without the spirit [or breath] is dead, so faith without works is dead also" (James 2:22,24,26).

In the book of Isaiah we read, "They that wait on the Lord shall renew their strength; they shall mount up on eagles' wings; they shall run, and not be weary; they shall walk, and not faint." Rev. J. R. Miller, a contemporary of Murray, says that, "Every true Christian needs daily 'silent times,' when all shall be still, when the busy activity of other hours shall cease, and when the heart, in holy hush, shall commune with God. With these sacred 'silent times' in every day of toil and struggle, we shall always be strong, and 'prepared unto every good work.' Waiting thus upon God, we shall daily renew our wasted strength, and be able to run and not be weary, to walk and not be faint, and to mount up with wings as eagles in bold spiritual flights."

Throughout the history of the Church there have been those who view a sovereign God in such an extreme way that they divorce themselves from their own choices in life. The responsibility for poor decisions is redefined as "the will of God" and they take little or no action towards "working out their own salvation with fear and trembling" (Philippians 2:12). Here we come face-to-face with the intertwining of the beauty and mystery of the Gospel. We see, in the divine process of sanctification, the sovereignty of God and the responsibility of man working side-by-side in the lives of God's people—all enabled by the constant interceding of the Holy Spirit through the power of the sacrificial blood of King Jesus. Oh, how could one ever think that this concept could ever be devised from the minds of men! Only the God we read about in the Bible could create such a plan! Could show such love!

"Waiting on God has its value in that it makes us strong in work for God. Yet the secret of this strength is revealed in the fact that 'God worketh for Him that waiteth for Him.' The waiting on God secures the working of God for us and in us, out of which our work must spring. Waiting on God lies at the root of all true working for God, so working for God must be the fruit of all true waiting on Him. Our great need is to hold the two sides of the truth in perfect harmony."

Rev. Murray says of the waiting, working, and perfecting in sanctification: "Without the work there can be no full development and manifestation and perfecting of the life. The work depends upon the life. And the life depends on the work for its growth and perfection."

"Let us think of the inconceivably glorious salvation God has wrought for us in Christ, and is now purposing to work out and to perfect in us by His Spirit."

"Life is perfected by work. The highest manifestation of its hidden nature and power comes out in its work."

"The perfect heart is a gift from God, given in the way of the obedience of faith. Begin at once to serve God with a perfect heart, and the perfect heart will be given to you."

"All Christians need to learn that waiting has working for its object that it is only in working that waiting can attain its full perfection and blessedness."

Throughout his ministry and his writings Andrew Murray seems to strike a beautiful balance between maintaining the solidly biblical theology of the Reformed faith amidst his deep conviction in the ruling power of the Holy Spirit to effect great and miraculous events in the lives of God's people. One contemporary writer says of the life and influence of Murray, "It was the power if the Holy Ghost upon the heart and life of Andrew Murray that caused his spiritual influence to be felt throughout Christendom, and his books about Christ and the spiritual life are like a spice-laden breeze carrying refreshment to the whole Christian world!"

As you read through the short biography of the author I trust you will find a man who truly practiced and preached what you read in these pages. His reflections here come from a lifetime of experience, with all it's sorrows and failures, of seeking to wait upon God, to better work for Him, and then to receive the perfecting influence of the Holy Spirit in his soul.

I would encourage you to read one chapter each day, and after three months you will have completed what I believe to be a blessed journey towards walking closer to God.

Affectionately, for His glory,
Gene Fedele
Editor
February 2008

BIOGRAPHY OF

ANDREW MURRAY
1828-1917

From the very beginning of his call to be a minister of the gospel of Jesus Christ in 1822, Andrew Murray, senior, had devoted every Friday night to praying for revival in the Church. His children always remembered how they sometimes stood outside his study door listening to his pleading to God for an outpouring of the Holy Spirit. Other like-minded ministers united with the elder Murray in a concert of prayer, waiting in faith—waiting for God's glorious answer to come. Little could he imagine that his prayers would be answered through the Lord's saving work in the heart and life of his own son.

Andrew Murray, junior, was born in South Africa in 1828. From the earliest age he was blessed by the godly influence of faithful missionary parents. His father also served as the pastor of a congregation in the Dutch Reformed Church at Graaff Reinet. Descending from noble stock, the ancestors of the Murray family were known as "Auld Lichts" or "Old Light" Presbyterians, a very godly race.

Andrew had many brothers and sisters, but his older brother, John, was his closest companion in early life and later became a fellow minister of the Gospel of Jesus Christ in the Dutch Reformed Church. In 1838, John and Andrew traveled to live with their father's brother, Uncle John, in Aberdeen, Scotland, and engage in arduous, profitable studies. Under his scholarly and holy guidance, the boys were trained to take a keen interest in the events of their day, and develop a clear, biblical world-view.

In their many journeys throughout Scotland the two brothers were exposed to the influence of many eminent men, such as Dr. Chalmers, Thomas McCrie, Robert Murray M'Cheyne, Dr. Candlish, and the Bonar brothers, Horatius and Andrew. During those years a great spiritual awakening was passing through Scotland and surrounding lands, much like an earlier revival in America under Jonathan Edwards. The influence and fellowship of such faithful men was instrumental in keeping the Murray brothers committed to the orthodox, reformed teachings they had learned and lived under in their earlier years. It also helped prepare them to be vessels "fit for the Master's use," as formidable forces against the erroneous teachings of rationalism and emotionalism that began to infect and divide the Church.

The Rev. William C. Burns was a great spiritual influence over the two Murray brothers, especially Andrew. He was greatly moved by the quiet confidence of Burns and his devotion to prayer and fasting. He seemed to always carry about him a sense of the presence of God. This all made a lasting impression upon him and was eventually used by God to lead him to himself.

His Conversion

God had long been preparing the heart of Andrew Murray to be a means of His reviving work in the Church. It all culminated just before his eighteenth birthday. Andrew writes to his parents of his conversion:

> November 14, 1845,
> My Dear Parents,
> It was with great pleasure that I received your letter today, containing the announcement of the birth of another brother. And equal to that, I'm sure, will be your delight when I tell you glad tidings, over which angels rejoice, that *your son has been born again!* It would be difficult for me to express what I feel in writing to you about this. Always in my letters, and even in my conversation, I hardly know how to speak about these things. When I look back to see how I have been brought to where I am now, I must acknowledge that "He hath brought the blind by a way that he knew not, and led him in a path he hath not known." For the last two or three years there has been a continual process going on in my soul, an exchange between seriousness and forgetfulness. Yet, upon our departure from Aberdeen, during the three days voyage at sea, I had opportunity to reflect upon recollections of the past. After arriving in Holland I was led to pray in earnest and came to realize "Whereas I was blind, but now I see." I was long troubled with the idea that I must have some deep sight of my sins before I could be converted, and though I cannot say I have any special insight into the guilt of sin, I trust I can say, I am confident that as a sinner I have been led to cast myself on Christ.

What can I say now, my dear parents, but to call on you to praise the Lord with me; "Bless the Lord, O my soul, and all that is within me bless His holy name." At present I am in a peaceful state. I cannot say that I experience any special seasons of joy, but I enjoy a true confidence in God. Though I can say that my heart at present is warm, yet whenever I begin to write or speak I fail. I often think how glorious it will be when it shall be impossible to do anything but ascribe praise to "Him that hath loved us and washed us from our sins with His blood and made us kings and priests unto God."

Through grace I have always been enabled to trust in Him who has begun the good work in me, and to believe He will perform what He has begun, out of His free love before I was born. Oh, that I might receive grace to walk more holily before Him.

In 1848, both John and Andrew were ordained as ministers in the Dutch reformed Church. John was appointed to the church in Burgersdorp, and Andrew was called to the small farming town of Bloemfontein. With this news was great rejoicing in the Murray household. Father and mother daily praised God for the answered prayers for sons marked by genuine piety, simplicity and unworldliness.

While traveling in Cape Town, in 1855, Andrew met the lovely Emma Rutherford, daughter of pious, God-fearing parents. Emma was dedicated to educating the poor and needy, and delighted in her role of giving Bible lessons. She was highly cultured and fluent in English, Greek, and Latin. She was an excellent musician and singer. But most of all, she proved to be a true helpmeet to her husband and whole-heartedly devoted to his work. Together they had a blessed marriage that ministered to many young couples contemplating the sacred institution.

Though he was much loved at Bloemfontein, and cherished to service he was called to, he was greatly discouraged by the lightheartedness and lack of conviction in his congregation. His earnest prayers for revival and true conviction of sin became a burden to him. But God was leading His servant onward, and opening up the secret of a life of true peace and victory, into the blessed call of a worldwide ministry.

Revivals and Missions
Andrew Murray was a minister who preached powerful, soul-stirring messages, eager to reach the hearts of even the simplest hearers. Yet he was a man intimately in touch with the sinfulness of his own heart, who so often felt unfit for the calling and sought to cultivate a deeper sense of humility and dependence on the leading of the Holy Spirit. And, as is so often the case, those who consider themselves the most unworthy are the very ones called by God to do such great things for His kingdom. Andrew Murray was no exception.

He writes to his Brother, John, "Oh, to know Him in the likeness of His death and the fellowship of His sufferings, for nothing but a crucified Jesus revealed in the soul can give a humble spirit. Pray for me, my dear brother."

Of the revival that began with him in Worchester, he writes:
> To my mind the most striking proof that we truly had the Holy Spirit among us, is to be seen in what He is now doing in stirring up in the hearts of believers a desire after more entire surrender to himself and His service.

Yesterday, I preached from the words, "Be filled with the Spirit," and am only strengthened in the conviction that it is our calling just to take God's Word setting forth what we are to be, as it stands, and seek and expect it, even though we cannot exactly comprehend what it means. In all experience of the blessings of the Gospel, the intellect must follow with a heart and life.

He was very much about the "holy work of the Spirit's ministry" and a man of fervent and regular prayer, yet from the very beginning of his ministry he was often disturbed by what he called the "carnal excitement" of some believers in connection with worship and revivals. While participating in a pastors' conference in Worchester, South Africa, Andrew Murray experienced, during a worship service, an incident very disturbing to him. The hall became exceedingly loud with the noise of simultaneous and disorderly sounds, prayers and whispers of many in the congregation. An eyewitness writes:

Rev. Andrew Murray had been preaching that evening in English, and when the service was over an elder passing the door of the hall heard a loud noise and looked in. He then hastened to call Mr. Murray, presently returning with him. Mr. Murray came forward and asked me what had happened. He then walked down the hall for some distance and called out as loudly as he could, "Silence!" But the noise continued. He then called out again, "I am your minister, sent from God. Silence!" but there was no cessation of the noise. Mr. Murray then returned to me and asked that I start a hymn. I did so, but the noise continued and the people went on. Mr. Murray then said, "God is a God of order, and here everything is in disorder," and he left the hall.

The fruits of the revival were evident in that congregation for many years. One of the most striking results was that fifty men decided to enter the ministry, when previously one could hardly be found for such a calling.

From there the revival spread throughout the whole country, and people from all races were richly blessed. He writes, "We are greatly grieved at the self-deceit to which emotional people are subject, but we cannot expect great revival that is not exposed to this danger. However this may be, we thank the Lord we have good reason to affirm that since the revival began many have been added to the Lord's flock."

Rev. and Mrs. Murray had a particular ministry to children. For over sixty years they had one or more young people living with them in the parsonage. His children's sermons were always popular, and a vehicle for leading many to Christ at an early age. The godly couple also had similar success in their ministry to parents. At Worchester, Mr. Murray began the custom of regular monthly baptismal services when he would preach directly to the parents of those children receiving the sacrament. His passion for the subject was the basis for his book, *The Children for Christ*, written in 1864. His thoughts on the subject are reflected in the following letter written to his wife in 1860:

> Did you ever observe the promise applicable to parents when God grants them children, "Whosoever receiveth a child in my name receiveth Me." If we only knew how to receive children in His name, as given by Him, to be educated for Him, and above all as bringing a blessing to the home where they are rightly welcomed—how rich the reward would be!"

The consciousness he had of the need for help of the many young converts of the Revival and of God's children was a key factor which contributed to the publishing of *Abide in Christ*, one of Murray's best known works.

The Call to Cape Town

In 1864, Murray received the call to the pastorate in Cape Town, while amidst a great conflict, which arose between the Modernists and Orthodox sects of the Synod. As moderator of the Synod, he discharged his duty faithfully, bringing a measure of resolution, and accepted the call to Cape Town. After accepting he said, "If God wills to bless, no instrument is too weak, and blessed it is to be the instrument which He condescends to use."

There were more than 3,000 communicant members in two churches he served. The work of the ministry was very heavy, even with three pastoral assistants. Murray's deep interest in the salvation of souls burdened him to spend a great amount of time in pastoral visitation. Yet, he became discouraged that a significant number were not regular participants of the means of grace.

Murray spent some time visiting friends and preaching in various churches in Holland, Scotland, and England. After his return to the Cape he received a call to the Marylebone Presbyterian Church in London. When his wife asked him whether he would accept the call he replied, "No, my church needs me, my people need me, my country needs me; I must sacrifice myself for them." He then threw himself into the sphere of work that opened for his people and country.

During his absence, a religious controversy ran high in Cape Town to which Murray invested himself upon his return. An opposition to the conservatism of the Dutch

Reformed Church of South Africa made damaging work in the Christian society. It culminated in the publication of a book titled, *Modern Theology*, by Rev. David Faure. In opposition to the warped spiritualism of Faure, Andrew Murray wrote and published his book, *Modern Unbelief*, followed by a week long series of lectures and sermons, that were described in the English newspapers as "keen in thought, scientific in treatment, and profoundly philosophical in essence as they were eloquent in expression."

The following sketch of Murray by his opponent is quite expressive:

> First let me speak of the men of the ultra-orthodox party, who pose as watchmen on the walls of Zion. Under this category I begin with Rev. Andrew Murray—a worthy leader. Eloquent, quick and talented, he has an acute mind and clear judgment. He instantly divines the weak points in his opponent's arguments and knows how to assail them. There is no member of the assembly who possesses more influence than Andrew Murray and certainly there is none among the conservatives who better deserves his influence.

In addition to his many regular responsibilities, the poor and sick were always very much on his heart. He conducted special services for them and developed a genuine fellowship and ministry among them. Shortly after his arrival in Cape Town he established a branch of the YMCA and threw himself heartily into it. Mr. Murray was exemplary in his faithful visitations to the poor and sick, even fearless amidst the severe smallpox epidemic, which claimed many victims in the area.

Pastor, Educator, Evangelist

In 1871, Andrew Murray was called to the pastorate of the small farming community of Wellington. In a letter to his brother he wrote, "I do think that I have honestly and with child-like simplicity said to the Father that if He would have me stay here I am ready and willing." So Mr. Murray came to the place where he was to spend the remaining forty-five years of his life, in the midst of the people he so dearly loved, and who warmly loved him in return.

His relationships there were ruled by love, and the poorest and unlearned had the same courteous interest shown to them as the rich and wise had received. He was always in great demand as an evangelist and his preaching on sin was deep and searching. He truly had a shepherd's heart for the people in his care, "I feel anxious to get God's people together to point out the need of intercession and entire consecration."

Murray's love for children was evident his entire life and ministry. The death of his darling little daughters became a means to putting forth renewed efforts on behalf of the youth. In 1874, with Mrs. Murray's direction and the help of a number of pious young women, he opened the Huguenot Seminary. It became an inexpressibly powerful religious influence in the hearts and lives of many young ladies.

In 1877, Mr. Murray was elected as Moderator of the Synod of the Dutch Reformed Church. With this new responsibility he would travel to various places in Europe and America. He had three primary objectives in his work:

1. To study the condition of the church
2. To enquire about education
3. To consider the spiritual life of the countries he visited

He became more convinced of the importance of the unity of the Church. "Believers are ONE!" he would often say. He did not merely talk about fellowship, but practiced it constantly. Few men have ever manifested a wider catholicity than Andrew Murray.

Murray spent time with D. L. Moody, and after fellowship at the home of one of Moody's parishioners writes, "In the house in which I stayed and in the intercourse with laymen, I noticed very distinctly the influence of Mr. Moody's work. There is much more readiness to talk out on spiritual things and much more warmth."

"Falling Asleep"

The closing years of Andrew Murray's life were filled with a mix of joys and sorrows, commensurate with a life of one preparing for the world to come. The death of his oldest son, Haldane, in the war brought bitterness and pain, but in spite of it his own spirit was entering into deep, sweet peace in God as his time to depart grew nearer.

In 1916, at the age of eighty-eight, Dr. Murray preached his last sermon, in Wellington. The death of his life-long companion, Emma, just the year before and his own failing health brought him to realize his work in this life was ending, and his eternal life was near at hand.

On January 18, 1917, Andrew Murray departed for his heavenly mansion, yet "though dead, he still speaks" through the many writings and books and the testimony of the labors of his life. As Murray would say, "Let us reap while the light lasts. Bring in the golden sheaves."

Andrew Murray
1828-1917

The house in which Andrew Murray was born,
known as "the old Parsonage," which later became
the home of his son Charles

Andrew Murray's father and mother

Andrew Murray as a young student

Marischal College, Aberdeen

Andrew Murray as
a young minister

John Murray,
Andrew's brother,
as a young minister

The Murray family in 1873.
Andrew is in the back row with his arm
affectionately around his wife Emma

1866 painting of Adderly Street, Cape Town, with the
Dutch Reformed Church in the background

Worcester, South Africa, about 1877.
The town of Andrew Murray's pastorate where great
revival broke out (1860–1864).

Andrew Murray,
43 years old,
accepts the call
to the parsonage
in the small
South African
town of Wellington

Andrew Murray (center) and his family about 1880

Andrew Murray's dwelling, "Clairvaux" (on right)
with the Training Institute for Missionaries (to the left)

Professor Murray age 70

Andrew and Emma Murray

Andrew Murray unveiling the monument to his two
colleagues, Professors J. Murray and N. Hofmeyr, 1915

Andrew Murray shortly before his death
on January 18, 1917

WAITING
ON GOD

WAIT THOU ONLY
UPON GOD

"My soul waiteth thou only upon God" (Psalm 62:5).

"A God ... which worketh for him that waiteth for Him"
(Isaiah 64:4).

"Wait only upon God;" my soul, be still,
And let thy God unfold His perfect will,
Thou fain would'st follow Him throughout this year,
Thou fain with listening heart His voice would'st hear,
Thou fain would'st be a passive instrument
Possessed by God, and ever Spirit-sent
Upon His service sweet—then be thou still,
For only thus can He in thee fulfill
His heart's desire. Oh, hinder not His hand
From fashioning the vessel He hath planned.
"Be silent unto God," and thou shalt know
The quiet, holy calm He doth bestow
On those who wait on Him; so shalt thou bear
His presence, and His life and light e'en where
The night is darkest, and thine earthly days
Shall show His love, and sound His glorious praise.
And He will work with hand unfettered, free,
His high and holy purposes through thee.

First on thee must that hand of power be turned,
Till in His love's strong fire thy dross is burned,
And thou come forth a vessel for thy Lord,
So frail and empty, yet, since He hath poured
Into thine emptiness His life, His love,
Henceforth through thee the power of God shall move
And He will work for thee. Stand still and see
The victories thy God will gain for thee;
So silent, yet so irresistible,
Thy God shall do the thing impossible.
Oh, question not henceforth what thou canst do;
Thou cans't do nought. But He will carry through
The work where human energy had failed
Where all thy best endeavours had availed
Thee nothing. Then, my soul, wait and be still;
Thy God shall work for thee His perfect will.
If thou wilt take no less, His best shall be
Thy portion now and through eternity.

—*Freda Hanbury*

PREFACE

Previous to my leaving home for England last year, I had been much impressed by the thought of how, in all our religion, personal and public, we need more of God. I felt that we needed to train our people in their worship more to wait on God, and to make the cultivation of a deeper sense of His presence, of more direct contact with Him, of entire dependence on Him, a definite aim of our ministry. At a welcome breakfast in Exeter Hall, I gave very simple expression to this thought in connection with all our religious work. I have already said elsewhere that I was surprised at the response the sentiment met with. I saw that God's Spirit had been working the same desire in many hearts.

The experiences of the past year, both personal and public, have greatly deepened the conviction. It is as if I myself am only beginning to see the deepest truth concerning God and our relation to Him center in this waiting on God, and how very little in our life and work we have been surrounded by its spirit. The following pages are the outcome of my conviction, and of the desire to direct the attention of all God's people to the one great remedy for all our needs. More than half the pieces were written on board ship. I fear they bear the marks of being somewhat crude and hasty. I have felt, in looking them over, as if I could wish to write them over again. But this I cannot now do. And so I send them out with the prayer that He who loves to use the feeble may give His blessing with them.

I do not know if it will be possible for me to put into a few words what are the chief things we need to learn. In a note at the close of the book on law I have mentioned some. But what I want to say here is this: The great lack of our religion is, we do not know God. The answer to every complaint of feebleness and failure, the message to every congregation or convention seeking instruction on holiness, ought to be simply, What is the matter? Have you not God? If you really believe in God, He will put all right. God is willing and able by His Holy Spirit. Cease from expecting the least good from yourself, or the least help from anything there is in man, and just yield yourself unreservedly to God to work in you and He will do all for you.

How simple this looks! And yet this is the gospel we so little know. I feel ashamed as I send forth these very defective meditations. I can only cast them on the love of my brethren, and of our God. May He use them to draw us all to himself, to learn in practice and experience the blessed art of waiting only upon God. Might we get some right conception of what the influence would be of a life given, not in thought, or imagination, or effort, but in the power of the Holy Spirit, wholly to waiting upon God.

With my greeting in Christ to all God's saints it has been my privilege to meet, and no less to those I have not met, I subscribe myself—your brother and servant,

Andrew Murray
Wellington, March 3, 1896

P.S. In this little book I have more than once spoken of our waiting on God in our conventions. I have been much interested in noticing in the life of Canon Battersly how prominent the thought was in his mind. In a paper preparing the way for Keswick, he speaks of three steps needful to the attainment of true holiness. The first two are: A clear view of the possibilities of Christian attainment, and a deliberate purpose to live the life. And then the third: "We must look up to, and wait upon our ascended Lord for all that we need to enable us to do this." In a letter written a few days after the first Keswick Convention in 1875, he writes again: "At the first meeting the keynote was struck which vibrated through all our meetings: 'My soul I wait thou only upon God, for my expectation is from Him' (Psalm 62:5). And farther, 'There is a very remarkable resemblance in all the testimonies which I have since received, viz. the ability given to make a full surrender to the Lord, and the consequent experience of an abiding peace.'"

WAITING ON GOD

DAY 1

WAITING ON THE GOD OF OUR SALVATION

*"My soul waiteth only upon God; from Him cometh my
salvation" (Psalms 62:1).*

If salvation indeed comes from God, and is entirely His
work, just as our creation was, it follows, as a matter of
course, that our first and highest duty is to wait on Him to
do that which pleases Him. Waiting becomes then the only
way to the experience of a full salvation, the only way to truly
know God as the God of our salvation. All the difficulties
that are brought forward as keeping us back from fully living
out our salvation, have their cause in the defective knowledge
and practice of waiting upon God. All that the Church and
its members need for the manifestation of the mighty power
of God in the world, is the return to our true place, the place
that belongs to us, both in creation and redemption, the place
of absolute and unceasing dependence upon God. Let us strive
to see what the elements are that make up this most blessed
and needful waiting upon God. It may help us to discover the
reasons why this grace is so little cultivated, and to feel how
infinitely desirable it is that the Church, that we ourselves,
should at any price learn its blessed secret.

The deep need for this waiting on God lies equally in the nature of man and the nature of God. God, as Creator, formed man, to be a vessel in which He could show forth His power and goodness. Man was not to have in himself a fountain of life, or strength, or happiness. The ever-living and only living One was each moment to be the Communicator to him of all that he needed. Man's glory and blessedness were not to be independent, or dependent upon himself, but dependent on a God of such infinite riches and love. Man was to have the joy of receiving every moment out of the fullness of God. This was his blessedness as an unfallen [before Adam's sin] creature.

When he fell from God, he was still more absolutely dependent on Him. There was not the slightest hope of his recovery out of his state of death, but in God, His power and mercy. It is God alone who began the work of redemption. It is God alone who continues and carries it on each moment in each individual believer. Even in the regenerate man there is no power of goodness in himself. He has and can have nothing that he does not each moment receive. Waiting on God is just as indispensable and must be just as continuous and unbroken as the breathing that maintains his natural life.

It is only because Christians do not know of their own absolute poverty and helplessness in their relationship with God, that they have no sense of the need of absolute and unceasing dependence, or of the unspeakable blessedness of continual waiting on God. But when a believer finally begins to see it, and consent to it, that he by the Holy Spirit must each moment receive what God each moment works, waiting on God becomes his brightest hope and joy. As he appreciates how God, as God, as Infinite Love, delights to impart His own nature to His child as fully as He can, how God is not weary of each moment keeping charge of his life and strength, he wonders that he ever thought otherwise of God than as a God to be waited on all the day. God unceasingly giving and working, His child unceasingly waiting and receiving: this is the blessed life.

"Truly my soul waiteth upon God; from Him cometh my salvation" (Psalms 62:1). First we wait on God for salvation. Then we learn that salvation is only to bring us to God, and teach us to wait on Him. Then we find what is better still that waiting on God is itself the highest salvation. It is the ascribing to Him the glory of being All. It is the experiencing that He is All to us. May God teach us the blessedness of waiting on Him.

"My soul waiteth only upon God!"

REFLECTION

1. Waiting on God is the absolute, unceasing, moment-by-moment dependence upon God! How do you display such dependence in your life? In what areas do you need to better exercise waiting?

2. Waiting on God becomes the full experience of salvation, as we are totally and completely dependent upon God. It is just as indispensable and must be just as continuous and unbroken as the breathing that maintains the natural life.

DAY 2

WAITING ON GOD: THE KEYNOTE OF LIFE

"I have waited for Thy salvation, O Lord!"
(Genesis 49:18).

It is not easy to say exactly in what sense Jacob used these words, in the midst of his prophecies in regard to the future of his sons. But they do certainly indicate that both for himself and for them his expectation was from God alone. It was God's salvation he waited for; a salvation which God had promised and which God himself alone could work out. He knew himself and his sons to be under God's charge. Jehovah the Everlasting God would show in them what His saving power is and does. The words point forward to that wonderful history of redemption that is not yet finished, and to the glorious future in eternity whither it is leading. They suggest to us how there is no salvation but God's salvation, and how waiting on God for that, whether for our personal experience or in wider circles, is our first duty, our true blessedness.

Let us think of the inconceivably glorious salvation God has wrought for us in Christ, and is now purposing to work out and to perfect in us by His Spirit. Let us meditate until we somewhat realize that every participation of this great salvation, from moment to moment, must be the work of God himself. God cannot part with His grace, or goodness, or strength, as an external thing that He gives us, as He gives the raindrops from heaven. No! He can only give it, and we can only enjoy it, as He works it himself directly and unceasingly. And the only reason that He does not work it more effectively and continuously is, that we do not let Him. We hinder Him either by our indifference or by our self-effort.

34

What He asks of us, in the way of surrender, and obedience, and desire, and trust, is all comprised in this one thought: waiting on Him, waiting for His salvation. It combines the deep sense of our entire helplessness to work what is divinely good, and the perfect assurance that our God will work it all in His divine power.

Again, I say, let us meditate on the divine glory of the salvation God purposes to work out in us, until we know the truth it implies. Our heart is the scene of a divine operation more wonderful than creation. We can do as little towards the work as towards creating the world, except as God works in us to will and to do. God only asks of us to yield, to consent, to wait upon Him, and He will do it all. Let us meditate and be still, until we see how appropriate and right and blessed it is that God alone does all, and our soul will of itself sink down in deep humility to say: "I have waited for your salvation, O Lord." And the deep blessed background of all our praying and working will be: "Truly my soul waits upon God."

The application of the truth to wider circles, to those we labor among or intercede for, to the Church of Christ around us, or throughout the world, is not difficult. There can be no good except what God works. To wait upon God, and have the heart filled with faith in His working, and in that faith to pray for His mighty power to come down, is our only wisdom. Oh for the eyes of our heart to be opened to see God working in us and in others, and to see how blessed it is to worship and just to wait for His salvation!

Our private and public prayer is our chief expression of our relation to God. It is in them chiefly that our waiting upon God must be exercised. If our waiting begins by quieting the activities of nature, and being still before God; if it bows and

35

seeks to see God in His universal and almighty operation, alone able and always ready to work all good; if it yields itself to Him in the assurance that He is working and will work in us; if it maintains the place of humility and stillness and surrender, until God's Spirit has quickened the faith that He will perfect His work, it will indeed become the strength and the joy of the soul. Life will become one deep blessed cry, "I have waited for Your salvation, O Lord."

"My soul waiteth only upon God!"

REFLECTION

1. Let us be still and meditate on the truth that our salvation is of nothing we can do, but only the work of our loving God.

2. We so often hinder the Lord by our self-effort. What He desires of us is complete surrender, obedience and trust to receive perfect assurance in His divine work.

DAY 3

WAITING ON GOD: THE TRUE PLACE
OF THE CREATURE

"These wait all upon Thee; That Thou mayest give them their meat in due season. That Thou givest unto them, they gather; Thou openest Thine hand, they are satisfied with good" (Psalm 104:27,28).

This Psalm, in praise of the Creator, has been speaking of the birds and the beasts of the forest; of the young lions, and man going forth to his work; of the great sea, wherein are things creeping innumerable, both small and great beasts. And it sums up the whole relation of all creation to its Creator, and its continuous and universal dependence upon Him in the one word: "These all wait upon You!" Just as much as it was God's work to create, it is His work to maintain. As little as the creature could create itself, is it left to provide for itself. The whole creation is ruled by the one unchangeable law of—waiting upon God!

The word is the simple expression of that for the sake of which alone the creature was brought into existence, the very groundwork of its constitution. The one object for which God gave life to creatures was that in them He might prove and show forth His wisdom, power, and goodness—and in His being each moment their life and happiness, and pouring forth unto them, according to their capacity, the riches of his goodness and power. And just as this is the very place and nature of God, to be unceasingly the supplier of every want in the creature, so the very place and nature of the creature is nothing but this—to wait upon God and receive from Him what He alone can give, what He delights to give.

If we are in this book at all to appreciate what waiting on God is to be to the believer, to practice it and to experience its blessedness, it is of consequence that we begin at the very beginning, and see the deep reasonableness of the call that comes to us. We shall understand how the duty is no arbitrary command. We shall see how it is not only rendered necessary by our sin and helplessness. It is simply and truly our restoration to our original destiny and our highest nobility, to our true place and glory as creatures blessedly dependent on the all-glorious God.

If once our eyes are opened to this precious truth, all nature will become a preacher, reminding us of the relationship which, founded in creation, is now taken up in grace. As we read this Psalm, and learn to look upon all life in nature as continually maintained by God himself, waiting on God will be seen to be the very necessity of our being. As we think of the young lions and the ravens crying to Him, of the birds and the fish and every insect waiting on Him, until He give them their meat in due season, we shall see that it is the very nature and glory of God that He is a God who is to be waited on. Every thought of what nature is, and what God is, will give new force to the call: "Wait thou only upon God."

"These all wait upon you, that you may give" (Psalms 104:27). It is God who gives all. Let this faith enter deeply into our hearts. Before we fully understand all that is implied in our waiting upon God, and before we ever have been able to cultivate the habit, let the truth enter our souls: waiting on God, unceasing and entire dependence upon Him, is, in heaven and earth, the one only true religion, the one unalterable and all-comprehensive expression for the true relationship to the ever-blessed One in whom we live.

Let us resolve at once that it shall be the one characteristic of our life and worship, a continual, humble, trustful waiting upon God. We may rest assured that He who made us for Himself, that He might give Himself to us and in us, that He will never disappoint us. In waiting on Him we shall find rest and joy and strength, and the supply of every need.

"My soul waiteth only upon God!"

REFLECTION
1. In what ways does the created world become a "preacher" to us?

2. Consider the reasons for which God brought man into this world?

DAY 4

WAITING ON GOD FOR SUPPLIES

"The Lord upholdeth all that fall, And raiseth up all those that be bowed down. The eyes of all wait upon Thee; And Thou givest them their meat in due season" *(Psalm 145:14,15).*

Psalms 104 is a Psalm of creation, and the words, "These all wait upon thee," were used with reference to the animal creation. Here we have a Psalm of the kingdom, and "The eyes of all wait upon thee" appears especially to point to the needs of God's saints, of all that fall and them that be bowed down. What the universe and the animal creation does unconsciously, God's people are to do intelligently and voluntarily. Man is to be the interpreter of Nature. He is to prove that there is nothing more noble or more blessed in the exercise of our free will than to use it in waiting upon God.

If an army has been sent out to march into an enemy's country and tidings are received that it is not advancing, the question is at once asked, "What may be the cause of delay?" The answer will very often be, "Waiting for supplies." All the stores of provisions or clothing or ammunition have not arrived; without these they dare not proceed. It is no different in the Christian life. Day by day, at every step, we need our supplies from above. And there is nothing so needful as to cultivate that spirit of dependence on God and of confidence

39

in Him, which refuses to go on without the needed supply of grace and strength.

If the question be asked, whether this is any different from what we do when we pray, the answer is, that there may be much praying with but very little waiting on God. In praying we are often occupied with ourselves, with our own needs, and our own efforts in the presentation of them. In waiting upon God, the first thought is of the God upon whom we wait. We enter His presence and feel we need just to be quiet, so that He, as God, can overshadow us with himself. God longs to reveal himself, to fill us with himself. Waiting on God gives Him time in His own way and divine power to come to us.

It is especially at the time of prayer that we ought to set ourselves to cultivate this spirit. Before you pray, bow quietly before God, and seek to remember and realize who He is, how near He is, how certainly He can and will help. Just be still before Him, and allow His Holy Spirit to awaken and stir up in your soul the childlike disposition of absolute dependence and confident expectation. Wait upon God as a living being, as the living God, who notices you, and is just longing to fill you with His salvation. Wait on God until you know you have met Him; prayer will then become so different.

And when you are praying, let there be intervals of silence, reverent stillness of soul, in which you yield yourself to God, in case He may have aught He wishes to teach you or to work in you. Waiting on Him will become the most blessed part of prayer, and the blessing thus obtained will be doubly precious as the fruit of such fellowship with the Holy One. God has so ordained it, in harmony with His holy nature, and with ours, that waiting on Him should be the honor we give Him. Let us bring Him the service gladly and truthfully. He will reward it abundantly.

"The eyes of all wait upon thee, and thou givest them their meat in due season." Dear soul, God provides in nature for the creatures He has made. How much more will He provide in grace for those He has redeemed. Learn to say of every want, and every failure, and every lack of needful grace; I have waited too little upon God, or He would have given me in due season all I needed. And say then, too:

"My soul waiteth only upon God!"

REFLECTION

1. How does waiting on God direct our perspective in times of prayer? Are we truly about God's business or our own?

2. As we wait patiently on God, it gives Him time to come to us, and opens our ears to hear Him.

DAY 5

WAITING ON GOD FOR INSTRUCTION

"Show me thy ways, O Lord; Teach me Thy paths. Lead me in Thy truth, and teach me; For Thou art the God of my salvation; On Thee do I wait all the day" (Psalms 25:4,5).

I spoke of an army, on the point of entering an enemy's territories, answering the question as to the cause of delay, "Waiting for supplies." The answer might also have been, "Waiting for instructions," or, "Waiting for orders." If the last dispatch had not been received, with the final orders of the commander-in-chief, the army dared not move. So it is in the Christian life—as deep as the need of waiting for supplies, is that of waiting for instructions.

See how beautifully this comes out in Psalms 25. The writer knew and loved God's law exceedingly, and meditated in that law day and night. But he knew that this was not enough. He knew that for the right spiritual understanding of the truth, and for the right personal application of it to his own peculiar circumstances, he needed a direct divine teaching.

This psalm has at all times been a favorite one, because of its reiterated expression of the felt need of the Divine teaching, and of the childlike confidence that such teaching would be given. Study the psalm until your heart is filled with the two thoughts—the absolute need and the absolute certainty of divine guidance. And notice, then, how entirely it is in this connection that he speaks, "On You do I wait all the day." Waiting for guidance, waiting for instruction, all the day, is a very blessed part of waiting upon God.

The Father in heaven is so interested in His child, and so longs to have his life at every step in His will and His love, that He is willing to keep his guidance entirely in His own hand. He knows so well that we are unable to do what is really holy and heavenly, except as He works it in us. He means His very demands to become promises of what He will do in watching over and leading us all the day. Not only in special difficulties and times of perplexity, but in the common course of everyday life, we may count upon Him to teach us His way and show us His path.

And what is needed in us to receive this guidance? One thing: Waiting for instructions, waiting on God. "On You do I wait all the day." We want in our times of prayer to give clear expression to our sense of need, and our faith in His help. We want definitely to become conscious of our ignorance as to what God's way may be, and the need of the divine light shining within us, if our way is to be as of the sun, shining more and more unto the perfect day. And we want to wait quietly before God in prayer, until the deep, restful assurance fills us. It will be given—"the meek will He guide in the way."

"On You do I wait all the day." The special surrender to the divine guidance in our seasons of prayer must cultivate, and be followed up by, the habitual looking upwards 'all the day.' As simple as it is, to one who has eyes, to walk all the day in the light of the sun, so simple and delightful can it become to a soul practiced in waiting on God, to walk all the day in the enjoyment of God's light and leading. What is needed to help us to such a life is the real knowledge and faith of God as the one only source of wisdom and goodness, as ever ready, and longing much to be to us all that we can possibly require—yes! This is the one thing we need. If we saw our God in His love, if we believed that He waits to be gracious, that He waits to be our life and to work all in us—how this waiting on God would become our highest joy, the natural and spontaneous response of our hearts to His great love and glory!

O God! Teach us, above everything, the blessed lesson, that all the day, and every moment of it, You are around and within us, working out Your work of love. Show us that You only ask of us that we wait on You. And so teach us to say, "On You do I wait all the day."

"My soul waiteth only upon God!"

43

REFLECTION

1. As we pray, may God see our genuine sense of need and resignation to His will.

2. Lord, as we wait upon you, may we receive your instructions and will for us.

DAY 6

WAITING ON GOD FOR ALL SAINTS

"Let none that wait on Thee be ashamed" (Psalm 25:3).

In our meditation today, let us each now forget ourselves, to think of the great company of God's saints throughout the world, who are all with us waiting on Him. And let us all join in the fervent prayer for each other, "Let none that wait on Thee be ashamed."

Just think for a moment of the multitude of waiting ones who need prayer. How many are sick and weary, to whom it seems their prayers are not being answered, and who sometimes begin to fear that their hope will be put to shame. And then, how many servants of God, ministers or missionaries, teachers or workers, whose hopes in their work have been disappointed, and whose longing for power and blessing remains unsatisfied. And then think of how many, who have heard of a life of rest and perfect peace, of abiding light and fellowship, of strength and victory, and who cannot find the path. With all these, it is only that they have not yet learned the secret of full waiting upon God. They just need what we all need—the living assurance that waiting on God can never be in vain. Let us remember all who are in danger of fainting or being weary, and all unite in the cry, "Let none that wait on You be ashamed!"

If this intercession for all who wait on God becomes part of our waiting on Him for ourselves, we shall help to bear each other's burdens, and so fulfill the law of Christ. As we wait on God we will be introduced to that element of unselfishness and love, which is the path to the highest blessing, and the fullest communion with God. Love to the brethren and love to God are inseparably linked. In God, the love to His Son and to us are one: "That the love wherewith You have loved Me, may be in them" (John 17:26). In Christ, the love of the Father to Him, and His love to us, are one: "... As the Father loved me, so have I loved you." In us, He asks that His love to us shall be ours to the brethren: "As I have loved you, that you love one another" (John 13:34). All the love of God, and of Christ, are inseparably linked with love to the brethren. And how can we, day by day, prove and cultivate this love except by daily praying for each other? Christ did not seek to enjoy the Father's love for Himself. He passed it all on to us. All true seeking of God and His love for ourselves will be inseparably linked with the thought and the love of our brethren in prayer for them.

"Let none that wait on You be ashamed." Twice in the psalm David speaks of his waiting on God for himself. Here he thinks of all who wait on Him. Let this page take the message to all God's tried and weary ones, that there are more praying for them than they know. Let it stir us, in our waiting, to make a point of forgetting ourselves at times, and to enlarge our hearts and say to the Father, "These all wait upon You, and You give them their meat in due season" (Psalms 104:27). Let it inspire us all with new courage—for who is there who is not ready at times to faint and be weary? "Let none that wait on You be ashamed" is a promise in a prayer, "They that wait on You shall not be ashamed!" From many witnesses the cry comes to everyone who needs the help. Brother, sister, tried one, "Wait on the Lord; be of good courage, and He shall strengthen your heart; wait, I say, on the Lord. Be of good courage, and He shall strengthen your heart, all you that wait on the Lord."

Blessed Father! We humbly beseech You, Let none that wait on You be ashamed. No, not one. Some are weary and the time of waiting appears long. And some are feeble and scarcely know how to wait. And some are so entangled in the effort of their prayers and their work, they think that they can find no time to wait continually. Father! Teach us all how to wait. Teach us to think of each other and pray for each other. Teach us to think of You, the God of all waiting ones. Father! Let none that wait on You be ashamed. For Jesus' sake. Amen.

"My soul waiteth only upon God!"

REFLECTION

1. The path to highest blessing is a prayer life that includes the needs and burdens of the brethren. Unselfish intercession brings forth rich reward.

2. Let us think of the multitude of friends, family, ministers, teachers, and missionaries, who need the interceding prayers of our lips to reach heaven.

DAY 7

WAITING ON GOD: A PLEA IN PRAYER

"Let integrity and uprightness preserve me; for I wait on Thee" (Psalms 25:21).

For the third time in this psalm we have the word wait. As before in verse 5, "On Thee do I wait all the day," so here, too, the believing supplicant appeals to God to remember that he is waiting on Him, looking for an answer. It is a great thing for a soul not only to wait upon God, but to be filled with such a consciousness that its whole spirit and position is that of a waiting one, that it can, in childlike confidence, say, Lord! You know, I wait on You. It will prove a mighty plea in prayer, giving ever-increasing boldness of expectation to claim the promise, "They that wait on Me shall not be ashamed!"

The prayer in connection with which the plea is put forth here is one of great importance in the spiritual life. If we draw near to God, it must be with a true heart. There must be perfect integrity, wholeheartedness, in our dealing with God. As we read in the next Psalm, "Judge me, O Lord, for I have walked in my integrity" (Psalms 26:1), "As for me, I will walk in my integrity," there must be perfect uprightness or single-heartedness before God. As it is written, "His righteousness is for the upright in heart." The soul must know that it allows nothing sinful, nothing doubtful. If it is indeed to meet the Holy One and receive His full blessing, it must be with a heart wholly and singly given up to His will. The whole spirit that animates us in the waiting must be, "Let integrity and uprightness"—You see that I desire to come so to You, You know I am looking to You to work them perfectly in me. Let them "preserve me, for I wait on You."

And if at our first attempt truly to live the life of fully and always waiting on God, we begin to discover how much that perfect integrity is wanting, this will just be one of the blessings which the waiting was meant to work. A soul cannot seek close fellowship with God, or attain the abiding consciousness of waiting on Him all the day, without a very honest and entire surrender to all His will.

"For I wait on You." It is not only in connection with the prayer of our text but with every prayer that this plea may be used. To use it often will be a great blessing to us. Let us therefore study the words well until we know all their bearings. It must be clear to us what we are waiting for. There may be very different things. It may be waiting for God in our times of prayer to take his place as God, and to work in us the sense of His holy presence and nearness. It may be some special petition, to which we are expecting an answer. It may be our whole inner life, in which we are on the lookout for God's putting forth of His power. It may be the whole state of His Church and saints, or some part of His work, for which our eyes are looking toward Him. It is good that we sometimes count exactly what the things are we are waiting for, and as we say definitely of each of them, "On You do I wait," we shall be emboldened to claim the answer, "For on You do I wait."

It must also be clear to us on whom we are waiting. Not an idol, a God of whom we have made an image by our conceptions of what He is. No, but the living God, such as He really is in His great glory, His infinite holiness, His power, wisdom, and goodness, in His love and nearness. It is the presence of a beloved or a dreaded master that wakens up the whole attention of the servant who waits on him. It is the presence of God, as He can in Christ by His Holy Spirit make Himself known, and keep the soul under its covering

48

and shadow. This will awaken and strengthen the true waiting spirit. Let us be still and wait and worship until we know how near He is, and then say, "On You do I wait."

And then, let it be very clear, too, that we are waiting. Let that become so much our consciousness that the utterance comes spontaneously, "On You I do wait all the day; I wait on You." This will indeed imply sacrifice and separation, a soul entirely given up to God as its all, its only joy. This waiting on God has hardly been acknowledged as the only true Christianity. And yet, if it be true that God alone is goodness and joy and love; if it be true that our highest blessedness is in having as much of God as we can; if it be true that Christ has redeemed us wholly for God, and made a life of continual abiding in His presence possible, nothing less ought to satisfy than to be ever breathing this blessed atmosphere, "I wait on You."

"My soul waiteth only upon God!"

REFLECTION

1. In waiting on God in prayer our primary focus should be in surrendering our will to His. Is that the course of our prayers? Or are we only occupied with ourselves and our own needs and interests?

DAY 8

STRONG AND OF GOOD COURAGE

*"Wait on the Lord: be of good courage, and He shall
strengthen thine heart: wait, I say, on the Lord"
(Psalms 27:14).*

The psalmist had just said, in the previous verse, "I had
fainted, unless I had believed to see the goodness of the
Lord in the land of the living." If it had not been for his faith
in God, his heart would have fainted. But in the confident
assurance in God which faith gives, he urges himself and us
to remember one thing above all—to wait upon God. One of
the chief needs in our waiting upon God, one of the deepest
secrets of its blessedness and blessing, is a quiet, confident
persuasion that it is not in vain; courage to believe that God
will hear and help; that we are waiting on a God who never
could disappoint His people.

"Be of good courage." These words are frequently found
in connection with some great and difficult enterprise, in
prospect of the combat with the power of strong enemies,
and the utter insufficiency of all human strength. Is waiting
on God a work so difficult, that such words are needed? Yes,
indeed. The deliverance, for which we often have to wait,
is from enemies, in presence of whom we are impotent. The
blessings for which we plead are spiritual and all unseen;
things impossible with men; heavenly, supernatural, divine
realities. Our souls are so little accustomed to hold fellowship
with God, the God on whom we wait so often appears to hide
himself. We who have to wait are often tempted to fear that
we do not wait aright, that our faith is too feeble, that our
desire is not as upright or as earnest as it should be, that our
surrender is not complete. Our heart may well faint and fail.

With all these causes of fear or doubt, how blessed to hear the voice of God, "Wait on the Lord: be of good courage!" YES, WAIT ON THE LORD! Let nothing in heaven or earth or hell keep you from waiting on your God in full assurance that it cannot be in vain.

The one lesson our text teaches us is this: that when we set ourselves to wait on God, we should resolve that it will be with the most confident expectation of God's meeting and blessing us. We ought to make up our minds to this, that nothing was ever so sure, as that waiting on God will bring us untold and unexpected blessing. We are so accustomed to judge God and His work in us by what we feel, that it is very likely that when we begin to cultivate the waiting on Him, we shall be discouraged, because we do not find any special blessing from it. The message comes to us, "Above everything, when you wait on God, do so in the spirit of abounding hopefulness. It is God in His glory, in His power, in His love longing to bless you that you are waiting on."

If you say that you are afraid of deceiving yourself with vain hope, because you do not see or feel any warrant in your present state for such special expectations, my answer is, it is God, who is the warrant for your expecting great things. Oh, do learn the lesson. You are not going to wait on yourself to see what you feel and what changes come to you. You are going to wait on God, to know first, what He is, and then, after that, what He will do. The whole duty and blessedness of waiting on God has its root in this; that He is such a blessed Being full to overflowing, of goodness and power and life and joy, that we, however wretched, cannot for any time come into contact with Him, without that life and power secretly, silently beginning to enter into us and blessing us. God is Love! That is the one only and all-sufficient warrant of your expectation. Love seeks not

51

its own. God's love is just His delight to impart himself and His blessedness to His children. No matter how feeble you feel, just come and wait in His presence. As a feeble, sickly invalid is brought out into the sunshine to let its warmth go through him, come with all that is dark and cold in you into the sunshine of God's holy, omnipotent love, and sit there and wait, with the one thought: Here I am, in the sunshine of His love. As the sun does its work in the weak one who seeks its rays, God will do His work in you. Oh, do trust Him fully. "Wait on the Lord: be of good courage, and He shall strengthen thine heart: wait, I say, on the Lord."

"My soul waiteth only upon God!"

REFLECTION

1. If we resolve to wait on God, we can confidently expect He will meet with us and bless us.

2. God's infinite and perfect love is the confidence of our expecting to meet with Him as we wait on Him.

DAY 9

WAIT ON GOD WITH THE HEART.

"Be of good courage, and He shall strengthen thine heart, all ye who hope in the Lord" (Psalms 31:24).

These words are nearly the same as in our last meditation. But I gladly avail myself of them again to press home a much needed lesson for all who desire to learn truly and fully what it is to wait on God. It is with the heart we must wait upon God. "Be of good courage." All our waiting depends upon the state of the heart. As a man's heart is, so is he before God. We can advance no further or deeper into the holy place of God's presence to wait on Him there, than our heart is prepared for it by the Holy Spirit. The message is, "Be of good courage, and He shall strengthen thine heart, all ye who hope in the Lord."

The truth appears so simple, that some may ask, "Do not all admit this? Where is the need of insisting on it so specially?" Because very many Christians have no sense of the great difference between the religion of the mind and the religion of the heart, and the former is far more diligently cultivated than the latter. They know not how infinitely greater the heart is than the mind. It is in this that one of the chief causes must be sought of the feebleness of our Christian life, and it is only as this is understood that waiting on God will bring its full blessing.

Proverbs 3:5 may help to make my meaning plain. Speaking of a life in the fear and favor of God, it says, "Trust in the Lord with all your heart, and lean not upon your own understanding." In all religion we have to use these two powers. The mind has to gather knowledge from God's word, and prepare the food by which the heart with the inner life is to be nourished. But herein lies a terrible danger—our leaning to our own understanding, and trusting in our understanding of divine things. People imagine that if they are occupied with the truth, the spiritual life will of its own be strengthened. And this is by no means the case. The understanding deals with conceptions and images of divine things, but it cannot reach the real life of the soul. It is with the heart that man believes and comes in touch with God. It is in the heart God has given His Spirit, to be there to us the presence and the power of God working in us. In all our religion it is the heart that must trust and love and worship and obey. My mind is utterly impotent in creating

53

or maintaining the spiritual life within me. The heart must wait on God for Him to work it in me.

It is same as in the physical life. My reason may tell me what to eat and drink, and how the food nourishes me. But in the eating and feeding my reason can do nothing. The body has its organs for that special purpose. Just so, reason may tell me what God's word says, but it can do nothing to the feeding of the soul on the bread of life—this the heart alone can do by faith and trust in God. A man may be studying the nature and effects of food or sleep; when he wants to eat or sleep he sets aside his thoughts and study, and uses the power of eating or sleeping. And so the Christian needs ever, when he has studied or heard God's word, to cease from his thoughts, to put no trust in them, and to awaken his heart to open itself before God—seeking the living fellowship with Him.

This is now the blessedness of waiting upon God, that I confess the impotence of all my thoughts and efforts, and set myself still to bow my heart before Him in holy silence, and to trust Him to renew and strengthen His own work in me. And this is just the lesson of our text, "Be of good courage, and He shall strengthen thine heart, all ye who hope in the Lord." Remember the difference between knowing with the mind and believing with the heart. Beware of the temptation of leaning upon your understanding, with its clear, strong thoughts. They only help you to know what the heart must get from God: in themselves they are but images and shadows. Present it before Him as that wonderful part of your spiritual nature in which God reveals Himself, and by which you can know Him. Cultivate the greatest confidence that, though you cannot see into your heart, God is working there by His Holy Spirit. Let the heart wait at times in perfect silence and quiet; in its hidden depths God will work. Be sure of this and just wait on Him.

No knowledge of the air or the food around me can nourish me, except it enters into my inward life. And no knowledge of the truths of God can profit me, except as He, by His Spirit, enters into my inmost being and dwells within me. It is with the heart I must wait upon God. It is into the heart I must receive God. It is in the heart God will give His Spirit and every spiritual blessing in Christ. Give your whole heart, with its secret workings, into God's hands continually. He wants the heart and takes it, and as God, dwells in it. "Be of good courage, and He shall strengthen thine heart, all ye who hope in the Lord."

"My soul waiteth only upon God!"

REFLECTION

1. We can advance no further or deeper into the holy place of God's presence to wait on Him there, than our heart is prepared for it by the Holy Spirit.

2. What is the difference between religion of the mind and religion of the heart? Because many Christians have no sense of the great difference between the two, the former is far more diligently cultivated than the latter.

3. Is it with the heart or the mind that man believes and comes in touch with God? Or is it both?

DAY 10

WAITING ON GOD IN HUMBLE FEAR AND HOPE

"Behold, the eye of the Lord is upon them that fear Him, upon them that hope in His mercy; to deliver their soul from death, and to keep them alive in famine. Our soul waiteth for the Lord; He is our help and our shield, for our heart shall rejoice in Him, because we have trusted in His holy name. Let thy mercy, O Lord, be upon us, according as we hope in thee" (Psalms 33:18-22).

God's eye is upon His people and their eye is upon Him. In waiting upon God, our eye, looking up to Him, meets His looking down upon us. This is the blessedness of waiting upon God—that takes our eyes and thoughts away from ourselves, even our needs and desires, and occupies us with our God. We worship Him in His glory and love, with His all-seeing eye watching over us, that He may supply our every need. Let us consider this wonderful meeting between God and His people, and mark well what we are taught here of those on whom God's eye rests, and of Him on whom our eye rests.

"Behold, the eye of the Lord is upon them that fear Him, upon them that hope in His mercy" (Psalms 33:18).

Fear and hope are generally thought to be in conflict with each other. In the presence and worship of God they are found side by side in perfect and beautiful harmony; and this is because in God himself all apparent contradictions are reconciled. Righteousness and peace, judgment and mercy, holiness and love, infinite power and infinite gentleness, a majesty that is exalted above all heaven, and a condescension that bows very low, meet and kiss each other. There is indeed a fear that has torment that is cast out entirely by perfect love. But there is a fear that is found in the very heavens. In the song of Moses and the Lamb they sing, "Who shall not fear You, O Lord, and glorify Thy name?" And out of the very throne the voice came, "Praise our God, all ye His servants, and ye that fear Him" (Revelation 19:5). Let us in our waiting ever seek to fear the glorious and fearful name, the Lord your God. The deeper we bow before His holiness in holy fear and adoring awe, in deep reverence and humble self-abasement, even as the angels veil their faces before the throne, the more will His holiness rest upon us, and the soul be fitted to have God reveal himself. The deeper we enter into the truth "that no flesh glory in His presence," will it be given us to see His glory. "The eye of the Lord is on them that fear Him."

"On them that hope in His mercy." So far will the true fear of God be from keeping us back from hope, it will stimulate and strengthen it. The lower we bow, the deeper we feel we have nothing to hope in but His mercy. The lower we bow, the nearer God will come and make our hearts bold to trust Him. Let every exercise of waiting, let our whole habit of waiting on God be pervaded by abounding hope—a hope as bright and boundless as God's mercy. The fatherly kindness of God is such that, in whatever state we come to Him, we may confidently hope in His mercy.

Such are God's waiting ones. And now, think of the God on whom we wait. "The eye of the Lord is on them that fear Him, on them that hope in His mercy; to deliver their soul from death, and to keep them alive in famine." Not to prevent the danger of death and famine—this is often needed to stir us up to wait on Him—but to deliver and to keep alive. The dangers are often very real and dark. The situation, whether in the temporal or spiritual life, may appear to be utterly hopeless, yet there is always one hope; God's eye is on them. That eye sees the danger, and sees in tender love His trembling waiting child, and sees the moment when the heart is ripe for the blessing, and sees the way in which it is to come. This living, mighty God, oh, let us fear Him and hope in His mercy. And let us humbly but boldly say, "Our soul waits for the Lord; He is our help and our shield. Let Your mercy be upon us, O Lord, according as we hope in You."

Oh, the blessedness of waiting on such a God! He is a very present help in time of trouble; a shield and defense against every danger. Children of God, will you not learn to sink down in entire helplessness and impotence, and in stillness to wait and see the salvation of God? In the utmost spiritual famine, and when death appears to prevail, oh, wait on God. He does deliver. He does keep alive. Say it not only in solitude, but say it to each other; the psalm speaks not of one but of God's people. "Our soul waits on the Lord: He is our help and our shield." Strengthen and encourage each other in the holy exercise of waiting, that each may not only say it of himself, but of his brethren, "We have waited for Him. We will be glad and rejoice in His salvation."

"My soul, wait thou only upon God!"

REFLECTION

1. Lord, I confess the impotence of all my thoughts and efforts, and bow my heart before You in holy silence, and trust You to renew and strengthen Your own work in me.

2. Do not think of waiting on God until you are willing to walk in His path.

DAY 11

WAITING ON GOD PATIENTLY

"Rest in the Lord, and wait patiently for Him. Those that wait upon the Lord, they shall inherit the earth"
(Psalm 37:7,9).

"In your patience possess ye your souls" (Luke 21:9).

"You have need of patience, that, after ye have done the will of God, ye might receive the promise"
(Hebrews 10:36).

"Let patience have its perfect work, that ye may be perfect and entire, wanting nothing" (James 1:4).

Such words of the Holy Spirit show us what an important element in the Christian life and character patience is. And nowhere is there a better place for cultivating or displaying it than in waiting on God. There we discover how impatient we are, and what our impatience means. We confess at times that we are impatient with men and circumstances that hinder us, or with our slow progress in the Christian life. If we truly set ourselves to wait upon God, we shall find that it is with Him we are impatient, because He does not at once, or as soon as we wish, do our bidding. It is in waiting upon God that our eyes are opened to believe in His wise and sovereign will, and to see that the sooner and the more completely we yield absolutely to it, the more surely His blessing can come to us.

"So then it is not of him that willeth, nor of him that runneth, but of God that showeth mercy" (Romans 9:16). We have as little power to increase or strengthen our spiritual life,

59

as we had to originate it. We "were born not of blood, nor of the will of the flesh, nor of the will of man, but of God" (John 1:13). Even so, our willing and running, our desire and effort, works for nothing. All is "of God that shows mercy." All the exercises of the spiritual life, our reading and praying, our willing and doing, have their very great value. But they can go no farther than this, that they point the way and prepare us in humility to look to and to depend alone upon God Himself, and in patience to await His good time and mercy. The waiting is to teach us our absolute dependence upon God's mighty working, and to make us in perfect patience place ourselves at His disposal. They that wait on the Lord shall inherit the land—the promised land and its blessing. The heirs must wait, they can afford to wait.

"Rest in the lord, and wait patiently for Him." The margin reference gives for "Rest in the Lord," "Be silent to the Lord," or "Be still before the Lord." It is resting in the Lord, in His will, His promise, His faithfulness, and His love, that makes patience easy. And the resting in Him is nothing but being silent unto Him, still before Him. Having our thoughts and wishes, our fears and hopes, hushed into calm and quiet in that great peace of God that passes all understanding. That peace keeps the heart and mind when we are anxious for anything, because we have made our request known to Him. The rest, the silence, the stillness, and the patient waiting, all find their strength and joy in God Himself.

The reasonableness and the blessedness of patience will be opened up to the waiting soul. Our patience will be seen to be the counterpart of God's patience. He longs far more to bless us fully than we can desire it. But, as the husbandman has great patience until the fruit becomes ripe, so God bows Himself to our slowness and bears long with us. Let us remember this, and wait patiently. With each promise and every answer to prayer the word is true, "I the Lord will hasten it in its time."

"Rest in the Lord, and wait patiently for Him." Yes, for Him. Seek not only the help, the gift you need; but seek Himself; wait for Him. Give God His glory by resting in Him, by trusting him fully, by waiting patiently for Him. This patience honors Him greatly. It leaves Him, as God on the throne, to do His work. It yields self wholly into His hands. It lets God be God. If your waiting is for some special request, wait patiently. If your waiting is more the exercise of the spiritual life seeking to know and have more of God—wait patiently. Whether it is in the shorter specific periods of waiting, or as the continuous habit of the soul, rest in the Lord, be still before the Lord, and wait patiently. "They that wait on the Lord shall inherit the earth."

"My soul waiteth only upon God!"

REFLECTION

1. What are other words for *waiting, patience, suffering, and endurance*?

2. What does it mean to "Rest in the Lord?"

DAY 12

WAITING ON GOD: KEEPING HIS WAYS

"Wait upon the Lord, and keepeth His way, And He shalt exalt thee to inherit the earth" (Psalms 37:34).

If we desire to find a man whom we long to meet, we inquire where the places and the ways are where he is to be found. When waiting on God, we need to be very careful that we keep His ways. Out of these we never can expect to find Him. "Thou meeteth him that rejoiceth and worketh righteousness, those that remember thee in thy ways" (Psalms 64:5). We may be sure that God is never and nowhere to be found but in His ways. And that there, by the soul who seeks and patiently waits, He is always most surely to be found. "Wait upon the Lord, and keepeth His ways, and He shall exalt thee."

See how close is the connection between the two parts of the injunction. "Wait on the Lord,"—that has to do with worship and disposition; "and keep His ways,"—that deals with walk and work. The outer life must be in harmony with the inner, and the inner must be the inspiration and the strength for the outer. It is our God who has made known His ways in His Word for our conduct, and invites our confidence for His grace and help in our heart. If we do not keep His ways, our waiting on Him cannot bring blessing. The surrender to a full obedience to His will is the secret of full access to all the blessings of His fellowship.

Notice how strongly this comes out in the psalm. It speaks of the evildoer who prospers in his way and calls on the believer not to fear. When we see men around us prosperous and happy while they forsake God's ways, and ourselves left in difficulty or suffering, we are in danger of first fretting at what appears unfair, and then gradually yielding to seek our prosperity in their path. The psalm says, "Fret not yourself; trust in the Lord, and do good. Rest in the Lord, and wait patiently for Him; cease from anger, and forsake wrath. Depart from evil, and do good; the Lord forsaketh not His saints. The righteous shall inherit the earth. The law of his God is in his heart; none of his steps shall slide." And then follows—the word occurs for the third time in the psalm—"Waiteth upon the Lord, and keepeth His ways." Do what God asks you to do. God will do more than you can ask Him to do.

And let no one give way to the fear that says, I cannot keep His ways. It is this that robs us of our confidence. It is true you do not have the strength yet to keep all His ways. But keep carefully those for which you have received strength already. Surrender yourself willingly and trustingly to keep all God's ways, in the strength which will come in waiting on Him. Give up your whole being to God without reserve and without doubt. He will prove Himself God to you, and work in you that which is pleasing in His sight through Jesus Christ. Keep His ways, as you know them in the Word. Keep His ways, as nature teaches them, in always doing what appears right. Keep His ways, as Providence points them out. Keep His ways, as the Holy Spirit suggests. Do not think of waiting on God while you say you are not willing to walk in His path. However weak you feel, only be willing, and He who has worked to will, will work to do everything by His power.

"Waiteth upon the Lord, and keepeth His ways." It may be that the consciousness of shortcoming and sin makes our text look more like a hindrance than a help in waiting on God. Let it not be so. Have we not said more than once, the very starting-point and groundwork of this waiting is utter and absolute impotence? Why then not come with everything evil you feel in yourself, every memory of unwillingness, unwatchfulness, unfaithfulness, and all that causes such unceasing self-condemnation? Put your trust in God's omnipotence, and find in waiting on God your deliverance. Your failure has been owing to only one thing; you sought to conquer and obey in your own strength. Come and bow before God until you learn that He is the God who alone is good, and alone can work any good thing. Believe that in you, and all that nature can do, there is no true power. Be content to receive from God each moment the in-working of His mighty grace and life, and waiting on God will become the renewal of your strength to run in His ways and not be weary, to walk in His paths and never faint. "Waiteth upon the Lord, and keepeth His ways" will be command and promise in one.

"My soul waiteth thou only upon God!"

REFLECTION

1. How does our consciousness of sin keep us from waiting on God?

2. Consider how the outer and inner life must be in harmony.

DAY 13

WAITING ON GOD FOR MORE THAN WE KNOW

"And now, Lord, what wait I for? My hope is in Thee.
Deliver me from all my transgressions" (Psalms 39:7,8).

There may be times when we feel as if we knew not what we are waiting for. There may be other times when we think we do know, and when it would just be so good for us to realize that we do not know what to ask as we ought. God is able to do for us exceeding abundantly above what we ask or think, and we are in danger of limiting Him, when we confine our desires and prayers to our own thoughts of them. It is a great thing at times to say, as our psalm says: "And now, Lord, what wait I for? I scarce know or can tell; this only I can say—'My hope is in You.'"

How we see this limiting of God in the case of Israel! When Moses promised them meat in the wilderness, they doubted, saying, "Can God furnish a table in the wilderness? Behold, He smote the rock that the water gushed out, and the streams overflowed; can He give bread also? Can He provide flesh for His people?" (Psalm 78:19,20). If they had been asked whether God could provide streams in the desert, they would have answered, "Yes. God had done it, and He could do it again." But when the thought came of God doing something new, they limited Him. Their expectation could not rise beyond their past experience or their own thoughts of what was possible. Even so we may be limiting God by our conceptions of what He has promised or is able to do. Do let us beware of limiting the Holy One of Israel in our very prayer. Let us believe that every promise of God we plead has a divine meaning, infinitely beyond our thoughts of them. Let us believe that His fulfillment of them can be,

65

in a power and an abundance of grace, beyond our largest grasp of thought. And let us therefore cultivate the habit of waiting on God, not only for what we think we need, but for all His grace and power are ready to do for us.

In every true prayer there are two hearts in exercise. The one is your heart, with its little, dark, human thoughts of what you need and God can do. The other is God's great heart, with its infinite, its divine purposes of blessing. What do you think? To which of these two ought the larger place to be given in your approach to Him? Undoubtedly, to the heart of God; everything depends upon knowing and being occupied with that. But how little this is done. This is what waiting on God is meant to teach you. Just think of God's wonderful love and redemption, in the meaning these words must have to Him. Confess how little you understand what God is willing to do for you, and say each time as you pray "And now, what wait I for?" My heart cannot say. God's heart knows and waits to give. "My hope is in You." Wait on God to do for you more than you can ask or think.

Apply this to the prayer that follows; "Deliver me from all my transgressions." You have prayed to be delivered from temper, or pride, or self-will. It is as if it is in vain. May it not be that you have had your own thoughts about the way or the extent of God's doing it, and have never waited on the God of glory, according to the riches of His glory, to do for you what has not entered the heart of man to conceive? Learn to worship God as the God who does wonders, who wishes to prove in you that He can do something supernatural and divine. Bow before Him, wait upon Him, until your soul realizes that you are in the hands of a divine and almighty worker. Consent not to know what and how He will work, expect it to be something altogether god-like, something to be waited for in deep humility, and received only by His divine power. Let the, "And now, Lord, what wait I for? My hope is in You" become the spirit of every longing and every prayer. He will in His time do His work.

Dear soul, in waiting on God you may often be ready to be weary, because you hardly know what you have to expect. I pray you, be of good courage—this ignorance is often one of the best signs. He is teaching you to leave all in His hands, and to wait on Him alone. "Wait on the Lord! Be strong, and let your heart take courage. Yes, wait on the Lord."

"My soul waiteth only upon God!"

REFLECTION

1. In our prayers, there is often two hearts in conflict, the heart that focuses on "my needs and wants," and the other that seeks God's glory and will. How do we get more of the latter in our prayer life?

DAY 14

WAITING ON GOD: THE WAY TO THE NEW SONG

"I waited patiently for the Lord, and He inclined unto me, and heard my cry ... And He hath put a new song in my mouth, even praise unto our God" (Psalms 40:1-3).

Come and listen to the testimony of one who can speak from experience of the sure and blessed outcome of patient waiting upon God. True patience is so foreign to our self-confident nature, it is so indispensable in our waiting upon God, it is such an essential element of true faith, that

67

we may well once again meditate on what the word has to teach us.

The word patience is derived from the Latin word for suffering. It suggests the thought of being under the constraint of some power from which we want to be free. At first we submit against our will. Experience teaches us that when it is vain to resist, patient endurance is our wisest course. In waiting on God it is of infinite consequence that we not only submit, because we are compelled to, but because we lovingly and joyfully consent to be in the hands of our blessed Father. Patience then becomes our highest blessedness and our highest grace. It honors God, and gives Him time to have His way with us. It is the highest expression of our faith in His goodness and faithfulness. It brings the soul perfect rest in the assurance that God is carrying on His work. It is the token of our full consent that God should deal with us in such a way and time as He thinks best. True patience is the losing of our self-will in His perfect will.

Such patience is needed for the true and full waiting on God. Such patience is the growth and fruit of our first lessons in the school of waiting. To many it will appear strange how difficult it is to truly wait upon God. The great stillness of soul before God that sinks into its own helplessness and waits for Him to reveal Himself; the deep humility that is afraid to let its own will or its own strength work aught except as God works to will and to do; the meekness that is content to be and to know nothing except as God gives His light; the entire resignation of the will that only wants to be a vessel in which His holy will can move and mold—all these elements of perfect patience are not found at once. But they will come in measure as the soul maintains its position, and says: "Truly my soul waits upon God; from Him comes my salvation. He only is my rock and my salvation."

Have you ever noticed what proof we have that patience is a grace for which very special grace is given, in these words of Paul: "Strengthened with all might, according to His glorious power, unto all" —what? "patience and long-suffering with joyfulness" (Colossians 1:11). Yes, we need to be strengthened with all God's might, and that according to the measure of His glorious power, if we are to wait on God in all patience. It is God revealing himself in us as our life and strength that will enable us with perfect patience to leave all in His hands. If we are inclined to despond, because we have not such patience, let us be of good courage. It is in the course of our feeble and very imperfect waiting that God himself by His hidden power strengthens us and works out in us the patience of the saints, the patience of Christ himself.

Listen to the voice of one who was deeply tried, "I waited patiently for the Lord, and He inclined unto me, and heard my cry." Hear what he passed through, "He brought me up also out of an horrible pit, out of the miry clay, and set my feet upon a rock, and established my goings. And He hath put a new song in my mouth, even praise unto our God" (Psalms 40:2,3). Patient waiting upon God brings a rich reward; the deliverance is sure; God himself will put a new song into your mouth. O soul! Be not impatient, whether it be in the exercise of prayer and worship that you find it difficult to wait, or in the delay in respect of definite requests, or in the fulfilling of your heart's desire for the revelation of God himself in a deeper spiritual life—fear not, but rest in the Lord, and wait patiently for Him. And if you sometimes feel as if patience is not your gift, then remember it is God's gift, and take that prayer, "The Lord direct thine hearts into the patience of Christ" (2 Thessalonians 3:5). Into the patience with which you are to wait on God, He himself will guide you.

"My soul waiteth thou only upon God!"

25

REFLECTION

1. Patience is one of the most difficult graces for us to practice, but one of the most indispensable when our sanctification is in view. How may we cultivate more patience?

2. True patience is losing self-will for God's will.

DAY 15

WAITING ON GOD FOR HIS COUNSEL

"They soon forgot His works: they waited not for His counsel: ... they provoked Him with their counsel"
(Psalms 106:13,43).

This is said of the sin of God's people in the wilderness. He had wonderfully redeemed them, and was prepared as wonderfully to supply their every need. But, when the time of need came, "they waited not for His counsel." They thought not that the Almighty God was their Leader and Provider. They asked not what His plans might be. They simply thought the thoughts of their own heart and tempted and provoked God by their unbelief. "They waited not for His counsel."

How this has been the sin of God's people in all ages! In the land of Canaan, in the days of Joshua, the only three failures of which we read were owing to this one sin. In going up against Ai, in making a covenant with the Gibeonites, in settling down without going up to possess the whole land, they waited not for His counsel. And so even the advanced believer is in danger from this most subtle of temptations— taking God's word and thinking his own thoughts of them, and not waiting for His counsel. Let us take the warning and see what Israel teaches us. And let us very specially regard it not only as a danger to which the individual is exposed, but as one against which God's people, in their collective capacity, need to be on their guard.

Our whole relation to God is rooted in the fact that His will is to be done in us and by us as it is in heaven. He has promised to make known His will to us by His Spirit, the Guide into all truth. And our position is to be that of waiting for His counsel, as the only guide of our thoughts and actions. In our church worship, in our prayer-meetings, in our conventions, in all our gatherings as managers, or directors, or committees, or helpers in any part of the work for God, our first object ought ever to be to ascertain the mind of God. God always works according to the counsel of His will. The more that counsel of His will is sought and found and honored, the more surely and mightily will God do His work for us and through us.

The great danger in all such assemblies is that in our consciousness of having our Bible, and our past experience of God's leading, and our sound creed, and our honest wish to do God's will, we trust in these, and do not realize that with every step we need and may have a heavenly guidance. There may be elements of God's will, applications of God's word, experiences of the close presence and leading of God, manifestations of the power of His Spirit, of which we know nothing as yet. God may be willing, no, God is willing to open up these to the souls who are intently set upon allowing Him to have His way entirely, and who are willing in patience to wait for His making it known. When we come together praising God for all He has done and taught and given, we may at the same time be limiting Him by not expecting greater things. It was when God had given the water out of the rock that they did not trust Him for bread. It was when God had given Jericho into his hands that Joshua thought the victory over Ai was sure. And so, while we think that we know and trust the power of God for what we may expect, we may be hindering Him by not giving time, and not definitely cultivating the habit of waiting for His counsel.

A minister's most solemn duty is in teaching people to wait upon God. Why was it that in the house of Cornelius, when "Peter spoke these words, the Holy Ghost fell upon all that heard him?" They had said, "We are here before God to hear all things that are commanded you of God." We may come together to give and to listen to the most earnest exposition of God's truth with little spiritual profit if there be not the waiting for God's counsel. In all our gatherings we need to believe in the Holy Spirit as the Guide and Teacher of God's saints when they wait to be led by Him into the things that God has prepared, and which the heart cannot conceive.

More stillness of soul to realize God's presence; more consciousness of ignorance of what God's great plans may be; more faith in the certainty that God has greater things to show us; more longing that He himself may be revealed in new glory: these must be the marks of the assemblies of God's saints, if they would avoid the reproach, "They waited not for His counsel."

"My soul waiteth thou only upon God!"

REFLECTION
1. How are we listening to God's counsel?

2. What are the means by which God has ordained to reveal His will to us?

DAY 16

WAITING ON GOD FOR HIS LIGHT IN THE HEART

"I wait for the Lord, my soul doth wait, and in His word do I hope. My soul waiteth for the Lord more than they that watch for the morning: yea, more than they that watch for the morning" (Psalms 130:5,6).

With what intense longing the morning light is often waited for. By the mariners in a shipwrecked vessel; by a benighted traveler in a dangerous country; by an army that finds itself surrounded by an enemy. The morning light will show what hope of escape there may be. The morning may bring life and liberty. And so the saints of God in darkness have longed for the light of His countenance, more than watchmen for the morning. They have said, "More than watchmen for the morning, my soul waiteth for the Lord." Can we say that too? Our waiting on God can have no higher object than simply having His light shine on us, and in us, and through us, all the day.

God is Light. God is a Sun. Paul says; "God has shined in our hearts to give the light" (2 Corinthians 4:6). What light? "The light of the glory of God, in the face of Jesus Christ." Just as the sun shines its beautiful, life-giving light on and into our earth, so God shines into our hearts the light of His glory, of His love, in Christ His Son. Our heart is meant to have that light filling and gladdening it all the day. It can have it, because God is our sun, and it is written, "Your sun shall no more go down forever." God's love shines on us without ceasing.

But can we indeed enjoy it all the day? We can. And how can we? Let nature give us the answer. Those beautiful trees and flowers, with all this green grass, what do they do to keep the sun shining on them? They do nothing. They simply bask in the sunshine when it comes. The sun is millions of miles away, but over all that distance it sends its own light and joy. The tiniest flower that lifts its little head upwards is met by the same exuberance of light and blessing as floods the widest landscape. We need not care for the light we need for our day's work. The sun cares, provides and shines the light around us all the day. We simply count upon it, and receive it, and enjoy it.

The only difference between nature and grace is what the trees and the flowers do unconsciously, as they drink in the blessing of the light, to be with us a voluntary and a loving acceptance. Faith, simple faith in God's Word and love, is to be the opening of the eyes, the opening of the heart, to receive and enjoy the unspeakable glory of His grace. And even as the trees, day by day, and month by month, stand and grow into beauty and fruitfulness, just welcoming whatever sunshine the sun may give, so it is the very highest exercise of our Christian life just to abide in the light of God, and let it, and let Him, fill us with the life and the brightness it brings.

And if you ask, "Can I truly rejoice in God's light all the day, even as naturally and heartily as I recognize and rejoice in the beauty of a bright sunny morning?" I can, indeed. From my breakfast-table I look out on a beautiful valley, with trees and vineyards and mountains. In our spring and autumn months the light in the morning is exquisite, and almost involuntarily we say, "How beautiful!" And the question comes, is it only the light of the sun that is to bring such continual beauty and joy? And is there no provision for the light of God being just as much an unceasing source of joy and gladness? There is, indeed, if the soul will only be still and wait on Him, will only let God shine.

Dear soul! Learn to wait on the Lord, more than watchers for the morning. All within you may be very dark. Is that not the very best reason for waiting for the light of God? The first beginnings of light may be just enough to discover the darkness, and painfully to humble you on account of sin. Can you not trust the light to expel the darkness? Do believe it will. Just bow, even now, in stillness before God, and wait on Him to shine into you. Say, in humble faith: God is light, infinitely brighter and more beautiful than that of the sun. God is light. He is the Father, the eternal, inaccessible, and incomprehensible light. He is the Son, the light concentrated, and embodied, and manifested. He is the Spirit, the light entering and dwelling and shining in our hearts. God is light, and is here shining on my heart. I have been so occupied with my own thoughts and efforts, I have never opened the shutters to let His light in. Unbelief has kept it out. I bow in faith: God's light is shining into my heart. The God of whom Paul wrote, "God has shined into our heart," is my God. What would I think of a sun that could not shine? What shall I think of a God that does not shine? No, God shines! God is light! I will take time, and just be still, and rest in the light of God. My eyes are feeble, and the windows are not clean, but I will wait on the Lord. The light shines, yes, the light will shine in me, and make me full of light. And I shall learn to walk all the day in the light and joy of God. My soul waits on the Lord, more than watchers for the morning.

"My soul waiteth thou only upon God!"

REFLECTION

1. Waiting on God may simply be "having His light shine on us, and in us, and through us, throughout the day." Do we exercise this grace in our daily walk?

2. Sometimes when it's darkest, light is just around the corner.

DAY 17

WAITING ON GOD IN TIMES OF DARKNESS

"I will wait upon the Lord, that hideth His face from the house of Jacob; and I will look for Him" (Isaiah 8:17).

Here we have a servant of God, waiting upon Him, not on behalf of himself, but of his people, from whom God was hiding his face. It suggests to us how our waiting upon God, though it commences with our personal needs, with the desire for the revelation of himself, or of the answer to personal petitions, need not, may not, stop there. We may be walking in the full light of God's countenance, and yet God could be hiding His face from His people around us. Far from our being content to think that this is nothing but the just punishment of their sin, or the consequence of their indifference, we are called with tender hearts to think of their sad estate, and to wait on God on their behalf. The privilege of waiting upon God is one that brings great responsibility. Even as Christ, when He entered God's presence, at once used His place of privilege and honor as intercessor for His people. Likewise, if we know what it is really to enter in and wait upon God, must use our access for our less favored brethren. "I will wait upon the Lord, who hideth His face from the house of Jacob."

You worship with a certain congregation. Possibly there is not the spiritual life or joy either in the preaching or in the fellowship that you seek. You belong to a Church, with its many congregations. There is so much of error or worldliness, of seeking after human wisdom and culture, of trust in ordinances and observances, that you do not wonder that God hides His face, in many cases, and that there is little power for conversion or true edification. Then there are branches of Christian work with which you are connected—a Sunday school, a gospel hall, a young men's association, a mission work abroad—in which the feebleness of the Spirit's working appears to indicate that God is hiding His face. You think that you know the reason. There is too much trust in men and money. There is too much formality and self-indulgence. There is too little faith and prayer; too little love and humility; too little of the spirit of the crucified Jesus. At times you feel as if things are hopeless and nothing will help.

Do believe that God can help and will help. Let the spirit of the prophet come into you, as you take his words, and set yourself to wait on God, on behalf of His erring children. Instead of the tone of judgment or condemnation, of despondency or despair, realize your calling to wait upon God. If others fail in doing it, give yourself wholly to it. The deeper the darkness, the greater the need of appealing to the one and only Deliverer. The greater the self-confidence around you, that knows not that it is poor and wretched and blind, the more urgent the call on you who profess to see the evil and to have access to Him who alone can help, to be at your post, waiting upon God. As often as you are tempted to complain, say ever afresh: 'I will wait on the Lord, who hides His face from the house of Jacob.'

There is a still larger circle—the Christian Church throughout the world. Think of Greek, Roman Catholic, and Protestant churches, and the state of the millions that belong to them. Or think only of the Protestant churches with their open Bible and orthodox creeds. How much nominal profession and formality! How much of the rule of the flesh and of man in the very temple of God! And what abundant proof that God does hide His face!

What are those to do who see and mourn this? The first thing to be done is, "... wait on the Lord, who hides His face from the house of Jacob." Let us wait on God, in the humble confession of the sins of His people. Let us take time and wait on Him in this exercise. Let us wait on God in tender, loving intercession for all saints, our beloved brethren, however wrong their lives or their teaching may appear. Let us wait on God in faith and expectation, until He shows us that He will hear. Let us wait on God, with the simple offering of ourselves to himself, and the earnest prayer that He would send us to our brethren. Let us wait on God, and give Him no rest until He makes Zion a joy in the earth. Yes, let us rest in the Lord, and wait patiently for Him who now hides His face from so many of His children. And let us say of the lifting up of the light of His countenance we desire for all His people, "I wait for the Lord, my soul waits, and my hope is in His word. My soul waits for the Lord, more than the watchers for the morning; yea, the watchers for the morning."

"My soul waiteth thou only upon God!"

REFLECTION

1. There is much formalism and nominal Christianity practiced in the world. Is this our course? Or are we engaged in the patient waiting, and prayers for the cause of Christ on the earth?

DAY 18

WAITING ON GOD TO REVEAL HIMSELF

"And it shall be said in that day, Lo, this is our God; we have waited for Him, and He will save us: this is the Lord; we have waited for Him, we will rejoice and be glad in His salvation" (Isaiah 25:9).

In this passage we have two precious thoughts. The one is that it is the language of God's people who have been united and are waiting on Him. The other is that the fruit of their waiting has been that God has so revealed himself, that they could joyfully say, "Lo, this is our God: This is the Lord." The power and the blessing of united waiting is what we need to learn.

Note the repeated, "We have waited for Him." In some time of trouble the hearts of the people had been drawn together, and ceasing from all human hope or help, with one heart set themselves to wait for their God. Is not this just what we need in our churches and conventions and prayer meetings? Is not the need of the Church and the world great enough to demand it? Are there not in the Church of Christ evils to which no human wisdom is equal? Have we not ritualism and rationalism, formalism and worldliness, robbing the Church of its power? Have we not culture and money and pleasure threatening its spiritual life? Are not the powers of the Church utterly inadequate to cope with the powers of infidelity and iniquity and wretchedness in Christian countries and in heathendom? And is there not in the promise of God, and in the power of the Holy Spirit, a provision made that can meet the need, and give the Church the restful assurance that she is doing all her God expects of her? And would not a united waiting upon God for the

79

supply of His Spirit most certainly seem the needed blessing? We cannot doubt it.

The object of a more definite waiting upon God in our gatherings would be very much the same as in personal worship. It would mean a deeper conviction that God must and will do all. It means a more humble and abiding entrance into our deep helplessness, and the need of entire and unceasing dependence upon Him. It means a more living consciousness that the essential thing is giving God His place of honor and of power. It means a confident expectation that to those who wait on Him, God will, by His Spirit, give the secret of His acceptance and presence, and then, in due time, the revelation of His saving power. The great aim would be to bring every one in a praying and worshipping company under a deep sense of God's presence, so that when they part there will be the consciousness of having met God himself, of having left every request with Him, and of now waiting in stillness while He works out His salvation.

It is this experience that is indicated in our text. The fulfillment of the words may, at times, be in such striking interpositions of God's power that all can join in the cry, "Lo, this is our God; this is the Lord." They may equally become true in spiritual experience, when God's people in their waiting times become so conscious of His presence that in holy awe souls feel, "Lo, this is our God; this is the Lord!"

It is this truth that is too much missed in our meetings for worship. The godly minister has no more difficult, no more solemn, no more blessed task, than to lead his people out to meet God, and before ever he preaches, to bring each one into contact with Him. "We are now here in the presence of God." These words of Cornelius show the way in which Peter's audience was prepared for the coming of the Holy Spirit. Waiting before God, and waiting for God, and waiting on God, is the one condition of God showing His presence.

A company of believers gathered with the one purpose, helping each other by little intervals of silence, to wait on God alone, opening the heart for whatever God may have of new discoveries of evil, of His will, of new openings in work or methods of work, would soon have reason to say, 'Lo, this is our God.' We have waited for Him, and He shall save us. This is the Lord and we have waited for Him. We will be glad and rejoice in His salvation.'

"My soul, waiteth thou only upon God!"

REFLECTION
1. Has not money, pleasure and power been robbing the Church of it's power and spiritual influence? What can we do individually and as a body of believers to combat this trend?

DAY 19
WAITING ON GOD AS A GOD OF JUDGMENT

"Yea, in the way of Thy judgments, O Lord, have we waited for Thee: ... for when Thy judgments are on the earth, the inhabitants of the world learn righteousness" (Isaiah 26:8,9).

"The Lord is a God of judgment: blessed are all they that waiteth for Him" (Isaiah 30:18).

God is a God of mercy and a God of judgment. Mercy and judgment are ever together in His dealings. In the flood, in the deliverance of Israel out of Egypt, in the overthrow

81

of the Canaanites, we constantly see mercy in the midst of judgment. Within the inner circle of His people, we see it as well. The judgment punishes the sin, while mercy saves the sinner. Or, rather, mercy saves the sinner, not in spite of, but by means of, the very judgment that came upon his sin. In waiting on God, we must beware of forgetting this. As we wait we must expect Him as a God of judgment.

"In the way of Your judgments, have we waited for You." That will prove true in our inner experience. If we are honest in our longing for holiness, in our prayer to be wholly the Lord's, His holy presence will stir up and discover hidden sin, and bring us very low in the bitter conviction of the evil of our nature, its opposition to God's law, its impotence to fulfill that law. The words will come true, "Who may abide the day of His coming ... for He is like a refiner's fire" (Malachi 3:2). "Oh that thou wouldest rend the heavens, that thou wouldest come down ... as when the melting fire burns!" (Isaiah 64:1,2). In great mercy God executes, within the soul, His judgments upon sin, as He makes it feel its wickedness and guilt. Many a one tries to flee from these judgments: the soul that longs for God, and for deliverance from sin, bows under them in humility and in hope. In silence of soul it says, "Arise, O Lord: save me, O my God!" (Psalm 3:7); "Let Thy enemies be scattered" (Psalms 68:1); "Yea, in the way of Thy judgments, O Lord, have we waited for Thee" (Isaiah 26:8).

Let no one who seeks to learn the blessed art of waiting on God, wonder if at first the attempt to wait on Him only discovers more of his own sin and darkness. Let no one despair because unconquered sins, or evil thoughts, or great darkness appear to hide God's face. Was not, in His Beloved Son, the gift and bearer of His mercy on Calvary, the mercy as if hidden and lost in the judgment? Oh, submit and sink down deep under the judgment of your every sin. Judgment prepares the way and breaks out in wonderful mercy. It is written, "Zion shall be redeemed with judgment" (Isaiah 1:27). Wait on God, in the faith that His tender mercy is working out in you His redemption in the midst of judgment. Wait for Him and He will be gracious to you.

Yet, there is still another application of unspeakable solemnity. We are expecting God, in the way of His judgments, to visit this earth. We are waiting for Him. What a thought! We know of these coming judgments. We know that there are tens of thousands of our professing Christians who live on in carelessness, and who, if no change comes, must perish under God's hand. Oh, shall we not do our utmost to warn them, to plead for them, that God may have mercy on them. If we feel our want of boldness, want of zeal, want of power, shall we not begin to wait on God more definitely and persistently as a God of judgment, asking Him to reveal himself in the judgments that are coming, that we may be inspired with a new fear of Him and them, and constrained to speak and pray as never before? Truly, waiting on God is not meant to be a spiritual self-indulgence. Its object is to let God and His holiness, Christ and the love that died on Calvary, the Spirit and fire that burns in heaven and came to earth, get possession of us, to warn and arouse men with the message that we are waiting for God in the way of His judgments. O Christian! Prove that you really believe in the God of judgment.

"My soul waiteth thou only upon God!"

REFLECTION
1. Genuine waiting on God is not about self, or personal inclinations, but a meditation on God's holiness and love

83

for us through the work of Christ on Calvary. How can we show we truly believe this?

DAY 20

WAITING ON GOD WHO WAITS ON US

"And therefore will the Lord wait, that He may be gracious unto thee; and therefore will He be exalted, that He may have mercy upon thee: for the Lord is a God of judgment: blessed are all they that waiteth upon Him" *(Isaiah 30:18).*

We must not only think of our waiting upon God, but also of what is more wonderful still, of God's waiting upon us. The vision of Him waiting on us, will give new impulse and inspiration to our waiting upon Him. It will give an unspeakable confidence that our waiting cannot be in vain. If He waits for us, then we may be sure that we are more than welcome and that He rejoices to find those for whom He has been seeking. Let us seek even now, at this moment, in the spirit of lowly waiting on God, to find out something of what it means when He says, "Therefore will the Lord wait, that He may be gracious unto thee." We shall accept and echo back the message, "Blessed are all they that waiteth upon Him."

Look up and see the great God upon His throne. He is Love—an unceasing and inexpressible desire to communicate His own goodness and blessedness to all His creatures. He longs and delights to bless. He has inconceivably glorious purposes concerning every one of His children, by the power of His Holy Spirit, to reveal in them His love and power. He waits with all the longings of a father's heart. He waits that He may be gracious unto you. And each time you come to wait upon Him, or seek to maintain in daily life the holy habit of waiting, you may look up and see Him ready to meet you, waiting that He may be gracious unto you. Yes, connect every exercise, every breath of the life of waiting, with faith's vision of your God waiting for you.

And if you ask, how is it, if He waits to be gracious, that even after I come and wait upon Him, He does not give the help I seek, but waits on longer and longer? There is a double answer. The one is that God is a wise husbandman, "who waits for the precious fruit of the earth, and has long patience for it." He cannot gather the fruit until it is ripe. He knows when we are spiritually ready to receive the blessing to our profit and His glory. Waiting in the sunshine of His love is what will ripen the soul for His blessing. Waiting under the cloud of trial and suffering that breaks in showers of blessing, is as needful. Be assured that if God waits longer than you could wish, it is only to make the blessing doubly precious. God waited four thousand years, until the fullness of time, before He sent His Son. Our times are in His hands. He will avenge His elect speedily and He will make haste for our help, not delaying one hour too long.

The other answer points to what has been said before. The giver is more than the gift. God is more than the blessing; and our being kept waiting on Him is the only way for our learning to find our life and joy in Him. Oh, if God's children only knew what a glorious God they have and what a privilege it is to be linked in fellowship with himself, then they would rejoice in Him, even when He keeps them waiting. They would learn to understand better than ever, "Therefore will the Lord wait, that He may be gracious unto thee." His waiting will be the highest proof of His graciousness.

"Blessed are all they that waiteth upon Him." Our Queen has her ladies-in-waiting. The position is one of subordination and service, and yet it is considered one of the highest dignity and privilege, because a wise and gracious sovereign makes them companions and friends. What a dignity and blessedness to be attendants-in-waiting on the Everlasting God, ever on the watch for every indication of His will or favor, ever conscious of His nearness, His goodness, and His grace! "The Lord is good to them that waiteth upon Him." "Blessed are all they that wait for Him." Yes, it is blessed when a waiting soul and a waiting God meet each other. God cannot do His work without His and our waiting His time; let waiting be our work, as it is His. And if His waiting is nothing but goodness and graciousness, let ours be nothing but a rejoicing in that goodness, and a confident expectancy of that grace. And let every thought of waiting become to us simply the expression of unmingled and unutterable blessedness, because it brings us to a God who waits that He may make himself known to us perfectly as the Gracious One.

"My soul waiteth thou only upon God!"

REFLECTION

1. What is the relationship between our waiting on God, and His waiting upon us?

2. Waiting in the sunshine of His love ripens our soul for His blessings.

3. Consider that He knows when we are spiritually ready to receive His blessing for our good and His glory.

DAY 21

WAITING ON GOD THE ALMIGHTY ONE

"They that wait upon the Lord shall renew their strength; they shall mount up with wings as eagles; they shall run and not be weary; they shall walk and not faint" (Isaiah 40:31).

Waiting always partakes of the character of our thoughts of the one on whom we wait. Our waiting on God will depend greatly on our faith of what He is. In our text we have the close of a passage in which God reveals himself as the Everlasting and Almighty One. It is as that revelation enters our soul that the waiting will become the spontaneous expression of what we know Him to be—a God altogether most worthy to be waited upon.

Listen to the words, "Why sayest thou, O Jacob, my way is hid from the Lord?" (Isaiah 40:27). Why do you speak as if God does not hear or help?

"Hast thou not known, hast thou not heard, that the Everlasting One, the Lord, the Creator of the ends of the earth, fainteth not, neither is weary?" So far from it, "He giveth power to the faint, and to them that have no might He increaseth strength. Even the youths" and "the glory of young men is their strength"—"even the youths shall faint, and the young men shall utterly fall" (Isaiah 40:28-30). All that is accounted strong with man shall come to nought. "But they that wait on the Lord," on the Everlasting One, who does not faint, neither is weary, they "shall renew their strength; they shall mount up with wings as eagles; they shall run and,"—listen now, they shall be strong with the strength of God, and even as He, "shall not be weary; they shall walk and," even as He, "not faint."

Yes, "they shall mount up with wings as eagles." You know what eagles' wings mean. The eagle is the king of birds, it soars the highest into the heavens. Believers are to live a heavenly life, in the very presence and love and joy of God. They are to live where God lives. They need God's strength to rise there. To them that wait on Him it shall be given.

You know how the eagle's wings are obtained: Only by the eagle birth. You are born of God. You have the eagle's wings. You may not have known it. You may not have used them, but God can and will teach you to use them.

You know how the eagles are taught the use of their wings. See yonder cliff rising a thousand feet out of the sea. See high up a ledge on the rock, where there is an eagle's nest with its treasure of two young eaglets. See the mother bird come and stir up her nest, and with her beak push the timid birds over the precipice. See how they flutter and fall and sink toward the depth. See now (Deuteronomy 32: 11): "... how she fluttereth over her young, spreadeth abroad her wings, taketh them, beareth them on her wings," and so, as they ride upon her wings, brings them to a place of safety. And so she does once and again, each time casting them out over the precipice, and then again taking and carrying them. "So the Lord alone did lead him." Yes, the instinct of that eagle mother was God's gift, a single ray of that love in which the Almighty trains His people to mount as on eagles' wings.

He stirs up your nest. He disappoints your hopes. He brings down your confidence. He makes you fear and tremble, as all your strength fails, and you feel utterly weary and helpless. And all the while He is spreading His strong wings for you to rest your weakness on, and offering His everlasting Creator-strength to work in you. And all He asks is that you should sink down in your weariness and wait on Him, and allow Him in His Jehovah-strength to carry you as you ride upon the wings of His Omnipotence.

Dear child of God! I pray, lift up your eyes, and behold your God! Listen to Him who says that He faints not, neither is weary, the One who promises that you too shall not faint or be weary, who asks nothing but this one thing—that you should wait on Him. Oh! Will you not do what God asks. Just be quiet and let Him work and let your answer be, with such a God, so mighty, so faithful, so tender,

"My soul waiteth thou only upon God!"

REFLECTION

1. To wait effectively we must first reflect on who He is, and to take into our souls the truth of His love and His worthiness to be waited upon.

DAY 22

THE CERTAINTY OF BLESSING
OF WAITING ON GOD

"Thou shalt know that I am the Lord; for they shall not be ashamed that waiteth upon Me" (Isaiah 49:23).

"Blessed are all they that waiteth for Him" (Isaiah 30:18).

What promises! How God seeks to draw us to waiting on Him by the most positive assurance that it never can be in vain; "They shall not be ashamed that waiteth for Me." How strange that, though we should so often have experienced it, we are yet so slow of learning that this blessed waiting must and can be as the very breath of our life, a continuous resting in God's presence and His love, an unceasing yielding of ourselves for Him to perfect His work in us. Let us once again listen and meditate, until our heart says with new conviction; "Blessed are they that waiteth for Him!" Our sixth day's lesson we found in the prayer of Psalms 25: "Let none that wait on Thee be ashamed." The very prayer shows how we fear lest it might be. Let us listen to God's answer until every fear is banished and we send back to heaven the words God speaks. Yes, Lord, we believe what You say: "All they that waiteth for Me shall not be ashamed." Blessed are all they that waiteth for Him."

The context of each of these two passages points us to times when God's Church was in great straits, and to the human eye there was no possibility of deliverance. But God interposes with His word of promise and pledges His Almighty Power for the deliverance of His people. And it is as the God who has himself undertaken the work of their redemption, that He invites them to wait on Him, and assures them that disappointment is impossible. We, too, are living in days in which there is much in the state of the Church, with its profession and its formalism that is indescribably sad. Amidst all we praise God for, there is much to mourn over! Were it not for God's promises we might well despair. But in His promises the Living God has given and bound Himself to us. He calls us to wait on Him. He assures us we shall not be put to shame. Oh that our hearts might learn to wait before Him, until He Himself reveals to us what His promises mean, and in the promises reveals Himself in His hidden glory! We shall be irresistibly drawn to wait on Him alone. God increase the company of those who say, "Our soul waiteth for the Lord. He is our Help and our Shield" (Psalms 33:20).

This waiting upon God on behalf of His Church and people will depend greatly upon the place that waiting on Him has taken in our personal life. The mind may often have beautiful visions of what God has promised to do, and the lips may speak of them in stirring words, but these are not really the measure of our faith or power. No, it is what we really know of God in our personal experience—conquering the enemies within, reigning and ruling, revealing himself in His holiness and power in our inmost being—this will be the real measure of the spiritual blessing we expect from Him, and bring to our fellow men. It is as we know how blessed the waiting on God has become to our own souls that we shall confidently hope in the blessing to come on the Church around us, and the keyword of all our expectations will be as He has said: "All they that wait on Me shall not be ashamed." From what He has done in us, we shall trust Him to do mighty things around us.

"Blessed are all they that waiteth for Him." Yes, blessed even now in the waiting. The promised blessings, for ourselves,

91

or for others, may tarry. The unutterable blessedness of knowing and having Him who has promised, the Divine Blesser, the Living Fountain of the coming blessings, is even now ours. Do let this truth get full possession of your souls. Waiting on God is itself the highest privilege of the creature, the highest blessedness of His redeemed child.

Even as the sunshine enters with its light and warmth, with its beauty and blessing, into every little blade of grass that rises upward out of the cold earth, so the Everlasting God meets, in the greatness and the tenderness of His love, each waiting child, to shine in his heart "the light of the knowledge of the glory of God in the face of Jesus Christ." Read these words again, until your heart learns to know what God waits to do to you. Who can measure the difference between the great sun and that little blade of grass? And yet the grass has all of the sun it can need or hold. Do believe that in waiting on God, His greatness and your littleness suit and meet each other most wonderfully. Just bow in emptiness and poverty and utter impotence, in humility and meekness and surrender to His will, before His great glory, and be still. As you wait on Him, God draws near. He will reveal Himself as the God who will fulfill mightily His every promise. And let your heart ever again take up the song, "Blessed are all they that waiteth for Him."

"My soul waiteth thou only upon God!"

REFLECTION

1. How are we listening and meditating with renewed conviction upon waiting?

2. Do we really believe that God will never disappoint us if we truly wait on Him?

DAY 23

WAITING ON GOD FOR UNLOOKED-FOR THINGS

"For since the beginning of the world men have not heard, nor perceived by the ear, neither hath the eye seen, O God, beside Thee, what He hath prepared for him that waiteth for Him" (Isaiah 64:4).

The *Revised Version* says, "Neither hath the eye seen a God beside Thee, which worketh for him that waiteth for Him." In the *Authorized Version* the thought is that no eye hath seen the thing which God hath prepared. In the R.V. no eye hath seen a God, beside our God, who worketh for him that waiteth for Him. To both the two thoughts are common: That our place is to wait upon God, and that there will be revealed to us what the human heart cannot conceive. The difference is that in the R.V. it is the God who works, in the A.V. it is the thing He is to work. In 1 Corinthians 2:9, the citation is in regard to the things which the Holy Spirit is to reveal, as it is in the A.V., and in this meditation we keep to that.

The previous verses refer to the low state of God's people. The prayer has been poured out, "Look down from heaven" (Isaiah 63:15); "Why hast Thou hardened my heart from Thy fear? Return for Thy servants' sake" (Isaiah 63:19); and still more urgent, "Oh that Thou wouldest rend the heavens, that thou wouldest come down,... as when the melting fire burneth, to make Thy name known to Thy adversaries!" (Isaiah 64:1). Then follows the plea from the past, "When Thou didst terrible things we looked not for, Thou camest down, the mountains flowed down at Thy presence." "For"—this is now the faith that has been awakened by the thought of things we looked not for, He is still the same God

93

—"eye hath not seen beside Thee, O God, what He hath prepared for him that waiteth for Him." God alone knows what He can do for His waiting people. As Paul expounds and applies it: "The things of God knoweth no man, save the Spirit of God. But God hath revealed them to us by His Spirit."

The need of God's people, and the call for God's interposition is as urgent in our days as it was in the time of Isaiah. There is now, as there was then, as there has been at all times, a remnant that seeks after God with their whole heart. But if we look at Christendom as a whole, at the state of the Church of Christ, there is infinite cause for beseeching God to rend the heavens and come down. Nothing but a special interposition of Almighty Power will avail. I fear we have no right conception of what the so-called Christian world is in the sight of God. Unless God comes down "as the melting fire burneth, to make known His name to His adversaries," our labors are comparatively fruitless. Look at the ministry—how much it is in the wisdom of man and of literary culture; how little in demonstration of the Spirit and of power. Think of the unity of the body—how little there is of the manifestation of the power of a heavenly love binding God's children into one. Think of holiness—the holiness of Christ-like humility and crucifixion to the world, and how little the world sees that they have men among them who live in Christ in heaven, in whom Christ and heaven live.

What is to be done? There is only one thing. We must wait upon God. And what for? We must cry, with a cry that never rests, "Oh that Thou wouldest rend the heavens and come down, that the mountains might flow down at Thy presence." We must desire and believe, we must ask and expect, that God will do unlooked-for things. We must set our faith on a God of whom men do not know what He has prepared for them that wait for Him. The wonder-doing God, who can surpass all our expectations, must be the God of our confidence.

Yes, let God's people enlarge their hearts to wait on a God able to do exceeding abundantly above what we can ask or think. Let us band ourselves together as His elect who cry day and night to Him for things men have not seen. He is able to arise and to make His people a name, and a blessing in the earth. "He will wait, that He may be gracious unto you; blessed are all they that waiteth for Him."

"My soul waiteth thou only upon God!"

REFLECTION
1. As we wait on God, may our soul find the secret of entering the quiet goodness of the Lord, and receive the blessed work that will satisfy our every need.

DAY 24

WAITING ON GOD TO KNOW HIS GOODNESS

"The Lord is good unto them that waiteth for Him"
(Lamentations 3:25).

"Oh how great is Thy goodness, which Thou hast laid up for them that fear Thee" (Psalms 31:19); "Oh, taste and see that the Lord is good!" (Psalms 34:8).

And here is now the true way of entering into and rejoicing in this goodness of God—waiting upon Him. The Lord is good—even His children often do not know it when they do not wait in quietness for Him to reveal it. But to those who persevere in waiting, whose souls do wait, it will come true. One might think that it is just those who have to wait who might doubt it. But this is only when they do not wait, but become impatient. The truly waiting ones will all be able to say, "The Lord is good to them that wait for Him." If you would fully know the goodness of God, give yourself more than ever to a life of waiting on Him.

At our first entrance into the school of waiting upon God, the heart is chiefly set upon the blessings, which we wait for. God graciously uses our need and desire for help to educate us for something higher than we were thinking of. We were seeking gifts, and He, the Giver, longs to give himself and to satisfy the soul with His goodness. It is just for this reason that He often withholds the gifts and the time of waiting is made so long. He is always seeking to win the heart of His child for himself. He wishes that we would not only say, when He bestows the gift, "How good is God," but even if it never comes, we would all the time be experiencing, "It is good that a man should quietly wait." "The Lord is good to them that waiteth for Him."

What a blessed life the life of waiting then becomes, the continual worship of faith, adoring and trusting His goodness. As the soul learns its secret, every act or exercise of waiting just becomes a quiet entering into the goodness of God, to let it do its blessed work and satisfy our every need. And every experience of God's goodness gives the work of waiting new attractiveness, and instead of only taking refuge in time of need, there comes a great longing to wait continually and all the day. And however duties and engagements occupy the time and the mind, the soul gets more familiar with the secret art of always waiting. Waiting becomes the habit and disposition, the very second nature and breath of the soul.

Dear Christian! Do you not see that waiting is not one among a number of Christian virtues, to be thought of from time to time, but that it expresses that disposition which lies at the very root of the Christian life? It gives a higher value and a new power to our prayer and worship, to our faith and surrender, because it links us in unalterable dependence to God himself. And it gives us the unbroken enjoyment of the goodness of God. "The Lord is good to them that waiteth for Him."

Let me press upon you once again to take time and trouble to cultivate this so much needed element of the Christian life. We get too much second-hand religion from the teaching of men. That teaching has great value if, even as the preaching of John the Baptist sent his disciples away from himself to the Living Christ, it leads us to God himself. What our religion needs is more of God. Many of us are too much occupied with our work. As with Martha, the very service we want to render the Master separates from Him. It is neither pleasing to Him nor profitable to ourselves. The more work, the more need of waiting upon God. The doing of God's will would then be our meat and drink, nourishment, and refreshment and strength. "The Lord is good to them that waiteth for Him." None will know how good, but those who prove it in waiting on Him. None can fully tell how good, but those who have proved Him to the utmost.

"My soul waiteth thou only upon God!"

REFLECTION

1. Don't we see that waiting is not just some Christian virtue that we exercise from time to time, but must be constantly a part of our consciousness and root of all our daily activities— "the unbroken enjoyment of the goodness of God."

DAY 25

WAITING ON GOD QUIETLY

*"It is good that a man should both hope and quietly wait
for the salvation of the Lord" (Lamentations 3:26).*

*"Take heed and be quiet: fear not, neither be faint-
hearted" (Isaiah 7:4); "In quietness and in confidence shall
be your strength" (Isaiah 30:15).*

Such words reveal to us the close connection between
quietness and faith, and show us what a deep need there
is of quietness, as an element of true waiting upon God. If
we are to have our whole heart turned towards God, we
must have it turned away from the creature, from all other
occupations and interests, whether of joy or sorrow. God is
a being of such infinite greatness and glory, and our nature
has become so estranged from Him, that it needs our whole
heart and desires set upon Him, even in some little measure
to know and receive Him. Everything that is not God, that
excites our fears, or stirs our efforts, or awakens our hopes,
or makes us glad, hinders us in our perfect waiting on Him.
The message is one of deep meaning: "Take heed and be
quiet;" "In quietness shall be your strength;" "It is good that
a man should quietly wait."

How the very thought of God in His majesty and holiness
should silence us, Scripture abundantly testifies: "The Lord is
in His holy temple; let all the earth keep silence before Him"
(Habakkuk 2: 20). "Hold thy peace at the presence of the
Lord God" (Zephaniah 1:7); "Be silent, O all flesh, before
the Lord; for He is raised up out of His holy habitation"
(Zechariah 2:13).

As long as the waiting on God is chiefly regarded as an end towards more effectual prayer, and the obtaining of our petitions, this spirit of perfect quietness will not be obtained. But when it is seen that the waiting on God is itself an unspeakable blessedness, one of the highest forms of fellowship with the Holy One, the adoration of Him in His glory will of necessity humble the soul into a holy stillness, making way for God to speak and reveal himself. Then it comes to the fulfillment of the precious promise, that all of self and self-effort shall be humbled. "The lofty looks of man shall be humbled, and the haughtiness of men shall be bowed down, and the Lord alone shall be exalted in that day" (Isaiah 2:11).

Let everyone who would learn the art of waiting on God remember the lesson, "Take heed, and be quiet;" "It is good that a man quietly wait." Take time to be separate from all friends and all duties, all cares and all joys; time to be still and quiet before God. Take time not only to secure stillness from man and the world, but also from self and its energy. Let the Word and prayer be very precious; but remember, even these may hinder the quiet waiting. The activity of the mind in studying the Word, or giving expression to its thoughts in prayer, the activities of the heart, with its desires and hopes and fears, may so engage us that we do not come to the still waiting on the All-Glorious One. Though at first it may appear difficult to know how we are to quietly wait, with the activities of mind and heart for a time subdued, every effort after it will be rewarded. We shall find that it grows upon us and the little season of silent worship will bring a peace and a rest that gives a blessing not only in prayer, but each and every day.

"It is good that a man should quietly wait for the salvation of the Lord." Yes, it is good. The quietness is the confession of our impotence. With all our willing and running, and with all our thinking and praying, it will not be done. We must receive it from God. It is the confession of our trust that God will, in His time, come to our help—the quiet resting in Him alone. It is the confession of our desire to sink into our nothingness, and to let Him work and reveal himself. Do let us wait quietly. In daily life let there be a quiet reverence and an abiding watchfulness against deep engrossment in the world. In the soul that is waiting for God to do His wondrous work, the whole character will come to bear the beautiful stamp: Quietly waiting for the salvation of God.

"My soul waiteth thou only upon God!"

REFLECTION

1. True waiting upon God requires quietness and faith. Activity from the world around us distracts from the exercise of waiting. The unbroken enjoyment of the goodness of God is at stake.

2. Contrary to the thoughts of some, waiting on God is not to be viewed as an end towards more effectual prayer or the obtaining of our petitions. But simply waiting is often the means of rich blessings and meaningful fellowship with God.

DAY 26

WAITING ON GOD IN HOLY EXPECTATION

"Therefore will I look to the Lord; I will wait for the God of my salvation; my God will hear me" (Micah 7:7).

Have you ever read the beautiful little book, *Expectation Corner*? If not, get it. You will find in it one of the best sermons on our text. It tells of a king who prepared a city for some of his poor subjects. Not far from them were large storehouses, where everything they could need was supplied if they would just send in their requests. But on one condition—that they should be on the outlook for the answer, so that when the king's messengers came with the gifts they had desired, they would always be found waiting and ready to receive them. The sad story is told of one despondent person who never expected to get what he asked, because he was too unworthy. One day he was taken to the king's storehouses, and there, to his amazement, he saw, with his address on them, all the packages that had been made up for him and sent. There was the garment of praise, and the oil of joy, and the eye salve, and so much more. They had been to his door, but found it closed. He was not on the outlook. From that time on he understood the lesson Micah would teach us today; "I will look to the Lord; I will wait for the God of my salvation; my God will hear me."

We have more than once said, "Waiting for the answer to prayer is not the whole of waiting, but only a part." Today we want to take in this blessed truth: It is a part, and a very important one. When we have special petitions, in connection with waiting on God, our waiting must be very definitely in the confident assurance: "My God will hear me." A holy, joyful expectancy is the very essence of true waiting.

101

And this not only in reference to the many varied requests every believer has to make, but most especially to the one great petition which ought to be the chief thing every heart seeks for itself—that the life of God in the soul may have full sway, that Christ may be fully formed within, and that we may be filled to all the fullness of God. This is what God has promised. This is what God's people too little seek, very often because they do not believe it is possible. This is what we ought to seek and dare to expect, because God is able and waiting to work it in us.

But God himself must work it. And for this end our working must cease. We must see how entirely it is to be the faith of the operation of God who raised Jesus from the dead—just as much as the resurrection, the perfecting of God's life in our souls is to be directly His work. And waiting has to become more than ever a tarrying before God in stillness of soul, counting upon Him who raises the dead, and calls the things that are not as though they were.

Just notice how the threefold use of the name of God in our text points us to himself as the one from whom alone is our expectation. "I will look to the Lord; I will wait for the God of my salvation; my God will hear me." Everything that is salvation, everything that is good and holy, must be the direct mighty work of God himself within us. For every moment of a life in the will of God, there must be the immediate operation of God. And the one thing I have to do is to look to the Lord; to wait for the God of my salvation; to hold fast the confident assurance, "My God will hear me."

God says, "Be still, and know that I am God" (Psalms 46:10). There is no stillness like that of the grave. In the grave of Jesus, in the fellowship of His death, in death to self with its own will and wisdom, its own strength and energy, there is rest. As we cease from self, and our soul becomes still to God, God will arise and show himself. "Be still, and know," then you shall know "that I am God." There is no stillness like the stillness Jesus gives when He speaks, "Peace, be still." In Christ, in His death, and in His life, in His perfected redemption, the soul may be still, and God will come in, and take possession, and do His perfect work.

"My soul, be thou still only unto God!"

REFLECTION

1. In what ways can we cultivate the art of waiting on God? How are patience, quietness, prayer, and trials a part of our waiting on God?

2. Consider how even the good and legitimate things can distract us from waiting upon God.

3. A holy, joyful expectancy is the very essence of true waiting.

DAY 27

WAITING ON GOD FOR REDEMPTION

"Simeon was just and devout, waiting for the consolation of Israel, and the Holy Ghost was upon him. Anna, a prophetess, ... spake of Him to all them that looked for redemption in Jerusalem" (Luke 2:25,38).

Here we have the mark of a waiting believer. Righteous in all his conduct; devoted to God, ever walking as in His presence; waiting for the consolation of Israel, looking for the fulfillment of God's promises; and the Holy Ghost was on him. In the devout waiting he had been prepared for the blessing. And Simeon was not the only one. Anna spoke to all that looked for redemption in Jerusalem. This was the one mark, amid surrounding formalism and worldliness, of a godly band of men and women in Jerusalem. They were waiting on God and looking for His promised redemption.

And now that the Consolation of Israel has come and the redemption has been accomplished, do we still need to wait? We do indeed. But will not our waiting, who look back to it as having come, differ greatly from those who looked forward to it as coming? It will, especially in two aspects. We now wait on God in the full power of the redemption, and we wait for its full revelation.

Our waiting is now in the full power of the redemption. Christ spoke, "In that day you shall know that you are in Me. Abide in Me." The Epistles teach us to present ourselves to God "as indeed dead to sin, but alive unto God through Jesus Christ our Lord" (Romans 6:11), "blessed with all spiritual blessings in heavenly places in Christ" (Ephesians 1:3). Our waiting on God may now be in the wonderful consciousness, wrought and maintained by the Holy Spirit within us, that we are accepted in the Beloved, that the love that rests on Him rests on us, that we are living in that love, in the very nearness and presence and sight of God. The old saints took their stand on the Word of God, and waited, hoping on that Word. We rest on the Word too. But, oh! Under what exceeding greater privileges as one with Christ Jesus. In our waiting on God, let our confidence be that in Christ we have access to the Father. How sure, therefore, may we be that our waiting cannot be in vain.

Our waiting differs also in that while they waited for redemption to come, we see it accomplished, and now wait for its revelation in us. Christ not only said, "Abide in Me, but also I in you." The Epistles not only speak of us in Christ, but of Christ in us, as the highest mystery of redeeming love. As we maintain our place in Christ day by day, God waits to reveal Christ in us, in such a way that He is formed in us, that His mind and disposition and likeness acquire form and substance in us, so that by each it can truly be said, "Christ lives in me."

My life in Christ up there in heaven and Christ's life in me down here on earth—these two are the complement of each other. And the more my waiting on God is marked by the living faith I have in Christ, the more the heart thirsts for and claims the Christ in me. And the waiting on God, which began with special needs and prayer, will increasingly be concentrated, as far as our personal life is concerned, on this one thing; Lord, reveal Your redemption fully in me. Let Christ live in me.

Our waiting differs from that of the old saints in the place we take, and the expectations we entertain. But at root it is the same—waiting on God, from who alone is our expectation.

Learn from Simeon and Anna one lesson. How utterly impossible it was for them to do anything towards the great redemption—towards the birth of Christ or His death. It was God's work. They could do nothing but wait. Are we as absolutely helpless regarding the revelation of Christ in us? We are indeed. God did not work out the great redemption in Christ as a whole, and leave its application in detail to us.

The secret thought that it is so lies at the root of all our feebleness. The revelation of Christ in every individual believer, and in each one the daily revelation, step by step and moment by moment, is as much the work of God's omnipotence as the birth or resurrection of Christ. Until this truth enters and fills us, and we feel that we are just as dependent upon God for each moment of our life in the enjoyment of redemption as they were in their waiting for it, our waiting upon God will not bring its full blessing. The sense of utter and absolute helplessness, the confidence that God can and will do all, these must be the marks of our waiting as of theirs. As gloriously as God proved himself to them the faithful and wonder-working God, He will to us also.

"My soul waiteth thou only upon God!"

REFLECTION

1. What does it mean to abide in Christ?

2. How can we wait on God for redemption?

DAY 28

WAITING ON GOD FOR THE COMING OF HIS SON

"Be ye yourselves like unto men that wait for their Lord"
(Luke 3:36).

"Until the appearing of our Lord Jesus Christ, which, in His own time, He shall show, who is the blessed and only Potentate, the King of kings, and Lord of lords"
(1 Timothy 6:14,15).

"... turned to God from idols to serve the living and true God, and to wait for His Son from heaven"
(1 Thessalonians 1:9,10).

Waiting on God in heaven, and waiting for His Son from heaven, these two God has joined together, and no man may put them asunder. The waiting on God for His presence and power in daily life will be the only true preparation for waiting for Christ in humility and true holiness. Waiting for Christ to come from heaven to take us to heaven will give the waiting on God its true tone of hopefulness and joy. The Father who in His own time will reveal His Son from heaven, is the God who, as we wait on Him, prepares us for the revelation of His Son. The present life and the coming glory are inseparably connected in God and in us.

There is sometimes a danger of separating them. It is always easier to be engaged with the religion of the past or the future than to be faithful in the religion of today. As we look to what God has done in the past, or will do in time to come, the personal claim of present duty and present submission to His working may be missed. Waiting on God must ever lead to waiting for Christ as the glorious consummation of His work. And waiting for Christ must ever remind us of the duty of waiting upon God, as our only proof that the waiting for Christ is in spirit and in truth. There is such a danger of our being so occupied with the things that are coming more than with Him who is to come. There is such scope in the study of coming events for imagination and reason and human ingenuity, that nothing but deeply humble waiting on God can save us from mistaking the interest and pleasure of intellectual study for the true love of Him and His appearing. All you that say you wait for Christ's coming, be sure that you wait on God now. All you who seek to wait on God now to reveal His Son in you, see to it that you do so as men waiting for the revelation of His Son from heaven. The hope of that glorious appearing will strengthen you in waiting upon God for what He is to do in you now. The same omnipotent love that is to reveal that eternal glory is working in you even now to fit you for it.

"The blessed hope and the appearing of the glory of our great God and Savior Jesus Christ" (Titus 2:13), is one of the great bonds of union given to God's Church throughout the ages. "He shall come to be glorified in His saints, and to be admired in all them that believe" (2 Thessalonians 1:10). Then we shall all meet and the unity of the body of Christ be seen in its divine glory. It will be the meeting-place and the triumph of divine love. Jesus receiving His own and presenting them to the Father. His own meeting Him and worshipping in speechless love that blessed face. His own meeting each other in the ecstasy of God's own love. Let us wait, long for, and love the appearing of our Lord and heavenly Bridegroom. Tender love to Him and tender love to each other is the true and only bridal spirit.

I fear greatly that this is sometimes forgotten. A beloved brother in Holland was speaking about the expectancy of faith being the true sign of the bride. I ventured to express a doubt. An unworthy bride, about to be married to a prince, might only be thinking of the position and the riches that she was to receive. The expectancy of faith might be strong, and true love utterly wanting. It is love in the bridal spirit. It is not when we are most occupied with prophetic subjects, but when in humility and love we are clinging close to our Lord and His brethren, that we are in the bride's place. Jesus refuses to accept our love except it is love to His disciples. Waiting for His coming means waiting for the glorious coming manifestation of the unity of the body, while we seek here to maintain that unity in humility and love. Those who love most are the most ready for His coming. Love to each other is the life and beauty of His bride, the Church.

And how is this to be brought about? Beloved child of God! If you would learn aright to wait for His Son from Heaven, live even now waiting on God in Heaven. Remember how Jesus lived ever waiting on God. He could do nothing of himself. It was God who perfected His Son through suffering and then exalted Him. It is God alone who can give you the deep spiritual life of one who is really waiting for His Son. Wait on God for it. Waiting for Christ himself is, oh, so different from waiting for things that may come to pass! The latter any Christian can do; but the former, God must work in you every day by His Holy Spirit. Therefore all you who wait on God, look to Him for grace to wait for His Son from heaven in the Spirit which is from heaven. And you who would wait for His Son, wait on God continually to reveal Christ in you.

The revelation of Christ in us, as it is given to them who wait upon God, is the true preparation for the full revelation of Christ in glory. It is Christ in us who is the hope of glory.

"My soul waiteth thou only upon God!"

REFLECTION

1. A preoccupation with end-times is a common error of many Christians in our day, and it will inevitably distract us from faithful service and holy waiting upon God as He wants us to in the here and now. "All you that say you wait for Christ's coming, be sure that you wait on God now."

DAY 29

WAITING ON GOD FOR THE
PROMISE OF THE FATHER

"He commanded them that they should not to depart from Jerusalem, but wait for the promise of the Father"
(Acts 1:4).

In speaking of the saints in Jerusalem at Christ's birth, with Simeon and Anna (Luke 2:34-38), we saw how, though the redemption they waited for has come, the call to waiting is no less urgent now than it was then. We wait for the full revelation in us of what came to them, but what they scarce could comprehend. Even so it is with waiting for the promise of the Father. In one sense, the fulfillment can never come again as it came at Pentecost. In another sense, and that in as deep reality as with the first disciples, we daily need to wait for the Father to fulfill His promise in us.

The Holy Spirit is not a person distinct from the Father in the way two persons on earth are distinct. The Father and the Spirit are never separate from each other. The Father is always in the Spirit and the Spirit works nothing except as the Father works in Him. Each moment the same Spirit that is in us, is in God too, and he who is most full of the Spirit will be the first to wait on God most earnestly, further to fulfill His promise, and still strengthen him mightily by His Spirit in the inner man. The Spirit in us is not a power at our disposal. Nor is the Spirit an independent power, acting apart from the Father and the Son. The Spirit is the real living presence and the power of the Father working in us; therefore, it is just he who knows that the Spirit is in him, who will wait on the Father for the full revelation and experience of what the Spirit's indwelling is—for His increase and abounding more and more.

We see this in the apostles. They were filled with the Spirit at Pentecost. When they were returning from the council, where they had been forbidden to preach, they prayed afresh for boldness to speak in His name—a fresh coming down of the Holy Spirit was the Father's fresh fulfillment of His promise.

At Samaria, by the word and the Spirit, many had been converted, and the whole city was filled with joy. At the apostles' prayer the Father once again fulfilled the promise. Even so it was to the waiting company, "We are all here before God," in Cornelius' house. And so it was in Acts 13. When men, filled with the Spirit, prayed and fasted, that the promise of the Father was afresh fulfilled, and the leading of the Spirit was given from heaven. "Separate Me Barnabas and Saul."

So also we find Paul in Ephesians, praying for those who have been sealed with the Spirit, that God would grant them the spirit of illumination. And later on, that He would grant them, according to the riches of His glory, to be strengthened with might by the Spirit in the inner man.

The Spirit given at Pentecost was not a something that God parted with in heaven, and sent away out of heaven to earth. God does not, cannot, give away anything in that way. When He gives grace, or strength, or life, He gives it by giving himself to work it—it is completely inseparable from himself. (See note on, *The Power of the Spirit*, by William Law, at the end of this volume.) Much more so is the Holy Spirit. He is God, present and working in us: the true position in which we can count upon that working with an unceasing power is as we, praising for what we have, still unceasingly wait for the Father's promise to be still more mightily fulfilled.

What new meaning and promise does this give to our life of waiting! It teaches us to always keep the place where the disciples tarried at the footstool of the throne. It reminds us that, as helpless as they were to meet their enemies, or to preach to Christ's enemies, until they were endued with power, we too, can only be strong in the life of faith, or the work of love, as we are in direct communication with God and Christ, and He maintains the life of the Spirit in us. It assures us that the omnipotent God will, through the glorified Christ, work in us a power that can bring to pass things unexpected, things impossible. Oh! Think what the Church will be able to do when her individual members learn to live their lives waiting on God, and when together, with all of self and the world sacrificed in the fire of love, they unite in waiting with one accord for the promise of the Father, once so gloriously fulfilled, but still unexhausted.

Come and let each of us be still in presence of the inconceivable grandeur of this prospect: the Father waiting to fill the Church with the Holy Ghost. And He is willing to fill me, let each of us say.

With this faith let there come over the soul a hush and a holy fear, as it waits in stillness to take it all in. And let life increasingly become a deep joy in the hope of the ever fuller fulfillment of the Father's promise.

"My soul waiteth thou only upon God!"

REFLECTION

1. Many errors have crept into the Church regarding the understanding of the work of the Holy Spirit, especially over

the past one hundred years. As Murray says, "The Spirit in us is not a power at our disposal." Simon the sorcerer made this mistake (Acts 8:9-14). Yet, there are not a few Christians and leaders in the Church who make outrageous claims that only lead to self-exaltation, spiritual pride, and inevitably lead to becoming a poor witness for the name of Christ in the world. How do you understand the workings of the Holy Spirit in the world and in the lives of God's people?

DAY 30

WAITING ON GOD CONTINUALLY

"Therefore turn thou to thy God: keep mercy and judgment, and wait on thy God continually" (Hosea12:6).

Continuity is one of the essential elements of life. Interrupt it for a single hour in a man, and it is lost, he is dead. Continuity, unbroken and ceaseless, is essential to a healthy Christian life. God wants me to be, and God waits to make me what I want to be. I wait on Him every moment to make me what He expects of me, and what is well-pleasing in His sight. If waiting on God is the essence of true religion, the maintenance of the spirit of entire dependence must be continuous. The call of God, "Wait on your God continually," must be accepted and obeyed. There may be times of special waiting. The disposition and habit of soul must be there unchangeably and uninterruptedly.

This waiting continually is indeed a necessity. To those who are content with a feeble Christian life, it appears a luxury, something beyond what is essential to being a good Christian. But all who are praying the prayer, "Lord! Make me as holy as a pardoned sinner can be made! Keep me as near to You as it is possible for me to be! Fill me as full of Your love as You are willing to do," feel at once that it is something that must be had. They feel that there can be no unbroken fellowship with God, no full abiding in Christ, no maintaining of victory over sin and readiness for service, without waiting continually on the Lord.

The waiting continually is a possibility. Many think that with the duties of life it is out of the question. They cannot be always thinking of it. Even when they wish to, they forget. They do not understand that it is a matter of the heart, and that what the heart is full of, occupies it, even when the thoughts are otherwise engaged. A father's heart may be filled continuously with intense love and longing for a sick wife or child at a distance, even though pressing business requires all his thoughts. When the heart has learned how entirely powerless it is for one moment to keep itself or bring forth any good, when it has understood how surely and truly God will keep it, when it has, in despair of itself, accepted God's promise to do for it the impossible, it learns to rest in God, and in the midst of occupations and temptations it can wait continually.

This waiting is a promise. God's commands are enabling gospel precepts that are all promises, a revelation of what our God will do for us. When you first begin waiting on God, it is with frequent intermission and frequent failure. But do believe God is watching over you in love and secretly strengthening you in it. There are times when waiting appears to be just losing time, but it is not so. Waiting, even in darkness, is unconscious advance, because it is God you have to do with, and He is working in you. God who calls you to wait on Him, sees your feeble efforts, and works it in you. Your spiritual life is in no respect your own work. As little as you began it, can you continue it. It is God's Spirit who has begun the work in you of waiting upon God. He will enable you to wait continually.

Waiting continually will be met and rewarded by God himself working continually. We are coming to the end of our meditations. Could it be that you and I might learn one lesson: God must, God will work continually. He ever does work continually, but the experience of it is hindered by unbelief. But He who by His Spirit teaches you to wait continually, will bring you to experience also how, as the Everlasting One, His work is never-ceasing. In the love and the life and the work of God there can be no break, no interruption.

Do not limit God in this by your thoughts of what may be expected. Do fix your eyes upon this one truth: in His very nature, God, as the only Giver of life, cannot do otherwise than work in His child every moment of every day. Do not look only at the one side; "If I wait continually, God will work continually." No, look at the other side. Place God first and say, "God works continually, so every moment I may wait on Him continually." Take time until you see the vision of your God working continually, without one moment's intermission, filling your being. Your waiting continually will then come into itself. Full of trust and joy, the holy habit of the soul will be, "On Thee do I wait all the day." The Holy Spirit will keep you ever waiting.

"My soul waiteth thou only upon God!"

MOMENT BY MOMENT

(Music in "Christian Endeavor Hymns" by I. D. Sankey)

"I the Lord do keep it: I will water it every moment.
Dying with Jesus, by death reckoned mine,
Living with Jesus a new life divine;
Looking to Jesus till glory doth shine,
Moment by moment, O Lord, I am Thine.

Chorus—
Moment by moment I'm kept in His love,
Moment by moment I've life from above;
Looking to Jesus till glory doth shine;
Moment by moment, O Lord, I am Thine.

Never a battle with wrong for the right,
Never a contest that He doth not fight;
Lifting above us His banner so white,
Moment by moment I'm kept in His sight.

Chorus

Never a trial that He is not there,
Never a burden that He doth not bear,
Never a sorrow that He does not share,
Moment by moment I'm under His care.

Chorus

Never a heartache, and never a groan,
Never a teardrop, and never a moan;
Never a danger but there on the throne
Moment by moment He thinks of His own.

Chorus

Never a weakness that He doth not feel,
Never a sickness that He cannot heal;
Moment by moment, in woo or in weal,
Jesus, my Savior, abides with me still.

REFLECTION

1. What promises come with faithful waiting?

2. What rewards come to those who faithfully wait on God?

3. How can we cultivate a holy sense of God's continual nearness and presence in our lives? How does this tie into waiting on God?

DAY 31
WAITING ON GOD ONLY

"My soul waiteth thou only upon God; for my expectation is from Him. He only is my rock and my salvation"
(Psalms 62:5,6).

It is possible to be waiting continually on God, but not only upon Him. There may be other secret confidences intervening and preventing the blessing that was expected. And so the word "only" must come to throw its light on the path to the fullness and certainty of blessing. "My soul waiteth thou only upon God. He only is my Rock."

Yes, "My soul waiteth thou only upon God." There is but one God, but one source of life and happiness for the heart.

117

He only is my Rock. My soul, wait thou only upon Him. You desire to be good. "There is none good but God," and there is no possible goodness but what is received directly from Him. You have sought to be holy: "There is none holy but the Lord," and there is no holiness but what He by His Spirit of holiness every moment breathes in you. You want to live and work for God and His kingdom, for men and their salvation. Hear how He says, "The Everlasting God, the Creator of the ends of the Earth." He alone "faints not, neither is weary. He gives power to the faint, and to them that have no might He increases strength. They that wait upon the Lord shall renew their strength." He only is God. He only is your Rock. "My soul waiteth thou only upon God."

You will not find many who can help you in this. There will be many of your brethren who will draw you to put your trust in churches and doctrines, in schemes and plans and human appliances, in means of grace and divine appointments. But, "My soul waiteth only upon God himself." His most sacred appointments become a snare when trusted in. The brazen serpent becomes Nehushtan; the ark and the temple a vain confidence. Let the living God alone, none and nothing but He, be your hope.

Eyes and hands and feet, mind and thought, may have to be intently engaged in the duties of this life; "My soul waiteth thou only upon God." You are an immortal spirit, created not for this world but for eternity and for God. O, my soul! Realize your destiny. Know your privilege, and "wait thou only upon God." Let not the interest of religious thoughts and exercises deceive you. They very often take the place of waiting upon God. My soul, you must wait; your very self, your inmost being, with all its power, "wait thou only upon God." God is for you, you are for God; wait only upon Him.

Yes, "my soul waiteth thou only upon God." Beware of your two great enemies—the world and self. Beware lest any earthly satisfaction or enjoyment, however innocent it appears, keep you back from saying, "I will go to God, my exceeding joy." Remember and study what Jesus says about denying self, "Let a man deny himself" (Matthew 16:24). Tersteegen says, "The saints deny themselves in everything." Pleasing self in little things may be strengthening it to assert itself in greater things. "My soul waiteth thou only upon God." Let Him be all your salvation and all your desire. Say continually and with an undivided heart, "From Him comes my expectation. He only is my Rock; I shall not be moved." Whatever be your spiritual or temporal need, whatever the desire or prayer of your heart, whatever your interest in connection with God's work in the Church or the world—in solitude or in the rush of the world, in public worship or other gatherings of the saints, "My soul waiteth thou only upon God." Let your expectations be from Him alone. HE ONLY IS YOUR ROCK.

Never forget the two foundational truths on which this blessed waiting rests. If ever you are inclined to think this "waiting only" is too hard or too high, they will recall you at once. They are your absolute helplessness, and the absolute sufficiency of your God. Oh! Enter deep into the entire sinfulness of all that is of self, and think not of letting self have anything to say one single moment. Enter deep into your utter and unceasing impotence ever to change what is evil in you, or to bring forth anything that is spiritually good. Enter deep into your relation of dependence as creature on God, to receive from Him every moment what He gives. Enter deeper still into His covenant of redemption, with His promise to restore more gloriously than ever what you had lost, and by His Son and Spirit to give within you unceasingly, His actual divine presence and power. And thus wait upon your God continually and only.

No words can tell, no heart can conceive, the riches of the glory of this mystery of the Father and of Christ. Our God, in the infinite tenderness and omnipotence of His love, waits to be our Life and Joy. Oh, my soul! Let it no longer be needed that I repeat the words, "Wait upon God," but let all that is in me rise and sing; "Truly my soul waits upon God. On Thee do I wait all the day."

"My soul waiteth thou only upon God!"

NOTE

My publishers have just issued a work of William Law on the Holy Spirit, *The Power of the Spirit*: *An humble earnest, and affectionate Address to the Clergy,* with Additional Extracts and Introduction, by Rev. Andrew Murray. (James Nisbet &Co.) In the Introduction I have said how much I owe to the book. I cannot but think that anyone who will take the trouble to read it thoughtfully will find rich spiritual profit in connection with a life of waiting upon God.

What he puts more clearly than I have anywhere else found are these cardinal truths:

1. That the very nature and being of God, as the only possessor and dispenser of any life there is in the universe, imply that He must every moment communicate to every creature the power by which it exists, and therefore also much more the power by which it can do that which is good.

2. That the very nature and being of a creature, as owing its existence to God alone and equally owing to Him each

moment the continuation of that existence, imply that its happiness can only be found in absolute unceasing momentary dependence upon God.

3. That the great value and blessing of the gift of the Spirit at Pentecost, as the fruit of Christ's redemption, is that it is now possible for God to take possession of His redeemed children and work in them as He did before the fall in Adam. We need to know the Holy Spirit as the presence and power of God in us restored to their true place.

4. That in the spiritual life our great need is the knowledge of two great lessons: One, our entire sinfulness and helplessness—our utter impotence by any effort of our own to do anything towards the maintenance and increase of our inner spiritual life. The other, the infinite willingness of God's love, which is nothing but a desire to communicate himself and His blessedness to us, to meet our every need, and every moment to work in us by His Son and Spirit what we need.

5. That the very essence of true religion, whether in heaven or upon earth, consists in an unalterable dependence upon God, because we can give God no other glory, than yielding ourselves to the love which created us to show forth in us its glory, that it may now perfect its work in us.

I need not point out how deep down these truths go to the very root of the spiritual life, and especially the life of waiting upon God. I am confident that those who are willing to take the trouble of studying this thoughtful writer will thank me for the introduction to his book.

REFLECTION

1. Is there anything or anyone else upon which we can wait in order to receive blessing?

2. Your absolute helplessness and God's absolute sufficiency is all you need to effectively and powerfully wait on God.

WORKING
FOR GOD

INTRODUCTION

The object of this little book is to remind all Christian workers of the greatness and the glory of the work in which God gives a share. It is nothing less than that work of bringing men back to God, at which God finds His highest glory and blessedness. As we see that it is God's own work we have to work out, that He works it through us, that in our doing it His glory rests on us and we glorify Him, we shall count it our joy to give ourselves to live only and wholly for it.

The aim of the book at the same time is to help those who complain, or perhaps do not even know to complain, that they are apparently laboring in vain, and to discover what may be the cause of so much failure. God's work must be done in God's way and in God's power. It is spiritual work to be done by spiritual men, in the power of the Spirit. The clearer our insight into, and the more complete our submission to, God's laws of work, the surer and richer will be our joy and reward in it.

Along with this I have had in view the great number of Christians who practically take no real part in the service of their Lord. They have not understood that as the chief characteristic of Divine life in God, and Christ's work of blessing men, the Divine life in us can show itself in no other way. I have tried to show that it is God's will that every believer without exception, whatever be his position in life, gives himself wholly to live and work for God.

I have also written in the hope that some who have the responsibility of training others in Christian life and work, may find thoughts that will be of use to them in teaching this imperative duty. That they might see the urgent need, the Divine blessedness of a life given to God's service, and to awaken within the consciousness of the power that works in them—the Spirit of the power of Christ himself.

To the great host of workers in churches and chapels, in mission-halls and open-air, in day schools and Sunday schools, and all the various forms of the ministry of love throughout the world, I lovingly offer these meditations, with fervent prayer that God, the Great Worker, may make us true fellow-workers with Himself.

—Andrew Murray
Wellington, February, 1901

WORKING FOR GOD

DAY 1

WAITING AND WORKING

*"They that wait upon the Lord shall renew their strength.
Neither hath the eye seen, O God, beside Thee, which
worketh for him that waiteth for Him"*
(Isaiah 40:31, 64:4).

Here we have two texts in which the connection between waiting and working is made clear. In the first we see that waiting brings the needed strength for working—that it fits for joyful and unwearied work. "They that wait on the Lord shall renew their strength; they shall mount up on eagles' wings; they shall run, and not be weary; they shall walk, and not faint." Waiting on God has its value in that it makes us strong in work for God. The second reveals the secret of this strength. "God worketh for Him that waiteth for Him." The waiting on God secures the working of God for us and in us, out of which our work must spring. The two passages teach the great lesson, that as waiting on God lies at the root of all true working for God, so working for God must be the fruit of all true waiting on Him. Our great need is to hold the two sides of the truth in perfect conjunction and harmony.

There are some who say they wait upon God, but who do not work for Him. For this there may be various reasons. There may be some who confound true waiting on God (in living direct intercourse with Him as the Living One), and the devotion to Him of the energy of the whole being, with the slothful, helpless waiting that excuses itself from all work until God, by some special impulse, has made work easy. Others wait on God more truly, regarding it as one of the highest exercises of the Christian life, and yet has never understood that at the root of all true waiting there must lie the surrender and the readiness to be wholly fitted for God's use in the service of men. Still others are ready to work as well as wait, but are looking for some great "movement" or "inflowing" of the Spirit's power to enable them to do mighty works, while they forget that as believers they already have the Spirit of Christ dwelling in them. They do not understand that more grace is only given to those who are faithful in the little, and that it is only in working that we can be taught by the Spirit how to do the greater works. All such, and all Christians, need to learn that waiting has working for its object, that it is only in working that waiting can attain its full perfection and blessedness. It is as we elevate working for God to its true place, as the highest exercise of spiritual privilege and power, that the absolute need and the divine blessing of waiting on God can be fully known.

On the other hand, there are some, there are many, who work for God, but know little of what it is to wait on Him. They have been led to take up Christian work, under the impulse of natural or religious feeling, at the bidding of a pastor or a society, with but very little sense of what a holy thing it is to work for God. They do not know that God's work can only be done in God's strength, by God himself working in us. They have never learned that, just as the Son of God could do nothing of himself, but that the Father in Him did the work, as He lived in continual dependence before Him, so the believer can do nothing except what God works in him. They do not understand that it is only as in utter weakness we depend upon Him, His power can rest on us. And so they have no conception of a continual waiting on God as being one of the first and essential conditions of successful work. And Christ's Church and the world are suffering today, oh, so terribly! Not only because so many of its members are not working for God, but because so much working for God is done without waiting on God.

Among the members of the body of Christ there is a great diversity of gifts and operations. Some, who are confined to their homes by reason of sickness or other duties, may have more time for waiting on God than opportunity of direct working for Him. Others, who are burdened by work, find it very difficult to find time and quiet for waiting on Him. These may mutually supply each other's lack. Let those who have time for waiting on God definitely link themselves to some who are working. Let those who are working as definitely claim the aid of those to whom the special ministry of waiting on God has been entrusted. So will the unity and the health of the body can be maintained. So will those who wait know that the outcome will be power for work, and those who work, that their only strength is the grace obtained by waiting. So will God work for His Church that waits on Him.

Let us pray that as we proceed in these 15 meditations on working for God, the Holy Spirit may show us how sacred and how urgent our calling is to work, how absolute our dependence is upon God's strength to work in us, how sure it is that those who wait on Him shall renew their strength, and how we shall find waiting on God and working for God to be indeed inseparably one.

REFLECTION

1. It is only as God works for me, and in me, that I can work for Him.

2. All His work for me is through His life in me.

3. He will most surely work, if I wait on Him.

4. All His working for me, and my waiting on Him, has but one aim: to fit me for His work of saving men.

5. What is the connection between waiting and working for God?

DAY 2

GOOD WORKS THE LIGHT OF THE WORLD

"Ye are the light of the world. Let your light shine before men, that they may see your good works, and glorify your Father which is in heaven" (Matthew 5:14,16).

A light is always meant for the use of those who are in darkness, that by it they may see. The sun shines upon the darkness of this world. A lamp is hung in a room to give it light. The Church of Christ is the light of men. The god of this world hath blinded their eyes. Christ's disciples are to shine into their darkness and give them light. As the rays of light stream forth from the sun and scatter that light all about, so the good works of believers are the light that streams out from them to conquer the surrounding darkness, with its ignorance of God and estrangement from Him.

What a high and holy place is given to our good works. What power is attributed to them. How much depends upon them. They are not only the light and health and joy of our own life, but in every deed the means of bringing lost souls out of darkness into God's marvelous light. They are even more. They not only bless men, but they glorify God, in leading men to know Him as the Author of the grace seen in His children. We propose studying the teaching of Scripture in regard to good works, and specially all work done directly for God and His kingdom. Let us listen to what these words of the Master have to teach us.

The Aim of Good Works

It is that God may be glorified. You remember how our Lord said to the Father: "I have glorified Thee on the earth, I have finished the work which Thou gavest Me to do" (John 17:4). We read more than once of His miracles, that the people glorified God. It was because what He had wrought was manifested by a Divine power. It is when our good works are something more than the ordinary virtues of refined men, and bear the impress of God upon them, that men will glorify God. They must be the good works of which the Sermon on the Mount is the embodiment—a life of God's children, doing more than others, seeking to be perfect as their Father in heaven is perfect. This glorifying of God by men may not mean conversion, but it is a preparation for it when an impression favorable to God has been made. The works prepare the way for the words, and are evidence to the reality of the Divine truth that is taught, while without them the world is powerless.

The whole world was made for the glory of God. Christ came to redeem us from sin and bring us back to serve and glorify Him. Believers are placed in the world with this one object, that they may let their light shine in good works, so as to win men to God. As truly as the light of the sun is meant to lighten the world, the good works of God's children are meant to be the light of those who know and love not God. What need that we form a right conception of what good works are, as bearing the mark of something heavenly and divine, and having a power to compel the admission that God is in them.

The Power of Good Works

Of Christ it is written, "In Him was life, and the life was the light of men" (John 1:4). The divine life gave out a divine light. Of His disciples Christ said:, "He that followeth Me shall not walk in darkness, but shall have the light of life" (John 8:12). Christ is our life and light. When it is said to us, "Let your light shine," the deepest meaning is, let Christ, who dwells in you, shine. As in the power of His life you do your good works, your light shines out to all who see you. And because Christ in you is your light, your works, however humble and feeble they are, can carry with them a power of divine conviction. The measure of the divine power that works them in you will be the measure of the power working in those who see them. Give way, O child of God, to the life and light of Christ dwelling in you, and men will see in your good works that for which they will glorify your Father which is in heaven.

The Urgent Need of Good Works in Believers

As needful as that the sun shines every day, so it is that every believer should let his light shine before men. For this we have been created anew in Christ, to hold forth the Word of Life, as lights in the world. Christ needs you urgently, my brother, to let His light shine through you. Perishing men around you need your light, if they are to find their way to God. God needs you, to let His glory be seen through you. As wholly as a lamp is given up to lighting a room, every believer ought to give himself up to be the light of a dark world.

Let us undertake the study of what working for God is, and what good works are as part of this, with the desire to follow Christ fully, and so to have the light of life shining into our hearts and lives and from us all around.

REFLECTION

1. "Ye are the light of the world"! The words express the calling of the Church as a whole. The fulfillment of her duty will depend upon the faithfulness with which each individual member loves and lives for those around him.

2. In all our efforts to awaken the Church to evangelize the world, our first aim must be to raise the standard of life for the individual believer of the teaching: As truly as a candle only exists with the object of giving light in the darkness, the one object of your existence is to be a light to men.
3. Pray God by His Holy Spirit to reveal it to you that you have nothing to live for but to let the light and love of the life of God shine upon souls.

DAY 3

SON, GO WORK

"Son, go work today in my vineyard" (Matt. 21:28).

The father had two sons. To each he gave the command to go and work in his vineyard. The one went, the other did not. God has given the command and the power to every child of His to work in His vineyard, with the world as the

133

field. The majority of God's children are not working for Him and the world is perishing.

Of all the mysteries that surround us in the world, is it not one of the strangest and most incomprehensible that after 1,800 years the very name of the Son of God should be unknown to a larger portion of the human race.

Just consider what this means. To restore the ruin sin had wrought, God, the Almighty Creator, actually sent His own Son to the world to tell men of His love, and to bring them His life and salvation. When Christ made His disciples partakers of that salvation, and the unspeakable joy it brings, it was with the express understanding that they would make it known to others, and so be the lights of the world. He spoke of all who through them should believe, having the same calling. He left the world with the distinct instruction to carry the Gospel to every creature, and teach all nations to observe all that He had commanded. He at the same time gave the definite assurance that all power for this work was in Him, that He would always be with His people, and that by the power of His Holy Spirit they would be able to witness to Him to the ends of the earth. And what do we see now? After 1,800 years so much of the human race has scarcely heard the name of Jesus.

Consider again what this means. All these dying millions, whether in Christendom or heathendom, have an interest in Christ and His salvation. They have a right to Him. Their salvation depends on their knowing Him. He could change their lives from sin and wretchedness to holy obedience and heavenly joy. Christ has a right to them. It would make His heart glad to have them come and be blessed in Him. But they are dependent on the service of His people to be the connecting link to bring them and Him together. And yet what His people do is as nothing to what needs to be done, to what could be done, to what ought to be done.

Just consider yet once again what this means. What a revelation of the state of the Church. The great majority of those who are counted believers are doing nothing towards making Christ known to their fellow men. Of the remainder, the majority are doing so little, and that little so ineffectually, by reason of the lack of wholehearted devotion, that they can hardly be said to be giving themselves to their Lord's service. And of the remaining portion, who have given themselves and all they have to Christ's service, so many are occupied with the hospital work of teaching the sick and the weakly in the Church, that the strength left free for aggressive work, and going forth to conquer the world, is terribly reduced. And so, with a finished salvation, and a loving Redeemer, and a Church set apart to carry life and blessing to men, many millions are still perishing.

There can be no question to the Church of more intense and pressing importance than this: What can be done to awaken believers to a sense of their holy calling, and to make them see that to work for God, that to offer themselves as instruments through whom God can do His work, ought to be the one aim of their life? The vain complaints that are continually heard of a lack of enthusiasm for God's kingdom on the part of the great majority of Christians, the vain attempts to waken anything like an interest in missions proportionate to their claim, or Christ's claim, make us feel that nothing less is needed than a revival that shall be a revolution, and shall raise even the average Christian to an entirely new type of devotion. No true change can come until the truth is preached and accepted, that the law of the kingdom is: Every believer to live only and wholly for God's service and work.

The father who called his sons to go and work in his vineyard did not leave it to their choice to do as much or as little as they chose. They lived in his home, they were his children, and he counted on what they would give him, their time and strength. This God expects much of His children. Until it is understood that each child of God is to give His whole heart to his Father's interest and work, until it is understood that every child of God is to be a worker for God, the evangelization of the world cannot be accomplished. Let every reader listen, and the Father will say to him personally, "Son, go work in My vineyard."

REFLECTION

1. Why is it that stirring appeals on behalf of missions often have so little permanent result? Because the command with its motives is brought to men who have not learned that absolute devotion and immediate obedience to their Lord is of the essence of true salvation.

2. If it is once seen, and confessed, that the lack of interest in missions is the token of a low and sickly Christian life, all who plead for missions will make it their first aim to proclaim the calling of every believer to live wholly for God. Every missionary meeting will be a consecration meeting to seek and surrender to the Holy Spirit's power.

3. The average standard of holiness and devotion cannot be higher abroad than at home, or in the Church at large than in individual believers.

4. Every one cannot go abroad, or give his whole time to direct work; but everyone, whatever his calling or circumstances, can give his whole heart to live for souls and the spread of the kingdom.

DAY 4

TO EACH ONE HIS WORK

*"As a man sojourning in another country, having
given authority to his servants, to each one his work,
commanded the porter also to watch" (Mark 13:34).*

What I have said in a previous chapter of the failure of
the Church to do her Master's work, or even clearly
to insist upon the duty of its being done by every member
has often led me to ask the question, "What must be done to
arouse the Church to a right sense of her calling?" This little
book is an attempt to give the answer. Working for God must
take a very different and much more definite place in our
teaching and training of Christ's disciples than it has done.

In studying the question I have been helped a great deal
by the life and writings of a great educationist. The opening
sentence of the preface to his biography tells us: "Edward
Thring was unquestionably the most original and striking
figure in the schoolmaster world of his time in England."
He himself attributes his own power and success to the
prominence he gave to a few simple principles, and the
faithfulness with which he carried them out at any sacrifice.
I have found them as suggestive in regard to the work of
preaching as of teaching, and to state them will help to make
plain some of the chief lessons this book is meant to teach.

The primary principle that distinguished his teaching
from what was current at the time was that every boy in
school, the dullest, must have the same attention as the
cleverest. At Eton, where he had been educated, and had been
first in his class, he had seen the evil of the opposite system.
The school kept up its name by training a number of men

137

for the highest prizes, while the majority was neglected. He maintained that this was dishonest, and that there could be no truth in a school that did not care for all alike. Every boy had some gift. Every boy needed special attention. Every boy could, with care and patience, be fitted to know and fulfill his mission in life.

Apply this to the Church. Every believer, the feeblest as much as the strongest, has the calling to live and work for the kingdom of his Lord. Every believer has a claim on the grace and power of the Holy Spirit, according to his gifts, to fit him for his work. And every believer has a right to be taught and helped by the Church for the service our Lord expects of him. It is when this truth—every believer from the feeblest to the strongest is to be trained as a worker for God—gets its true place that there can be any thought of the Church fulfilling its mission. Not one can be missed, because the Master gave to every one his work.

Another of Thring's principles was this: It is a law of nature that work is pleasure. See to make it voluntary and not compulsory. Do not lead the boys blindfold. Show them why they have to work, what its value will be, what interest can be awakened in it, what pleasure may be found in it. A little time stolen, as he says, for that purpose, from the ordinary teaching, will be more than compensated for by the spirit that will be thrown into the work.

What a field is opened out here for the preacher of the gospel in the charge he has of Christ's disciples—to unfold before them the greatness, the glory, the divine, blessedness of the work to be done. To show its value in the carrying out of God's will, and gaining His approval; in our becoming the benefactors and saviors of the perishing; in developing that spiritual vigor, that nobility of character, that spirit of self-sacrifice which leads to the true bearing of Christ's image.

A third truth Thring insisted on specially was the need of inspiring the belief in the possibility—the assurance—of success in gaining the object of pursuit. That object is not much knowledge. Not every boy can attain to this. The drawing out and cultivation of the power there is in himself—this is for everyone, and this alone is true education. As a learner's powers of observation grow under true guidance and teaching and he finds within himself a source of power and pleasure he never knew before, he feels a new self beginning to live, and the world around him gets a new meaning. "He becomes conscious of an infinity of unsuspected glory in the midst of which we go about our daily tasks, becomes lord of an endless kingdom full of light and pleasure and power."

If this is the law and blessing of a true education, what light is shed on the calling of all teachers and leaders in Christ's Church! That you are the temple of God—that Christ is in you—that the Holy Spirit dwells in you—acquire a new meaning. It tells us that the one thing that needs to be awakened in the hearts of Christians is the faith "in the power that worketh in us." As one comes to see the worth and the glory of the work to be done, as one believes in the possibility of his, too, being able to do that work well. As one learns to trust a Divine energy, the very power and spirit of God working in him, "he will, in the fullest sense become conscious of a new life, with an infinity of unsuspected glory in the midst of which we go about our daily task, and become lord of an endless kingdom full of light and pleasure and power." This is the royal life to which God has called all His people. The true Christian is one who knows God's power working in himself, and finds it his true joy to have the very

life of God flow into him, and through him, and out from
him to those around.

REFLECTION

1. We must learn to believe in the power of even little ones—of
the value of every individual believer. As people are saved one
by one, they must be trained one by one for work.

2. We must believe that work for Christ can become as
natural, as much an attraction and a pleasure in the spiritual
as in the natural world.

3. We must believe and teach that every believer can become
an effective worker in his sphere. Are you seeking to be filled
with love to souls?

DAY 5

TO EACH ACCORDING TO HIS ABILITY

*"The kingdom of heaven is as when a man, going into
another country, called his own servants, and delivered
them his goods. And unto one he gave five talents, to
another two, to another one; to each according to his
several ability" (Matthew 25:14).*

In the parable of the talents we have a most instructive
summary of our Lord's teaching in regard to the work
He has given to His servants to do. He tells us of His going
to heaven and leaving His work on earth to the care of His
Church. He speaks of His giving every one something to do,
however different the gifts might be, and of His expecting
to get back His money with interest; of the failure of him

who had received least; and of what it was that led to that terrible neglect.

"He called his own servants and delivered unto them his goods, and went on his journey" (Matthew 25:14). This literally is what our Lord did. He went to heaven, leaving His work with all His goods to the care of His Church. His goods were, the riches of His grace, the spiritual blessings in heavenly places, and His word and Spirit with all the power of His life on the throne of God. All these He gave in trust to His servants to be used by them in carrying out His work on earth. The work He had begun they were to prosecute. As some rich merchant leaves Cape Town to reside in London, while he leaves his business to be carried on by trustworthy servants, our Lord took His people into partnership with Himself, and entrusted His work on earth entirely to their care. Through their neglect it would suffer and through their diligence would be His enrichment. Here we have the true central principle of Christian service. Christ has made Himself dependent for the extension of His kingdom on the faithfulness of His people.

"Unto one he gave five talents, to another two, to another one; to each according to his several ability" (Matthew 25:15). Though there was a difference in the measure, every one received a portion of the master's goods. It is in connection with the service we are to render to each other that we read of "the grace given to each of us according to the measure of the gift of Christ." This truth, that every believer without exception has been set apart to take an active part in the work of winning the world for Christ, has almost been nearly lost. Christ was first a son, then a servant. Every believer is first a child of God, then a servant. It is the highest honor of a son to be a servant, to have the father's work entrusted to him. Neither the home nor the foreign missionary work of the

Church will ever be done right until every believer feels that the one object of his being in the world is to work for the kingdom. The first duty of the servants in the parable was to spend their life in caring for their master's interests.

"After a long time the lord of those servants cometh and maketh a reckoning with them" (Matthew 25:19). Christ keeps watch over the work He has left to be done on earth. His kingdom and glory depend upon it. He will not only hold us accountable when He comes again to judge, but comes unceasingly to inquire of His servants as to their welfare and work. He comes to approve and encourage, to correct and warn. By His word and Spirit He asks us to say whether we are using our talents diligently, and, as His devoted servants, living only and entirely for His work. Some He finds laboring diligently, and to them He frequently says, "Enter into the joy of thy Lord." Others He sees discouraged, and them He inspires with new hope. Some He finds working in their own strength; these He reproves. Still others He finds sleeping or hiding their talent. To such His voice speaks in solemn warning, "from him that hath shall be taken away even that he hath." Christ's heart is in His work. Every day He watches over it with the most intense interest.

"Lord, I was afraid and hid thy talent in the earth" (Matthew 25:25). That the man of the one talent should have been the one to fail, and to be so severely punished is a lesson of deep solemnity. It calls the Church to beware lest, by neglecting to teach the weaker ones, the one-talent men, that their service is needed, she allows them to let their gifts lie unused. In teaching the great truth that every branch is to bear fruit, special stress must be laid on the danger of thinking that this can only be expected of the strong and advanced Christian. When Truth reigns in a school the most backward pupil has the same attention as the more clever. Care must be taken that the feeblest Christians receive special training, so that they may joyfully have their share in the service of their Lord and all the blessedness it brings. If Christ's work is to be done, not one can be missed.

"Lord, I knew that thou art a hard man, and I was afraid." Wrong thoughts of God, looking upon His service as that of a hard master, are one chief cause of failure in service. If the Church is indeed to care for the weaker ones, who are apt to be discouraged by reason of their conscious weakness, we must teach them what God says of the sufficiency of grace and the certainty of success. They must learn to believe that the power of the Holy Spirit within them fits them for the work to which God has called them. They must learn to understand that God himself will strengthen them with might by His Spirit in the inner man. They must be taught that work is joy and health and strength. Unbelief lies at the root of sloth. Faith opens the eyes to see the blessedness of God's service, the sufficiency of the strength provided, and the rich reward. Let the Church awake to her calling to train the weakest of her members to know that Christ counts upon every redeemed one to live wholly for His work. This alone is true Christianity and full salvation.

REFLECTION

1. Is it possible to be waiting on God, but not working for Him?

2. What is the aim and purpose of doing good works?

3. What are some ways in which the unity of the church body can be maintained through waiting and working?

DAY 6

LIFE AND WORK

"My meat is to do the will of Him that sent Me, and to accomplish His work. I must work the works of Him that sent Me. I have glorified Thee on the earth; I have finished the work Thou gavest Me to do. And now, O Father, glorify Me with Thyself" (John 5:34, 9:4, 17:4).

Work is the highest form of existence. The highest manifestation of the Divine Being is in His work. Read carefully again the words of our Blessed Lord at the head of the chapter, and see what divine glory there is in His work. In His work Christ showed forth His own glory and that of the Father. It was because of the work He had done, and because in it He had glorified the Father, that He claimed to share the glory of the Father in heaven. The greater works He was to do in answer to the prayer of the disciples was, that the Father might be glorified in the Son. Work is indeed the highest form of existence, the highest manifestation of the Divine glory in the Father and in His Son.

What is true of God is true of His creature. Life is movement, is action, and reveals itself in what it accomplishes. The bodily life, the intellectual, the moral, the spiritual life—individual, social, national life—each of these is judged by its work. The character and quality of the work depends on the life. As goes the life, so goes the work. On the other hand the life depends on the work. Without this there can be no full development and manifestation and perfecting of the life. As goes the work, so goes the life.

This is especially true of the spiritual life—the life of the Spirit in us. There may be a great deal of religious work with its external activities, the outcome of human will and effort, with but little true worth and power, because the Divine life is feeble. When the believer does not know that Christ is living in him, does not know the Spirit and power of God working in him, there may be much earnestness and diligence, with little that lasts for eternity. There may, on the contrary, be much external weakness and apparent failure, and yet results that prove that the life is indeed of God.

The work depends upon the life. And the life depends on the work for its growth and perfection. All life has a destiny. It cannot accomplish its purpose without work. Life is perfected by work. The highest manifestation of its hidden nature and power comes out in its work. And so work is the great factor by which the hidden beauty and the divine possibilities of the Christian life are brought out. Not only for the sake of what it accomplishes through the believer as God's instrument, but what it affects on himself. Work must in the child of God take the same place it has in God Himself. As in the Father and the Son, so with the Holy Spirit dwelling in us, work is the highest manifestation of life.

Work must be restored to its right place in God's scheme of the Christian life as in very deed the highest form of existence—to be the intelligent willing channel of the power of God, to be capable of working the very work of God, to be animated by the divine Spirit of love, and in that to be allowed to work life and blessing to men. It is this that gives nobility to life, because it is for this that we are created in the image of God. As God never for a moment ceases to work His work of love and blessing in us and through us, so our working out what He works in us is our highest proof of being created anew in His likeness.

If God's purpose with the perfection of the individual believer, with the appointment of His Church as the body of Christ to carry on His work of winning back a rebellious world to His allegiance and love is to be carried out, waiting and working for God must have much greater prominence given to it as the true glory of our Christian calling. Every believer must be taught that, as work is the only perfect manifestation, and therefore the perfection of life in God and throughout the world, so our work is to be our highest glory. Shall it be so in our lives?

If this is to come true, we must remember two things. The one is that it can only come by beginning to work. Those who have not had their attention specially directed to it cannot realize how great the temptation is to make work a matter of thought and prayer and purpose, without its really being done. It is easier to bear than to think, easier to think than to speak, easier to speak than to act. We may listen and accept and admire God's will, and in our prayer profess our willingness to do—and yet not actually do. Let us, with such measure of grace as we have, and much prayer for more, take up our calling as God's working men, and do good hard work for Him. Doing is the best teacher. If you want to know how to do a thing, begin and do it.

Then you will feel the need of the second thing I wish to mention, and understand it—that there is sufficient grace in Christ for all the work you have to do. You will see with ever-increasing gladness how He, the Head, works all in you, the member, and how work for God may become your closest and fullest fellowship with Christ, your highest participation in the power of His risen and glorified life.

REFLECTION

1. Beware of separating life and work. The more work you have, the more your work appears a failure. The more unfit you feel for work, take all the more time and care to have your inner life renewed in close fellowship with God.

2. Christ living in me is the secret of joy and hope, and also of power for work. Care for the life, and the life will care for the work. "Be filled with the Spirit."

DAY 7

THE FATHER ABIDING IN ME DOETH THE WORK

"Jesus answered them, My Father worketh even until now, and I work." John 5:17-20. "Believest thou not that I am in the Father, and the Father in Me? The words that I speak I speak not of Myself: but the Father abiding in Me doeth the work" (John 14:10).

Jesus Christ became man that He might show us what a true man is, how God meant to live and work in man, and how man may find his life and do his work in God. In words like those above, our Lord opens up the inner mystery of His life, and discovers to us the nature and the deepest secret of His working. He did not come to the world to work instead of the Father; the Father was ever working and "worketh even until now." Christ's work was the fruit, the earthly reflection of the Heavenly Father working. And it was not as if Christ merely saw and copied what the Father willed or did: "The Father abiding in Me doeth the work." Christ did all His work in the power of the Father dwelling and working in Him. So complete and real was His dependence

147

on the Father, that in expounding it to the Jews, He used the strong expressions, "The Son can do nothing of himself, but what He seeth the Father doing." "I can do nothing of Myself" (John 5:19,30). As literally as what He said is true of us, "Apart from Me ye can do nothing," is it true of Him, too. "The Father abiding in Me doeth the work."

Jesus Christ became man that He might show us what is a true man, what is the true relation between man and God, and what is the true way of serving God and doing His work. When we are made new creatures in Christ Jesus, the life we receive is the very life that was and is in Christ, and it is only by studying His life on earth that we know how we are to live. "As the living Father hath sent me, and I live by the Father, so he that eateth Me, even he shall live by Me" (John 6:57). His dependence on the Father is the law of our dependence on Him and on the Father through Him.

Christ counted it no humiliation to be able to do nothing of himself, to be always and absolutely dependent on the Father. He counted it His highest glory, because all His works were the works of the all glorious God in Him. When shall we understand that to wait on God, to bow before Him in perfect helplessness, and let Him work all in us, is our true nobility, and the secret of the highest activity? This alone is the true Son-life, the true life of every child of God. As this life is known and maintained, the power for work will grow, because the soul is in the attitude in which God can work in us, as the God who "worketh for him that waiteth on Him." It is the ignorance or neglect of many great truths, that there can be no true work for God but as God works it in us, and that God cannot work in us fully except as we live in absolute dependence on Him, that is the explanation of the universal complaint of so much Christian activity with so little real result. The revival which many are longing and praying for must begin with the return of Christian ministers and workers to their true place before God—in Christ and like Christ, one of complete dependence and continual waiting on God to work in them.

Let me invite all workers, young and old, successful or disappointed, full of hope or full of fear, to come and learn from our Lord Jesus the secret of true work for God. "My Father worketh, and I work." "The Father abiding in Me doeth the works." Divine Fatherhood means that God is all, and gives all, and works all. Divine Sonship means continual dependence on the Father, and the reception, moment by moment, of all the strength needed for His work. Try to grasp the great truth that "it is God who worketh all in all." Your one need is, in deep humility and weakness, to wait for and to trust in His working. Learn from this that God can only work in us as He dwells in us. "The Father abiding in Me doeth the works." Cultivate the holy sense of God's continual nearness and presence, of your being His temple, and of His dwelling in you. Offer yourself for Him to work in you all His good pleasure. You will find that work, instead of being a hindrance, can become your greatest incentive to a life of fellowship and childlike dependence.

At first it may appear as if the waiting for God to work will keep you back from your work. It may indeed, but only to bring the greater blessing when you have learned the lesson of faith that counts on His working even when you do not feel it. You may have to do your work in weakness and fear and much trembling. You will know that it is all, that the excellency of the power may be of God and not of us. As you know yourself better and God better, you will be content that it should ever be "His strength made perfect in our weakness."

149

REFLECTION

1. "The Father abiding in Me doeth the work." There is the same law for the Head and the member, for Christ and the believer. "It is the same God that worketh all in all."

2. The Father not only worked in the Son when He was on earth, but now, too, that He is in heaven. As we believe in Christ in the Father's working in Him, we shall do even greater works (See John 14:10-12).

3. It is through the indwelling God, the Father abiding in us, that God works in us. Let the life of God in the soul be clear, the work will be sure.

4. Pray much for grace to say, in the name of Jesus, "The Father abiding in me doeth the work."

DAY 8

GREATER WORKS

"Verily, verily, I say unto You, He that believeth on Me, the works that I do shall he do also and greater works shall he do; because I go unto the Father. And whatsoever ye shall ask in My name, that will I do, that the Father may be glorified in the Son. If ye shall ask anything in My name, that will I do" (John 14:12-14).

In the words (verse 10), "The Father abiding in Me doeth the works," Christ had revealed the secret of His and of all Divine service—man yielding himself for God to dwell and to work in him. When Christ then promises, "He that believeth on Me, the works that I do shall he do also," the law of the Divine inner-working remains unchanged. In us, as much as in Him, one might even say a thousand times more than with Him, it must still ever be that the Father in me doeth the works. With Christ and with us, it is "the same God who worketh all in all."

How this can be, is taught to us in the words, "He that believeth on Me." This does not only mean for salvation, as a Savior from sin, but much more. Christ had just said, "Believe Me that I am in the Father, and the Father in Me: the Father abiding in Me doeth the works." We need to believe in Christ as Him in and through whom the Father unceasingly works. To believe in Christ is to receive Him into the heart. When we see the Father's working inseparably connected with Christ, we know that to believe in Christ, and receive Him into the heart, is to receive the Father dwelling in Him and working through Him. The works His disciples are to do cannot possibly be done in any other way than His own are done.

This becomes still clearer from what our Lord adds: "And greater works shall he do; because I go unto the Father." What the greater works are is evident. The disciples at Pentecost with three thousand baptized, and multitudes added to the Lord; Philip at Samaria, with the whole city filled with joy; the men of Cyprus and Cyrene, and later on, Barnabas at Antioch, with much people added to the Lord; Paul in his travels, and a countless host of Christ's servants down to our day, have in the ingathering of souls, done what the Master condescendingly calls greater works than He did in the days of His humiliation and weakness.

The reason why it should be so our Lord makes plain, "Because I go to the Father." When He entered the glory of the Father, all power in heaven and on earth was given to Him as our Redeemer. In a way more glorious than ever

151

the Father was to work through Him, and He then to work through His disciples. Even as His own work on earth "in the days of the weakness of the flesh" had been in a power received from the Father in heaven, so His people, in their weakness, would do works like His, and greater works in the same way, through a power received from heaven. The law of the divine working is unchangeable: God's work can only be done by God himself. It is as we see this in Christ, and receive Him in this capacity, as the One in and through whom God works all, and so yield ourselves wholly to the Father working in Him and in us, that we shall do greater works than He did.

The words that follow bring out still more strongly the great truths we have been learning, that it is our Lord himself who will work all in us, even as the Father did in Him, and that our posture is to be exactly what His was, one of entire receptivity and dependence. "Greater works shall he do, because I go to the Father, and whatsoever ye shall ask in My name, that will I do." Christ connects the greater works the believer is to do, with the promise that He will do whatever the believer asks. Prayer in the name of Jesus will be the expression of that dependence that waits on Him for His working, to which He gives the promise: Whatsoever ye ask, I will do, in you and through you. And when He adds, "that the Father may be glorified in the Son," He reminds us how He had glorified the Father, by yielding to Him as Father, to work all His work in himself as Son. In heaven Christ would still glorify the Father, by receiving from the Father the power, and working in His disciples what the Father would. The creature, as the Son himself can give the Father no higher glory than yielding to Him to work all. The believer can glorify the Father in no other way than the Son, by an absolute and unceasing dependence on the Son, in whom the Father works, to communicate and work in us all the Father's work. "If ye shall ask anything in My name, that will I do," and so you shall do greater works.

Let every believer strive to learn the one blessed lesson. I am to do the works I have seen Christ doing. I may even do greater works as I yield myself to Christ exalted on the throne, in a power He had not on earth. I may count on Him working in me according to that power. My one need is the spirit of dependence and waiting, and prayer and faith, that Christ abiding in me will do the works, even whatsoever I ask.

REFLECTION

1. How was Christ able to work the works of God? By God abiding in Him! How can I do the works of Christ? By Christ abiding in me!

2. What is Christ referring to when he says of the apostles that they shall do even greater works than He? How can I do greater works than Christ? By believing not only in Christ the incarnate and crucified, but Christ triumphant on the throne.

3. In work everything depends, O believer, on the life, the inner life, the Divine life. Pray to realize that work is vain except as it is in "the power of the Holy Spirit" dwelling in you.

DAY 9

CREATED IN CHRIST JESUS FOR GOOD WORKS

*"By grace have ye been saved through faith; not of works,
lest any man should glory. For we are His workmanship,
created in Christ Jesus for good works, which God afore
prepared that we should walk in them"
(Ephesians 2:8-10).*

We have been saved, not of works, but for good works.
How vast is this difference. How essential is the
apprehension of that difference to the health of the Christian
life. Not of works, which we have done, as the source from
where salvation comes, have we been saved. And yet for
good works, as the fruit and outcome of salvation, as part
of God's work in us, the one thing for which we have been
created anew. As worthless as are our works in procuring
salvation, so infinite is their worth as that for which God
has created and prepared us. Let us seek to hold these two
truths in their fullness of spiritual meaning. The deeper our
conviction that we have been saved, not of works, but of
grace, the stronger the proof we should give that we have
indeed been saved for good works.

"Not of works, for ye are God's workmanship." If works
could save us, there would be no need for our redemption.
Because our works were all sinful and vain, God undertook
to make us anew. We are now His workmanship, and all
the good works we do are His workmanship too. "His
workmanship, created us anew in Christ Jesus." So complete
had been the ruin of sin that God had to do the work of
creation over again in Christ Jesus. In Him, and especially
in His resurrection from the dead, He created us anew, after
His own image, into the likeness of the life, which Christ had

lived. In the power of that life and resurrection, we are able, we are perfectly fitted, for doing good works. As the eye, because it was created for the light, is most perfectly adapted for its work, as the vine-branch, because it was created to bear grapes, does its work so naturally, we who have been created in Christ Jesus for good work, may rest assured that a Divine capacity for good works is the very law of our being. If we could only know and believe in this as our destiny, if we but live our life in Christ Jesus, as we were new created in Him, we can and we will be fruitful unto every good work.

"Created for good works, which God hath afore prepared that we should walk in them" (Ephesians 2:10). We have been prepared for the works, and the works prepared for us. To understand this, think of how God foreordained His servants of old, Moses and Joshua, Samuel and David, Peter and Paul, for the work He had for them, and foreordained the works for them. The feeblest member of the body is equally cared for by the Head as the most honored. The Father has prepared for the humblest of His children their works as much as for those who are counted chief. For every child God has a life-plan, with work apportioned just according to the power, and grace provided just according to the work. And so just as strong and clear as the teaching, salvation not of works, is its blessed counterpart, salvation for good works, because God created us for them, and even prepared them for us.

And so the Scripture confirms the double lesson this little book desires to bring you. That good works are God's object in the new life He has given you, and ought therefore to be as distinctly your object. As every human being was created for work and endowed with the needful powers, and can only live out a true and healthy life by working, so every believer exists to do good works, that in them his life may be perfected, his fellowmen may be blessed, his Father in heaven be glorified.

We educate all our children with the thought that they must have their work in the world. When shall the Church learn that its great work is to train all believers to take their share in God's great work, and to abound in the good works for which they were created? Let each of us seek to take in the deep spiritual truth of the message, "Created in Christ Jesus for good works, which God hath afore prepared" for each one, and which are waiting for him to take up and fulfill.

The other lesson—that waiting on God is the one great thing needed on our part if we would do the good works God has prepared for us. Let us take up into our hearts these words in their divine meaning; "We are God's workmanship." Not by one act in the past, but in a continuous operation. We are created for good works, as the great means for glorifying God. The good works are prepared for each of us, that we might walk in them. Surrender to and dependence upon God's working is our one need. Let us consider how our new creation for good works is all in Christ Jesus, and abiding in Him, believing on Him, and looking for His strength alone will become the habit of our soul. Created for good works will reveal to us at once the divine command and the sufficient power to live a life in good works.

Let us pray for the Holy Spirit to work the word into the very depths of our consciousness—created in Christ Jesus for good works! In its light we shall learn what a glorious destiny, what an infinite obligation, what a perfect capacity is ours.

REFLECTION

1. Our creation in Adam was for good works. It resulted in failure and the entrance of sin into the world. Our new creation in Christ is for good works again. But with this difference: perfect provision has been made for securing them.

2. Created by God for good works; created by God in Christ Jesus; the good works prepared by God for us—let us pray for the Holy Spirit to show us and impart this to us.

3. Let the life in fellowship with God be true and the power for the work will be sure. As the life goes, so does the work.

DAY 10

WORK, FOR GOD WORKS IN YOU

"Work out your own salvation with fear and trembling; for it is God which worketh in you both to will and to work, for His good pleasure" (Philippians. 2:12, 13).

In our last chapter we saw what salvation is. It is our being God's workmanship, created in Christ Jesus for good works. It concludes, as one of its chief and essential elements, all that treasury of good works which God afore prepared that we should walk in them. In the light of this thought we get the true and full meaning of today's text. Work out your own salvation, such as God has meant it to be, a walk in all the good works, which God has prepared for you. Study to know exactly what the salvation is that God has prepared for you, all that He has meant and made it possible for you to be, and work it out with fear and trembling. Let the greatness of this divine and most holy life, hidden in Christ, your own absolute impotence, and the terrible dangers and temptations besetting you, make you work in fear and trembling.

And yet, that fear need never become unbelief, or that trembling discouragement, for it is God who works in you. Here is the secret of a power that is absolutely sufficient for everything we have to do, of a perfect assurance that we can do everything that God really means us to do. God works in us both to will and to work. First, to will; He gives the insight into what is to be done, the desire that makes the work pleasure, the firm purpose of the will that masters the whole being, and makes it ready and eager for action. He does not work to will, and then leave it unaided to work it out ourselves. The will may have seen and accepted the work, and yet the power be lacking to perform. The renewed will of Romans 7 delighted in God's law, and yet the man was impotent to do, until in Romans 8:2-4, by the law of the Spirit of life in Christ Jesus, he was set free from the law of sin and death; then first could the righteousness of the law be fulfilled in him, as one who walked not after the flesh but after the Spirit.

One great cause of the failure of believers in their work is that, when they think that God has given them over to their will, they undertake to work in the strength of that will. They have never learned the lesson, that because God has created us in Christ Jesus for good works, and has afore prepared the good works in which we are to walk, He will most certainly, himself work them all in us. They have never listened long to the voice speaking "It is God which worketh in you."

We have here one of the deepest, most spiritual, and most precious truths of Scripture—the unceasing operation of Almighty God in our heart and life. In virtue of the very nature of God, as a Spiritual Being not confined to any place, but everywhere present, there can be no spiritual life but as it is upheld by His personal indwelling.

Not without the deepest reason does Scripture say, He worketh all in all. Not only of Him are all things as their first beginning, and to Him as their end, but also through Him, who alone maintains them.

In the man Christ Jesus the working of the Father in Him was the source of all He did. In the new man, created in Christ Jesus, the unceasing dependence on the Father is our highest privilege, our true nobility. This is indeed fellowship with God. God himself working in us to will and to do.

Let us seek to learn the true secret of working for God. It is not, as many think, that we do our best, and then leave God to do the rest. By no means. But it is that we know God is working His salvation in us—this is the secret of our working it out. Salvation includes every work we have to do. The faith of God's working in us is the measure of our fitness to work effectively. The promises, "According to your faith be it unto you," and, "All things are possible to him that believeth," have their full application here. The deeper our faith in God's working in us, the more freely will the power of God work in us, the more true and fruitful will our work be.

Perhaps some Bible teacher or Sunday school worker may be reading this. Let me ask, have you really believed that your only power to do God's work is as one who has been created in Christ Jesus for good works, as one in whom God himself works to will and to work? Have you yielded yourself to wait for that working? Do you work because you know God works in you? Say not that these thoughts are too high. The work of leading young souls to Christ is too high for us indeed, but if we live as little children, in believing that God will work all in us, we shall do His work in His strength. Pray much to learn and practice the lesson in all you do. Work, for God worketh in you.

REFLECTION
1. I think we begin to feel that the spiritual apprehension of this great truth, "God worketh in you," is what all workers need the most.

2. The Holy Spirit is the mighty power of God, dwelling in believers for life and for work. Pray that God would reveal to you, that in all our service our first care must be the daily renewing of the Holy Spirit.

3. Obey the command to be filled with the Holy Spirit. Believe in His indwelling. Wait for His teaching. Yield to His leading. Pray for His mighty working. Live in the Spirit.

4. What the mighty power of God works in us we are surely able to do. Only give way to the power working in you.

DAY 11

FAITH WORKING BY LOVE

"In Christ Jesus neither circumcision availeth anything, nor uncircumcision; but faith working through love. Through love be servants one to another; for the whole law is fulfilled in this: Thou shalt love thy neighbors as thyself" (Galatians 5:6,13).

In Christ Jesus no external privilege avails. The Jew might boast of his circumcision, the token of God's covenant. The Gentile might boast of his uncircumcision, with an entrance into the kingdom free from the Jewish law. Neither availed aught in the kingdom of Heaven—nothing except as we have it in 6:15, a new creature, in which old things are passed away and all things become new. Or as we have it in our text—as a description of the life of the new creature—nothing but faith working by love, that makes us in love serve one another.

160

What a perfect description of the new life. First you have faith, as the root, planted and rooted in Christ Jesus. Then as its aim you have works as the fruit. And then between the two, as the tree, growing downwards into the root and bearing the fruit upward, you have love, with the life-sap flowing through it by which the root brings forth the fruit. Of faith we need not speak here. We have seen how believing on Jesus does the greater works; how the faith in the new creation, and in God working in us, is the secret of all work. Nor need we speak here of works—our whole book aims at securing for them the place in every heart and life that they have in God's heart and in His Word.

We have here to study especially the great truth that all work is to be love, that faith cannot do its work but through love, that no works can have any worth but as they come of love, and that love alone is the sufficient strength for all the work we have to do.

The power for work is love.

It was love that moved God to all His work in creation and redemption. It was love that enabled Christ as man to work and to suffer as He did. It is love that can inspire us with the power of a self-sacrifice that seeks not its own, but is ready to live and die for others. It is love that gives us the patience that refuses to give up the unthankful or the hardened. It is love that reaches and overcomes the most hopeless. Both in ourselves and those for whom we labor, love is the power for work. Let us love as Christ loved us.

The power for love is faith.

Faith roots its life in the life of Christ Jesus, which is all love. Faith knows, even when we cannot realize fully, the wonderful gift that has been given into our heart in the Holy Spirit shedding abroad God's love there. A spring in the

161

earth may often be hidden or stopped up. Until it is opened the fountain cannot flow out. Faith knows that there is a fountain of love within that can spring up into eternal life, and can flow out as rivers of living waters. It assures us that we can love, that we have a divine power to love within us, as an unalienable endowment of our new nature.

The power to exercise and show love is work.

There is no such thing as power in the abstract. It only acts as it is exercised. Power in repose cannot be found or felt. This is especially true of the Christian graces, hidden as they are amid the weakness of our human nature. It is only by doing that you know that you have. A grace must be acted in order that we can rejoice in its possession. This is the unspeakable blessedness of work, and makes it so essential to a healthy Christian life that it wakens up and strengthens love, and makes us partakers of its joy.

Faith working by love.

In Christ Jesus nothing avails but this. Workers for God! Let me press home this message, too, on those who have never yet or only just begun to think of working for God. Come and listen. Believe this and practice it. Thank God for the fountain of eternal love opened within you. Pray fervently and frequently that God may strengthen you with might by the power of His Spirit in your inner man, so that, with Christ dwelling in you, you may be rooted and grounded in love. Live then, your daily life, in your own home, in all your intercourse with men, in all your work, as a life of divine love. The ways of love are so gentle and heavenly, you may not learn them all at once. But be of good courage, only believe in the power that works in you, and yield yourself to the work of love. It will surely gain the victory.

You owe everything to God's love.

The salvation you have received is all love. God's one desire is to fill you with His love—for His own satisfaction, for your own happiness, for the saving of men. Now, I ask you, will you not accept God's wonderful offer to be filled with His love? Oh! Come and give up heart and life to the joy and the service of His love. Believe that the fountain of love is within you. It will begin to flow as you make a channel for it by deeds of love. Whatever work for God you try to do, seek to put love into it. Pray for the spirit of love. Give yourself to live a life of love; to think how you can love those around you, by praying for them, by serving them, by laboring for their welfare, temporal and spiritual. Faith working by love in Christ Jesus, this alone availeth much.

REFLECTION

1. "Faith, Hope, Love: the greatest of these is Love." There is no faith or hope in God. But God is love. The most God-like thing is love.

2. Love is the nature of God. When it is shed abroad in our hearts by the Holy Spirit love becomes our new nature. Give yourself over to it, and act it out.

3. Love is God's power to do His work. Love was Christ's power. To work for God pray earnestly to be filled with love for the souls of others!

4. Whatever work you do for God, seek to do it with love. What could be hindering you from this?

DAY 12

BEARING FRUIT IN EVERY GOOD WORK

"To walk worthily of the Lord unto all pleasing, bearing fruit in every good work, and increasing in the knowledge of God; strengthened with all power, according to the might of His glory, unto all patience" *(Colossians 1:10).*

There is a difference between fruit and work. Fruit is that which comes spontaneously, without thought or will, the natural and necessary outcome of a healthy life. Work, on the contrary, is the product of effort guided by intelligent thought and will. In the Christian life we have the two elements in combination. All true work must be fruit, the growth and product of our inner life, the operation of God's Spirit within us. And yet all fruit must be work, the effect of our deliberate purpose and exertion. In the words, "bearing fruit in every good work," we have the practical summing up of the truth taught in some previous chapters. Because God works by His life in us, the work we do is fruit. Because, in the faith of His working, we have to will and to work, the fruit we bear is work. In the harmony between the perfect spontaneity that comes from God's life and Spirit animating us, and our co-operation with Him as His intelligent fellow-laborers, lies the secret of all true work.

In the words that precede our text, "filled with the knowledge of His will in all wisdom and spiritual understanding," we have the human side, our need of knowledge and wisdom. In the words that follow, "strengthened with all power, according to the might of His glory," we have the Divine side. God teaching and strengthening, man learning to understand and patiently do

His will, Such is the double life that will be fruitful in every good work.

It has been said of the Christian life that the natural man must first become spiritual, and then again the spiritual man must become natural. As the whole natural life becomes truly spiritual, all our work will partake of the nature of fruit, the outgrowth of the life of God within us. And as the spiritual again becomes perfectly natural to us, a second nature in which we are wholly at home, all the fruit will bear the mark of true work, calling into full exercise every faculty of our being.

"Bearing fruit unto every good work." The words, suggest again the great thought that as an apple tree or a vine is planted solely for its fruit, so the great purpose of our redemption is that God may have us for His work and service. It has been well said: "The end of man is an 'action' and not a 'thought,' though it were of the noblest." It is in his work that the nobility of man's nature as ruler of the world is proved. It is for good works that we have been newly created in Christ Jesus. It is when men see our good works that our Father in Heaven will be glorified and have the honor, which is His due for His workmanship. In the parable of the vine our Lord insisted on this: "If ye abide in Me, and my words abide in you, ye shall ask what ye will, and it shall be done unto you. Herein is My Father glorified, that ye bear much fruit" (John 15:7,8). Nothing is more to the honor of a husbandman than to succeed in raising an abundant crop—much fruit is glory to God.

What every believer needs, even the feeblest branch of the Heavenly Vine, is to be encouraged and helped, and even trained, unto the bearing of much fruit. A little strawberry plant may, in its measure, be bearing a more abundant crop than a large apple-tree. The call to be fruitful in every good work is for every Christian without exception. Every fruitful branch in every good work is an essential part of God's Gospel.

"Bearing fruit in every good work." Let us study to get a full impression of the two sides of this divine truth. God's first creation of life was in the vegetable kingdom. There it was a life without anything of will or self-effort, all growth and fruit was simply His own direct work, the spontaneous outcome of His hidden working. In the creation of the animal kingdom there was an advance. A new element was introduced—thought and will and work. In man these two elements were united in perfect harmony. The absolute dependence of the grass and the lily on the God who clothes them with their beauty were to be the groundwork of our relationship—nature has nothing but what it receives from God. Our works are to be fruit, the product of a God-given power. But to this was added the true mark of our God-likeness the power of will and independent action. All fruit is to be our own work. As we grasp this we shall see how the most absolute acknowledgment of our having nothing in ourselves is consistent with the deepest sense of obligation and the strongest will to exert our powers to the utmost. We shall learn to study the prayer of our text as those who must seek all their wisdom and strength from God alone. And we shall boldly give ourselves, as those who are responsible for the use of that wisdom and strength, to the diligence and the sacrifice and the effort needed for a life bearing fruit in every good work.

Reflection

1. Is there a difference between fruit and work. If so, what is that difference?

2. Much depends, for quality and quantity, on the healthy life of the tree. The life of God, of Christ Jesus, of His Spirit, the divine life in you, is strong and sure.

3. That life is love. Believe in it. Act it out. Have it replenished day by day out of the fullness there is in Christ.

4. Let all your work be fruit. Let all your willing and working be inspired by the life of God. So you will walk worthily of the Lord with all pleasing.

DAY 13

ALWAYS ABOUNDING IN THE WORK OF THE LORD

"Wherefore, my beloved brethren, be ye steadfast, unmovable, always abounding in the work of the Lord, forasmuch as ye know that your labor is not in vain in the Lord" (1 Corinthians 15:58).

We all know the fifteenth chapter of 1 Corinthians, in its Divine revelation of the meaning of Christ's resurrection, with all the blessings of which it is the source.

It gives us a living Savior, who revealed himself to His disciples on earth, and to Paul from heaven. It secures to us the complete deliverance from all sin. It is the pledge of His final victory over every enemy, when He gives up the kingdom to the Father, and God is all in all. It assures us of the resurrection of the body, and our entrance on the heavenly life. Paul had closed his argument with his triumphant appeal to death and sin and the law: "O death, where is thy sting? O grave where is thy victory? The sting of seath is sin, and the strength of sin is the law. But thanks be to God, which giveth us the victory through our Lord Jesus Christ" (I Corinthians 15:55-57). And then follows, after fifty-seven verses of exultant teaching concerning the mystery and the glory of the resurrection life in our Lord and His people, just one verse of practical application: "Wherefore, my beloved brethren, be ye steadfast, unmovable, always abounding in the work of the Lord." The faith in a risen, living Christ, and in all that His resurrection is to us in time and eternity, is to fit us for, is to prove itself in abounding work for our Lord!

It cannot be otherwise. Christ's resurrection was His final victory over sin, and death, and Satan, and His entrance upon His work of giving the Spirit from heaven and extending His kingdom throughout the earth. Those who shared the resurrection joy at once received the commission to make known the joyful news. It was so with Mary and the women. It was so with the disciples the evening of the resurrection day. "As the Father sent Me, I send you." It was so with all to whom the charge was given: "Go into all the world, preach the Gospel to every creature." The resurrection is the beginning and the pledge of Christ's victory over all the earth. That victory is to be carried out to its complete manifestation through His people. The faith and joy of the resurrection life are the inspiration and the power for the work of doing it. And so the call comes to all believers without exception: "Wherefore, my beloved brethren, be ye always abounding in the work of the Lord!"

"In the work of the Lord." The connection tells us at once what that work is. Nothing else, nothing less than, telling others of the risen Lord, and proving to them what new life Christ has brought to us. As we indeed know and acknowledge Him as Lord over all we are, and live in the joy of His service, we shall see that the work of the Lord is but one work that of winning men to know and bow to Him.

Amid all the forms of lowly, living, patient service, this will be the one aim, in the power of the life of the risen Lord, to make Him Lord of all.

This work of the Lord is not an easy one. It cost Christ His life to conquer sin and Satan and gain the risen life. It will cost us our life, too, the sacrifice of the life of nature. It needs the surrender of all on earth to live in the full power of resurrection newness of life. The power of sin, and the world, in those around us is strong, and Satan does not yield his servants an easy prey to our efforts. It needs a heart in close touch with the risen Lord, truly living the resurrection life, to be steadfast, unmovable, always abounding in the work of the Lord. But that is a life that can be lived because Jesus lives.

Paul adds: "Forasmuch as ye know that your labor is not vain in the Lord." I have spoken more than once of the mighty influence that the certainty of reward for work, in the shape of wages or riches, exerts on the millions of earth's workers. And shall not Christ's workers believe that, with such a Lord, their reward is sure and great? The work is often difficult and slow, and apparently fruitless. We are apt to lose heart, because we are working in our strength and judging by our expectations. Let us listen to the message, O ye children of the resurrection life, be ye "always abounding in the work of the Lord, forasmuch as ye know your labor is not in vain in the Lord." Let not your hands be weak; your work shall be rewarded. "You know that your labor is not vain in the Lord."

"In the Lord." The expression is a significant one. Study it in Romans 16 where it occurs ten times, where Paul uses the expressions: "Receive here in the Lord," "my fellow-worker in Christ Jesus," "who are in Christ, in the Lord," "beloved in the Lord," "approved in Christ," "who labor in the Lord," and "chosen in the Lord." The whole life and fellowship and service of these saints had this one mark: They were, their labors were, in the Lord. Here is the secret of effectual service. Your labor is not "in vain in the Lord." As a sense of His presence and the power of His life are maintained, as all works are wrought in Him, His strength works in our weakness. Our labor cannot be in vain in the Lord. Christ said, "He that abideth in Me, and I in him, the same bringeth forth much fruit." Oh! Let not the children of this world, with their confidence that the masters whose work they are doing will certainly give them their due reward, put the children of light to shame. Let us rejoice and labor in the confident faith of the word, "Your labor is not in vain in the Lord. Wherefore, beloved brethren, be ye always abounding in the work of the Lord."

REFLECTION
1. The one great "work of the Lord" is telling others of the risen Savior. How is that work exercised in your life?

2. It is the work of all believers in Jesus Christ to minister the Gospel. How have you witnessed your faith?

DAY 14

ABOUNDING GRACE FOR ABOUNDING WORK

"And God is able to make all grace abound unto you, that ye may abound unto every good work"
(2 Corinthians 9:8).

In our previous meditation we had the great motive to abounding work—the spirit of triumphant joy which

Christ's resurrection inspires as it covers the past and the future. Our text today assures us that for this abounding work we have the ability provided. God is able to make all grace abound that we may abound to all good works. Every thought of abounding grace is to be connected with the abounding in good works for which it is given. And every thought of abounding work is to be connected with the abounding grace that fits for it.

Abounding grace has abounding work for its aim. It is often thought that grace and good works are at variance with each other. This is not so. What Scripture calls the works of the law, our own works, the works of righteousness which we have done, dead works—works by which we seek to merit or to be made fit for God's favour, these are indeed the very opposite of grace. But they are also the very opposite of the good works which spring from grace, and for which alone grace is bestowed. As irreconcilable as are the works of the law with the freedom of grace, so essential and indispensable are the works of faith, good works, to the true Christian life. God makes grace to abound, that good works may abound. The measure of true grace is tested and proved by the measure of good works. God's grace abounds in us that we may abound in good works. We need to have the truth deeply rooted in us: Abounding grace has abounding work for its aim.

Abounding work needs abounding grace as its source and strength. There often is abounding work without abounding grace. Just as any man may be very diligent in an earthly pursuit, or a heathen in his religious service of an idol, so men may be very diligent in doing religious work in their own strength, but with little thought of that grace which alone can do true, spiritual effective work. For all work that is to be really acceptable to God, and truly fruitful, not only for

171

some visible result here on earth, but for eternity, the grace of God is indispensable. Paul continually speaks of his own work as owing everything to the grace of God working in him. "I labored more abundantly than they all: yet not I, but the grace of God which was with me" (1 Corinthians 15:10). "According to the gift of that grace of God which was given me according to the working of His power" (Ephesians 3:7). And he as frequently calls upon Christians to exercise their gifts "according to the grace that was given us" (Romans 12:6). "The grace given according to the measure of the gift of Christ" (Ephesians 4:7). It is only by the grace of God working in us that we can do what are truly good works. It is only as we seek and receive abounding grace that we can abound in every good work.

"God is able to make all grace abound unto you, that ye may abound in all good works." With what thanksgiving every Christian ought to praise God for the abounding grace that is thus provided for him. And with what humiliation to confess that the experience of, and the surrender to, that abounding grace has been so defective. And with what confidence to believe that a life abounding in good works is indeed possible, because the abounding grace for it is so sure and so divinely sufficient.

And then, with what simple childlike dependence to wait upon God day by day to receive the more grace which He gives to the humble.

Child of God! Do take time to study and truly apprehend God's purpose with you that you abound in every good work! He means it! He has provided for it! Make the measure of your consecration to Him nothing less than His purpose for you. And claim, then, nothing less than the abounding grace He is able to bestow. Make His omnipotence and His faithfulness your confidence. And live ever in the practice of continual prayer and dependence upon His power working in you. This will make you abound in every good work. According to your faith may it be unto you.

Christian worker, learn here the secret of all failure and all success. Work in our own strength, with little prayer and waiting on God for His spirit, is the cause of failure. The cultivation of the spirit of absolute impotence and unceasing dependence will open the heart for the workings of the abounding grace. We shall learn to ascribe all we do to God's grace. We shall learn to measure all we have to do by God's grace. And our life will increasingly be in the joy of God's making His grace to abound in us, and our abounding in every good work.

REFLECTION

1. "That ye may abound to every good work." Pray over this now till you feel that this is what God has prepared for you.

2. If your ignorance and feebleness appear to make it impossible, present yourself to God, and say you are willing, if He will enable you to abound in good works, to be a branch that brings forth much fruit.

3. Take into your heart, as a living seed, the precious truth that God is able to make all grace abound in you. Trust His power and His faithfulness (Romans 4:20,21; 1 Thessalonians 5:24).

4. Begin at once by doing lowly deeds of love. As the little child in the kindergarten, learn by doing.

DAY 15

IN THE WORK OF MINISTERING

"And he gave some to be apostles; and some, prophets; and some, evangelists; and some, pastors and teachers; for the perfecting of the saints, unto the work of ministering, unto the building up of the body of Christ" (Ephesians 4:11,12).

The object with which Christ when He ascended to heaven and bestowed on His servants the various gifts that are mentioned is threefold. Their first aim is for the perfecting of the saints. Believers as saints are to be led on in the pursuit of holiness until they "stand perfect and complete in all the will of God." It was for this Epaphras labored in prayer. It is of this Paul writes, "Whom we preach, teaching every man in all wisdom that we may present every man perfect in Christ" (Colossians 1:28; 4:12).

This perfecting of the saints is, however, only a means to a higher end. The work of ministering is to fit all the saints to take their part in the service to which every believer is called. It is the same word as is used in texts as these: "They ministered to Him of their substance; Ye ministered to the saints and do minister." (See Luke 4:30, 8:3; 1 Corinthians 16:15; Hebrews 6:10; 1 Peter 4:11.)

And this, again, is also a means to a still higher end—the building up of the body of Christ. As every member of our body takes its part in working for the health and growth and maintenance of the whole, so every member of the body of Christ is to consider it his first great duty to take part in all that can help to build up the body of Christ. The great work of the Church is, through its pastors and teachers, to labor for the perfecting of the saints in holiness and love and fitness for service, that every one may take his part in the work of ministering, so that the body of Christ may be built up and perfected.

Of the three great objects with which Christ has given His Church apostles and teachers, the work of ministering stands in the middle. On the one hand, it is preceded by that on which it absolutely depends—the perfecting of the saints. On the other, it is followed by that which it is meant to accomplish—the building up of the body of Christ. Every believer without exception, every member of Christ's body, is called to take part in the work of ministering. Let every reader try and realize the sacredness of his holy calling.

Let us learn what the qualification is for our work. "The perfecting of the saints" prepares them for the "work of ministering." It is the lack of true sainthood, of true holiness, that causes such lack and feebleness of service. As Christ's saints are taught and truly learn what conformity to Christ means, a life like His, given up in self-sacrifice for the service and salvation of men, as His humility and love, His separation from the world and devotion to the fallen, are seen to be the very essence and blessedness of the life He gives. The work of ministering and the ministry of love will become the things we live for. Humility and love—these are the two great virtues of the saint—they are the two great powers for the work of ministering. Humility makes us willing to serve. Love makes us wise to know how to do it. Love is inventive; it seeks patiently and suffers long until it finds a way to reach its object. Humility and love are equally turned away from self and its claims. Let us pray, let the Church labor for "the perfecting of the saints" in humility and love, and the Holy Spirit will teach us how to minister.

175

The great work of each believer in Christ is to minister to each other. Place yourself at Christ's disposal for service to your fellow Christians. Count yourself their servant. Study their interests. Set yourself actively to promote the welfare of the Christians around you. Selfishness may hesitate, the feeling of feebleness may discourage, sloth and ease may raise difficulties. Ask your Lord to reveal to you His will, and give yourself up to it. All around you there are Christians who are cold and worldly and wandering from their Lord. Think about what you can do for them. Accept as the will of the Head that you as a member should care for them. Pray for the Spirit of love. Begin somewhere—only begin, and do not continue hearing and thinking while you do nothing. Begin "the work of ministering" according to the measure of the grace you have. He will give more grace.

Let us believe in the power that works in us as sufficient for all we have to do. As I think of the thumb and finger holding the pen with which I write this, I ask, How is it that during all these seventy years of my life they have always known just to do my will? It was because the life of the head passed into and worked itself out in them. "He that believeth on Me," as his Head working in him, "the works that I do shall he do also." Faith in Christ, whose strength is made perfect in our weakness will give the power for all we are called to do.

Let us cry to God that all believers may waken up to the power of this great truth: Every member of the body is to live wholly for the building up of the body.

REFLECTION

1. What is "the perfecting of the Saints?" And what is the believer's part?

2. To be a true worker, the first thing is close, humble fellowship with Christ the Head, and to be guided and empowered by Him.

3. The next is humble, loving fellowship with Christ's members serving one another in love. This prepares and fits us for service in the world.

DAY 16

ACCORDING TO THE WORKING OF EACH SEVERAL PART

"That we may grow up in all things into Him, which is the Head, even Christ; from whom all the body fitly framed and knit together through that which every joint together supplieth, according to the working in due measure of each several part, maketh the increase of the body unto the building up of itself in love" (Ephesians 4:15,16).

The apostle is here speaking of the growth, the increase, and the building up of the body. This growth and increase has, as we have seen, a double reference. It includes both the spiritual uniting and strengthening of those who are already members, so as to secure the health of the whole body. It also speaks of the increase of the body by the addition of all who are as yet outside of it, and are to be gathered in. Of the former we spoke in the previous chapter—the mutual interdependence of all believers, and the calling to care for each other's welfare. In this chapter we look at the growth from the other side—the calling of every member of Christ's body to labor for its increase by the labor of love that seeks to bring in them who are not yet part of it. This increase of

177

the body and building up of itself in love can only be by the working in due measure of each several part.

Think of the body of a child and how it reaches the stature of a full-grown man? This can happen in no other way but by the working in due measure of every part. As each member takes its part, by the work it does in seeking and taking and assimilating food, the increase is made by its building up itself. Not from without, but from within, comes the work that assures the growth. In no other way can Christ's body attain to the stature of the fullness of Christ. As it is unto Christ the Head we grow up, and from Christ the Head that the body makes increase of itself, so it is all through that which every joint supplies, according to the working in due measure of each several part. Let us see what this implies.

The body of Christ is to consist of all who believe in Him throughout the world. There is no possible way in which these members of the body can be gathered in, but it is by the body building itself up in love. Our Lord has made himself, as Head, absolutely dependent on His members to do this work. What nature teaches us of our own bodies, Scripture teaches us of Christ's body. The head of a child may have thought and plans of growth—they will all be vain, except as the members all do their part in securing that growth. Christ Jesus has committed to His Church the growth and increase of His body. He asks and expects that as wholly as He the Head lives for the growth and welfare of the body, every member of His body, the very feeblest, shall do the same, to the building up of the body in love. Every believer is to count it his one duty and blessedness to live and labor for the increase of the body, and the gathering in of all who are to be its members.

What is it that is needed to bring the Church to accept this calling, and to train and help the members of the body to know and fulfill it? One thing. We must see that the new birth and faith, that all insight into truth, with all resolve and surrender and effort to live according to it, is only a preparation for our true work. What is needed is that in every believer Jesus Christ be formed, dwelling in the heart, that His life in us shall be the impulse and inspiration of our love to the whole body, and our life for it. It is because self occupies the heart that it is so easy and natural and pleasing to care for ourselves. When Jesus Christ lives in us, it will be as easy and natural and pleasing to live wholly for the body of Christ. As readily and naturally as the thumb and fingers respond to the will and movement of the head will the members of Christ's body respond to the Head, as the body grows up in Him.

Let us sum up. For the great work the Head is doing in gathering in from throughout the world and building up His body, He is entirely dependent on the service of the members. Not only our Lord, but a perishing world is waiting and calling for the Church to awake and give herself wholly to this work—the perfecting of the number of Christ's members. Every believer, the very feeblest, must learn to know his calling—to live with this as the main object of earthly existence. This great truth will be revealed to us in power, and obtain the mastery, as we give ourselves to the work of ministering according to the grace we already have. We may confidently wait for the full revelation of Christ in us as the power to do all He asks of us.

REFLECTION
1. The life of Christ in us shall be the impulse and inspiration of our love to the whole body. How are we being an encouragement to the body of which we are part?

DAY 17

WOMEN ADORNED WITH GOOD WORK

*"Let women adorn themselves; not with braided hair,
and gold or pearls or costly raiment; but through good
works. Let none be enrolled as a widow under threescore
years old, well reported of for good works; ...if she hath
diligently followed every good work"*
(1 Timothy 2:10, 5:9,10).

In the three pastoral epistles, written to two young pastors
to instruct them in regard to their duties, "good works" are
more frequently mentioned than in Paul's other epistles. In
writing to the Churches, as in a chapter like Romans 12, he
mentions the individual good work by name. In writing to the
pastors he had to use this expression as a summary of what,
both in their own life and their teaching of others, they had
to aim at. A minister was to be prepared to every good work,
furnished completely to every good work, an example of
good works. And they were to teach Christians—the women
to adorn themselves with good works, diligently to follow
every good work, to be well reported of for good works.
Likewise, the men are to be rich in good works, zealous of
good works, ready to every good work, to be careful and to
learn to maintain good works. No portion of God's work
presses home more definitely the absolute necessity of good
works as an essential, vital element in the Christian life.

Our two texts speak of the good works of Christian
women. In the first place they are taught that their adorning
is to be not with braided hair, and gold or pearls or costly
raiment, but as becomes women preferring godliness, with
good works. We know what adornment is. A leafless tree in
winter has life. When spring comes it puts on its beautiful

garments, and rejoices in the adornment of foliage and blossom. The adorning of Christian women is not to be in hair or pearls or raiment, but in good works. Whether it be the good works that have reference to personal duty and conduct, or those works of beneficence that aim at the pleasing and helping of our neighbor or those that more definitely seek the salvation of souls—the adorning that pleases God, that gives true heavenly beauty, that will truly attract others to come and serve God, is what Christian women ought to seek after. John saw the holy city descend from heaven, "made ready as a bride adorned for her husband." "The fine linen is the righteous acts of the saints" (Rev. 21:2, 24:8). Oh! That every Christian woman might seek so to adorn herself as to please the Lord that loved her.

In the second passage we read of widows who were placed upon a roll of honor in the early Church, and to whom a certain charge was given over the younger women. No one was to be enrolled who was not "well reported of for good works." Some of these are mentioned. If she has been known for the careful bringing up of her children, for her hospitality to strangers, for her washing the saints' feet, for her relieving the afflicted. And then there is added, "if she hath diligently followed every good work." If in her home and out of it, in caring for her own children, for strangers, for saints, for the afflicted, her life has been devoted to good works, she may indeed be counted fit to be an example and guide to others. The standard is a high one. It shows us the place good works took in the early Church. It shows how woman's blessed ministry of love was counted on and encouraged. It shows how, in the development of the Christian life, nothing so fits for rule and influence as a life given to good works.

Good works are part and parcel of the Christian life, equally indispensable to the health and growth of the individual, and to the welfare and extension of the Church. And yet what multitudes of Christian women there are whose active share in the good work of blessing their fellow-creatures is little more than playing at good works. They are waiting for the preaching of a full gospel, which shall encourage and help and compel them to give their lives so to work for their Lord, that they may be well reported of as diligently following every good work. The time and money, the thought and heart given to jewels or costly raiment will be redeemed to its true object. Religion will no longer be a selfish desire for personal safety, but the joy of being like Christ, the helper and savior of the needy. Work for Christ will take its true place as indeed the highest form of existence, the true adornment of the Christian life. And as diligence in the pursuits of earth is honored as one of the true elements of character and worth, diligently to follow good works in Christ's service will be found to give access to the highest reward and the fullest joy of the Lord.

REFLECTION

1. We are beginning to awaken to the wonderful place women can take in church and school and mission. This truth needs to be brought home to every one of the King's daughters, that the adorning in which they are to attract the world, to please their Lord, and to enter His presence is good works.

2. Woman, as the image of "the weakness of God," and "the meekness and gentleness of Christ," is to teach man the beauty and the power of the long-suffering, self-sacrificing ministry of love.

3. The training for the service of love begins in the home life; is strengthened in the inner chamber; reaches out to the needy around, and finds its full scope in the world for which Christ died.

4. How does the role of women differ from men in the pursuit of good works, according to 1 Timothy 2:10 and 5:9,10?

DAY 18

RICH IN GOOD WORKS

"Charge them that are rich in the present world, that they do good, that they be rich in good works, that they be ready to distribute, willing to communicate, laying up for themselves a good foundation against the time to come, that they may lay hold on the life which is life indeed"
(1 Timothy 6:18).

If women are to regard good work as their adornment, men are to count them as regards their riches. As good works satisfy woman's eye and taste for beauty, they meet man's craving for possession and power. In the present world riches have great significance. They are often God's reward on diligence, industry, and enterprise. They represent and embody the life-power that has been spent in procuring them. As such they exercise power in the honor or service they secure from others. Their danger consists in their being of this world, in their drawing off the heart from the living God and the heavenly treasures. They may become a man's deadliest enemy. How hardly shall they that have riches enter the kingdom of heaven!

The gospel never takes away anything from us without giving us something better in its stead. It meets the desire for riches by the command to be rich in good works. Good works are the coin that is current in God's kingdom. According to these will be the reward in the world to come. By abounding in good works we lay up for ourselves treasures in heaven.

Even here on earth they constitute a treasure, in the testimony of a good conscience, in the consciousness of being well pleasing to God (1 John 3) in the power of blessing others.

There is more. Wealth of gold is not only a symbol of the heavenly riches; it is actually a means to it, though so opposite in its nature. "Charge them that are rich in this world, that they be not high-minded, nor trust in uncertain riches, but in the living God ... that they do good, that they be rich in good works, ready to distribute, willing to communicate, laying up in store for themselves a good foundation against the time to come, that they may lay hold on eternal life" (1 Timothy 6:17-19). "Make to yourselves friends by means of the mammon of unrighteousness, that, when it fails, they may receive you into everlasting habitations" (Luke 16:9). Even as the widow's mite, the gifts of the rich, when given in the same spirit, may be an offering with which God is well pleased (Hebrew 13:16). The man who is rich in money may become rich in good works, if he follows out the instructions Scripture lays down. The money must not be given to be seen of men "but as unto the Lord." Nor as from an owner, but a steward who administers the Lord's money, with prayer for His guidance. Nor with any confidence in its power or influence, but in deep dependence on Him who alone can make it a blessing. Nor as a substitute for, or bringing out from that personal work and witness, which each believer is to give. As all Christian work, so our money giving has its value alone from the spirit in which it is done, even the spirit of Christ Jesus.

What an opportunity exists in the world for accumulating these riches, these heavenly treasures. In relieving the poor, in educating the neglected, in helping the lost, in bringing the gospel to Christians and heathen in darkness, what investment might be made if Christians sought to be rich in good works, rich toward God. We may well ask the question, "What can be done to awaken among believers a desire for these true riches?" Men have made a science of the wealth of nations, and carefully studied all the laws by which its increase and universal distribution can be promoted. How can the charge to be rich in good works find a response in the hearts that its pursuit shall be even a greater pleasure and passion than the desire for the riches of the present world?

All depends upon the nature, the spirit, there is in man. To the earthly nature, earthly riches have a natural affinity and irresistible attraction. To foster the desire for the acquisition of what constitutes wealth in the heavenly kingdom, we must appeal to the spiritual nature. That spiritual nature needs to be taught and educated and trained into all the habits that go to make a man rich. There must be the ambition to rise above the level of a bare existence, the deadly contentment with just being saved. There must be some insight into the beauty and worth of good works as the expression of the divine life—God's working in us and our working in Him; as the means of bringing glory to God; as the source of life and blessing to men; as the laying up of a treasure in heaven for eternity. There must be a faith that these riches are actually within our reach, because the grace and Spirit of God are working in us. And then the outlook for every opportunity of doing the work of God to those around us, in the footsteps of Him who said, "It is more blessed to give than receive." Study and apply these principles. They will open the sure road to your becoming a rich man. A man who wants to be rich often begins on a small scale, but never loses an opportunity. Begin at once with some work of love, and ask Christ, who became poor, that you might be rich, to help you.

REFLECTION

1. Why is it that the appeal for money for missions meets with such insufficient response? Is it because of the low spiritual state of the Church? Christians have no due conception of their calling to live wholly for God and His kingdom.

2. How can the evil be remedied? Only when believers see and accept their divine calling to make God's kingdom their first care, and with humble confession of their sins yield themselves to God, will they truly seek the heavenly riches to be found in working for God.

3. Let us never cease to plead and labor for a true spiritual awakening throughout the Church.

DAY 19

PREPARED UNTO EVERY GOOD WORK

"If a man therefore cleanse himself from them, he shall be a vessel unto honor, sanctified, meet for the Master's use, prepared unto every good work" (2 Timothy 2:21).

Paul had spoken of the foundation of God standing sure (2:19), of the Church as the great house built upon that foundation, of vessels, not only of gold, silver, costly and lasting, vessels to honor, but also of wood and of earth, common and perishable, vessels to dishonor. He distinguishes between them of whom he had spoken, who gave themselves to striving about words and to vain babbling, and such as truly sought to depart from all iniquity. In our text he gives us the four steps in the path in which a man can become a vessel unto honor in the great household of God. These are, the cleansing from sin; the being sanctified; the readiness for the Master to use us as He wills; and finally, the spirit of preparedness for every good work. It is not enough that we desire or attempt to do good works. As we need training and care to prepare us for every work we are to do on earth, we need it no less—or rather we need it much more—to be what constitutes the chief mark of the vessels unto honor—to be prepared unto every good work.

"If a man cleanse himself from them"—from that which characterizes the vessels of dishonor—the empty profession leading to ungodliness, against which he had warned. In every dish and cup we use, how we insist upon it that it shall be clean. In God's house the vessels must be much cleaner. And every one who would be truly prepared unto every good work must see to this first of all, that he cleanse himself from all that is sin. Christ himself could not enter upon His saving work in heaven until He had accomplished the cleansing of our sins. How can we become partners in His work, unless there be with us the same cleansing first. Or else how could Isaiah say, "Here am I, send me"? The fire of heaven had touched his lips, and he heard the voice, "Thy sin is purged." An intense desire to be cleansed from every sin lies at the root of fitness for true service.

"He shall be a vessel of honor, sanctified." Cleansing is the negative side, the emptying out and removal of all that is impure. Sanctified, the positive side, the refilling and being possessed of the spirit of holiness, through whom the soul becomes God-possessed, and so partakes of His holiness. "Let us cleanse ourselves from all defilement of flesh and spirit"—this first, then, and so "perfecting holiness in the fear of the Lord." In the temple the vessels were not only to be clean, but holy, devoted to God's service alone. He that would truly work for God must follow after holiness; "a heart established in holiness" (1 Thessalonians 4:14), a holy habit

187

of mind and disposition, yielded up to God and marked by a sense of His presence, fit for God's work. The cleansing from sin secures the filling with the Spirit.

"Meet for the Master's use." We are vessels for our Lord to use. In every work we do, it is to be Christ using us and working through us. The sense of being a servant, dependent on the Master's guidance, working under the Master's eye, instruments used by Him and His mighty power, lies at the root of effectual service. It maintains that unbroken dependence, that quiet faith, through which the Lord can do His work. It keeps up that blessed consciousness of the work being all His, which leads the worker to become the humbler the more be is used. His one desire is—meet for the Master's use.

"Prepared unto every good work." Prepared. The word not only means equipment, fitness, but also the disposition, the alacrity which keeps a man on the outlook, and makes him earnestly desire and joyfully avail himself of every opportunity of doing his Master's work. As he lives in touch with his Lord Jesus, and holds himself as a cleansed and sanctified vessel, ready for Him to use, and he sees how good works are what he was redeemed for, and what his fellowship with his Lord is to be proved in, they become the one thing he is to live for. He is prepared unto every good work.

REFLECTION

1. "Meet for the Master's use," is the central thought. A personal relation to Christ, an entire surrender to His disposal, a dependent waiting to be used by Him, a joyful confidence that He will use us—such is the secret of true work.

2. Let the beginning of your work be a giving yourself into the hands of the Master, as your living, loving Lord.

DAY 20

FURNISHED COMPLETELY UNTO EVERY GOOD WORK

"Give diligence to present thyself approved unto God, a workman that needeth not to be ashamed, handling aright the word of truth'" (2 Timothy 2:15).

"Every scripture inspired of God is also profitable for teaching, for reproof, for correction, for instruction which is in righteousness; that the man of God may be complete, furnished completely unto every good work" (2 Timothy 3:16, 17).

"A workman that needeth not to be ashamed" is one who is not afraid to have the master come and inspect his work. In hearty devotion to it, in thoroughness and skill, he presents himself approved to him who employs him. God's workers are to give diligence to present themselves approved to Him and have their work worthy of Him unto all well-pleasing. They are to be as a workman "that needeth not to be ashamed." A workman is one who knows his work, who gives himself wholly to it, who is known as a working man, who takes delight in doing his work well. So every Christian minister, every Christian worker, is to be a workman that makes a study of it to invite and expect the Master's approval.

"Handling aright the word of truth." The word is a seed, a fire, a hammer, a sword, is bread, and is light. Workmen in any of these spheres can be our example. In work for God everything depends upon handling the word aright. Therefore it is that, in the second text quoted above, the personal subjection to the word, and the experience of its power, is spoken of as the one means of our being completely furnished to every good work. God's workers must know that the Scripture is inspired of God, and has the life and life-giving power of God in it. Inspired is Spirit-breathed—the life in a seed, God's Holy Spirit is in the word. The Spirit in the word and the Spirit in our heart is One. As by the power of the Spirit within us we take the Spirit-filled word we become spiritual men. This word is given for teaching, the revelation of the thoughts of God; for reproof, the discovery of our sins and mistakes; for correction, the removal of what is defective to be replaced by what is right and good; for instruction in righteousness, the communication of all the knowledge needed to walk before God in His ways. As one yields wholly and heartily to all this, and the true Spirit-filled word gets mastery of his whole being, he becomes a man of God, complete and furnished completely to every good work. He becomes a workman approved of God, who needs not to be ashamed, rightly handling the word of God. And so the man of God has the double mark—his own life wholly molded by the Spirit-breathed word—and his whole work directed by his rightly handling that word.

"That the man of God may be complete, thoroughly furnished unto every good work." In our previous meditation we learned how in the cleansing and sanctification of the personal life the worker becomes a vessel meet for the Masters use, prepared unto every good work. Here we learn the same lesson—it is the man of God who allows God's word to do its work of reproving and correcting and instructing in his own life who will be complete, completely furnished unto every good work. Complete equipment and readiness for every good work—which is what every worker for God must aim at.

If any worker, conscious of how defective his preparation is, ask how this complete furnishing for every good work is to be attained, the analogy of an earthly workman, who needs not be ashamed, suggests the answer. He would tell us that be owes his success, first of all, to devotion to his work. He gave it his close attention. He left other things to concentrate his efforts on mastering one thing. He made it a life-study to do his work perfectly. They who would do Christ's work as a second thing, not as the first, and who are not willing to sacrifice all for it, will never be complete or completely furnished to every good work.

The second thing he will speak of will be patient training and exercise. Proficiency only comes through painstaking effort. You may feel as if you know not how or what to work the right way. Fear not! All learning begins with ignorance and mistakes. Be of good courage. He who has endowed human nature with the wonderful power that has filled the world with such skilled and cunning workmen, will He not much more give His children the grace they need to be His fellow-workers? Let the necessity that is laid upon you—the necessity that you should glorify God that you should bless the world, that you should through work ennoble and perfect your life and blessedness, urge you to give immediate and continual diligence to be a workman completely furnished unto every good work.

It is only in doing we learn to do aright. Begin working under Christ's training. He will perfect His work in you, and so fit you for your work for Him.

REFLECTION

1. The work God is doing, and seeking to have done in the world, is to win it back to himself.

2. In this work every believer is expected to take part. What part are you taking?

3. God wants us to be skilled workmen, who give our whole heart to His work, and delight in it.

4. God does His work by working in us, inspiring and strengthening us to do His work.

5. What God asks is a heart and life devoted to Him in surrender and faith.

6. As God's work is all love, love is the power that works in us, inspiring our efforts and conquering its object.

DAY 21

ZEALOUS OF GOOD WORKS

"He gave Himself for us, that He might redeem us from all iniquity, and purify us for Himself, a people of His own, zealous of good works" (Titus 2:14).

In these words we have two truths. First, what Christ has done to make us His own; and second, what He expects of us. In the former we have a rich and beautiful summary of Christ's work for us. He gave himself for us, He redeemed us from all iniquity, He cleansed us for himself, He took us for a people, for His own possession. And all with the one object, that we should be a people zealous of good works.

The doctrinal half of this wonderful passage has had much attention bestowed on it. Let us devote our attention to its practical part. We are to be a people zealous of good works. Christ expects of us that we shall be zealots for good works— ardently, enthusiastically devoted to their performance.

This cannot be said to be the feeling with which most Christians regard good works. What can be done to cultivate this disposition? One of the first things that awakens zeal in work is a great and urgent sense of need. A great need awakens strong desire, stirs the heart and the will, and arouses all the energies of our being. It was this sense of need that awakened many to be zealous of the law. They hoped their works would save them. The Gospel has robbed this motive of its power. Has it taken away entirely the need of good works? No, indeed, it has given that urgent need a higher place than before. Christ desires our good works. We are His servants, the members of His body, with whom He has chosen to carry on His work on earth. The work is so great—with the hundreds of millions of the unsaved—that not one worker can be spared. There are thousands of Christians today who feel that their own business is urgent, and must be attended to, and have no conception of the urgency of Christ's work committed to them. The Church must wake up to teach this to each believer.

As urgently as Christ needs our good works the world needs them. There are around you men and women and children who need saving. To see men swept down past us in a river, stirs our every power to try and save them. Christ has placed His people in a perishing world, with the expectation that they will give themselves, heart and soul, to carry on His work of love. Oh! Let us sound forth the blessed Gospel message. He gave himself for us that He might redeem us for himself, a people of His own, to serve Him and carry on His work—zealous of good works.

A second great element of zeal in work is delight in it. An apprentice or a student mostly begins his work under a sense of duty. As he learns to understand and enjoy it, be does it with pleasure, and becomes zealous in its performance. The Church must train Christians to believe that when once we give our hearts to it, and seek for the training that makes us in some degree skilled workmen, there is no greater joy than that of sharing in Christ's work of mercy and beneficence. As physical and mental activity give pleasure, and call for the devotion and zeal of thousands, the spiritual service of Christ can waken our highest enthusiasm.

Then comes the highest motive, the personal one of attachment to Christ our Redeemer: "The love of Christ constraineth us." The love of Christ to us is the source and measure of our love to Him. Our love to Him becomes the power and the measure of our love to souls. This love, shed abroad in our hearts by the Holy Spirit, this love as a divine communication, renewed in us by the renewing of the Holy Ghost day by day, becomes a zeal for Christ that shows itself as a zeal for good works. It becomes the link that unites the two parts of our text, the doctrinal and the practical, into one. Christ's love, that gave himself for us, that redeemed us from all iniquity, that cleansed us for himself, that made us a people of His own in the bonds of an everlasting loving kindness, that love believed in, known, received into the heart, makes the redeemed soul of necessity zealous in good works.

"Zealous of good works!" Let no believer, the youngest or feeblest, look upon this grace as too high. It is Divine grace, provided for and assured in the love of our Lord. Let us accept it as our calling. Let us be sure it is the very nature of the new life within us. Let us, in opposition to all that nature or feeling may say, in faith claim it as an integral part of our redemption—Christ Himself will make it true in us.

REFLECTION

1. We are to be people zealous for good works. What can be done to cultivate this disposition?

2. Does our zeal for good works have any part in our salvation?

DAY 22

READY TO EVERY GOOD WORK

"Put them in mind to be ready for every good work"
(Titus 3:1).

"Put them in mind." The words suggest the need of believers to have the truths of their calling to good works ever again set before them. A healthy tree spontaneously bears its fruit. Even where the life of the believer is in perfect health, Scripture teaches us how its growth and fruitfulness only come through teaching, and the influence that exerts on mind and will and heart. For all who have charge of others the need is great of divine wisdom and faithfulness to teach and train all Christians, especially young and feeble Christians, to be ready for every good work. Let us consider some of the chief points of such training.

Teach them clearly what good works are. Lay the foundation in the will of God, as revealed in the law, and show them how integrity and righteousness and obedience are the groundwork of Christian character. Teach them how

195

in all the duties and relationships of daily life true religion is to be carried out. Lead them on to the virtues, which Jesus especially came to exhibit and teach—humility, meekness and gentleness and love. Open out to them the meaning of a life of love, self-sacrifice, and beneficence—entirely given to think of and care for others. And then carry them on to what is the highest, the true life of good works—the winning of men to know and love God.

Teach them what an essential part of the Christian life good works are. They are not, as many think, a secondary element in the salvation given by God. They are not merely to be done in token of our gratitude, or as a proof of the sincerity of our faith, or as a preparation for heaven. They are all this, but they are a great deal more. They are the very object for which we have been redeemed. We have been created anew unto good works. They alone are the evidence that man has been restored to his original destiny of working as God works, and with God, and because God works through him. God has no higher glory than His works, and especially His work of saving love. In becoming imitators of God, and walking and working in love, even as Christ loved us and gave himself for us, we have the very image and likeness of God restored in us. The works of a man not only reveal his life, they develop and exercise, strengthen and perfect it. Good works are of the very essence of the divine life in us.

Teach them, too, what a rich reward they bring. All labor has its market value. From the poor man who scarce can earn a shilling a day, to the man who has made his millions, the thought of the reward there is for labor has been one of the great incentives to undertake it. Christ appeals to this feeling when He says, "Great shall be your reward." Let Christians understand that there is no service where the reward is so rich as that of God. Work is bracing, work is strength, and cultivates the sense of mastery and conquest. Work wakens enthusiasm and calls out a man's noblest qualities. In a life of good works the Christian becomes conscious of his divine ministry of dispensing the life and grace of God to others.

They bring us into closer union with God. There is no higher fellowship with God than fellowship in His saving work of love. It brings us into sympathy with Him and His purposes. It fills us with His love and secures His approval. And great is the reward, too, on those around us. When others are won to Christ, when the weary and the erring and the desponding are helped and made partakers of the grace and life there are in Christ Jesus for them, God's servants share in the very joy in which our blessed Lord found His recompense.

The most important thing is to teach them to believe that it is possible for each of us to abound in good works. Nothing is so fatal to successful effort as discouragement or despondency. Nothing is more a frequent cause of neglect of good works than the fear that we have not the power to perform them. Put them in mind of the power of the Holy Spirit dwelling in them. Show them that God's promise and provision of strength is always equal to what He demands; that there is always grace sufficient for all the good works to which we are called. Strive to awaken in them a faith in "the power that worketh in us," and in the fullness of that life which can flow out as rivers of living water. Train them to begin at once their service of love. Lead them to see how it is all God working in them, and to offer themselves as empty vessels to be filled with His love and grace. And teach them that as they are faithful in a little, even amid mistakes and shortcomings, the acting out of the life will strengthen the life itself, and work for God will become in full truth a second nature.

God grant that the teachers of the Church may be faithful to its commission in regard to all her members—"Put them in mind to be ready for every good work." Not only teach them, but train them. Show them the work there is to be done by them. See that they do it, and encourage and help them to do it hopefully. There is no part of the office of a pastor more important or more sacred than this, or fraught with richer blessing. Let the aim be nothing less than to lead every believer to live entirely devoted to the work of God in winning men to Him. What a change it would make in the Church and the world!

REFLECTION

1. Get a firm hold of the great root-principle. Every believer, every member of Christ's body, has his place in the body solely for the welfare of the whole body.

2. Pastors have been given for the perfecting of the saints with the work of ministering, of serving in love.

3. In ministers and members of the churches, Christ will work mightily if they will wait upon Him.

DAY 23

CAREFUL TO MAINTAIN GOOD WORKS

"And these things I will that thou affirm constantly, that they which have believed in God might be careful to maintain good works. Let our people also learn to maintain good works for necessary uses, that they be not unfruitful" *(Titus 3:8,14).*

In earlier passages Paul charges Titus confidently to affirm the truths of the blessed Gospel to the end, with the express object that all who had believed should be careful to make a study of and maintain good works. Faith and good works were to be inseparable. The diligence of every believer in good works was to be a main aim of a pastor's work. In the second passage he reiterates the instruction, with the expression, let them learn, suggesting the thought that, as all work on earth has to be learned, so in the good works of the Christian life there is an equal need of thought and application and teachableness, to learn how to do them rightly and abundantly.

There may be more than one reader of this little book who has felt how little he has lived in accordance with all the teaching of God's word, prepared, thoroughly furnished, ready unto, and zealous of good works. It appears so difficult to get rid of old habits and break through the conventionalities of society, to know how to begin and really enter upon a life that can be full of good works, to the glory of God. Let me try and give some suggestions that may be helpful. They may also aid those who have the training of Christian workers, in showing in what way the teaching and learning of good works may best succeed. Come, all young workers and listen.

1. A learner must begin by beginning to work at once. There is no way of learning an art like swimming or music, a new language or a trade, but by practice. Let neither the fear that you cannot do it, nor the hope that something will happen that will make it easier for you, keep you back. Learn to do good works, the works of love, by beginning to do them. However insignificant they appear, do them. A kind word, a little help to someone in trouble, an act of loving attention to a stranger or a poor man, the sacrifice of

a seat or a place to some one who longs for it—practice these things. All plants we cultivate are small at first. Cherish the consciousness that, for Jesus' sake, you are seeking to do what would please Him. It is only in doing you can learn to do.

2. The learner must give his heart to the work, must take interest and pleasure in it. Delight in work ensures success. Let the tens of thousands around you in the world who throw their whole soul into their daily business, teach you how to serve your blessed Master. Think sometimes of the honor and privilege of doing good works, of serving others in love. It is God's own work, to love and save and bless men. He works it in you and through you. It makes you share the spirit and likeness of Christ. It strengthens your Christian character. Without actions, intentions lower and condemn a man instead of raising him. Only as much as you act out, do you really live. Think of the Godlike blessedness of doing good, of communicating life, of making happy. Think of the exquisite joy of growing up into a life of beneficence, and being the blessing of all you meet. Set your heart upon being a vessel meet for the Master's use, ready to every good work.

3. Be of good courage, and fear not. The learner who says, "I cannot," will surely fail. There is a divine power working in you. Study and believe what God's word says about it. Let the holy self-reliance of Paul, grounded on his reliance on Christ, be your example. "I can do all things in Christ which strengtheneth me" (Philipians 4:13). Study and take home to yourself the wonderful promises about the power of the Holy Spirit, the abundance of grace, Christ's strength made perfect in weakness, and see how all this can only be made true to you in working. Cultivate the noble consciousness that as you have been created to good works by God, He himself will fit you for them. And believe then that just as natural as it is to any workman to delight and succeed in his profession,

it can be to the new nature in you to abound in every good work. Having this confidence, you need never faint.

4. Above all, cling to your Lord Jesus as your teacher and master. He said, "Learn of Me, for I am meek and lowly in heart, and ye shall find rest unto your souls" (Matthew 11:29. Work as one who is a learner in His school, who is sure that none teaches like Him, and is therefore confident of success. Cling to Him, and let a sense of His presence and His power working in you make you meek and lowly, and yet bold and strong. He who came to do the Father's work on earth, and found it the path to the Father's glory, will teach you what it is to work for God.

REFLECTION
1. Yield yourself to Christ. Lay yourself on the altar, and say you wish to give yourself wholly to live for God's work.
2. Believe quietly that Christ accepts and takes charge of you for His work, and will fit you for it.

3. Pray much that God would open to you the great truth of His own working in you. Nothing else can give true strength.

4. Seek to cultivate a spirit of humble, patient, trustful dependence upon God. Live in loving fellowship with Christ, and obedience to Him. You can count upon His strength being made perfect in your weakness.

DAY 24

AS HIS FELLOW-WORKERS

"We are God's fellow-workers: ye are God's building"
(1 Corinthians 3:9).

"And working together with Him we entreat that ye
receive not the grace of God in vain" (2 Corinthians 6:1).

We have listened to Paul's teaching on good works. Let us turn now to his personal experience and see if we can learn from him some of the secrets of effective service.

He speaks here of the Church as God's building, which, as the Great Architect, He is building up into a holy temple and dwelling for himself. Of his own work, Paul speaks as of that of a master builder, to whom a part of the great building has been given in charge. He had laid a foundation in Corinth. To all who were working there he said, "Let each man take heed how he buildeth thereon." "We are God's fellow workers." The word is applicable not only to Paul, but to all God's servants who take part in His work; and because every believer has been called to give his life to God's service and to win others to His knowledge, every, even the feeblest, Christian needs to have the word brought to him and taken home. "We are God's fellow workers." How much it suggests in regard to our working for God!

As to the work we have to do. The eternal God is building for Himself a temple. Christ Jesus, God's Son, is the foundation; believers are the living stones. The Holy Spirit is the mighty power of God through which believers are gathered out of the world made fit for their place in the temple, and built up into it. As living stones, believers are at the same time the living workmen, whom God uses to carry out His work. They are equally God's workmanship and God's fellow-workers. The work God is doing He does through them. The work they have to do is the very work God is doing. God's own work, in which He delights, on which His heart is set, is saving men and building them into His temple. This is the one work on which the heart of every one who would be a fellow-worker with God must be set. It is only as we know how great, how wonderful, this work of God is—giving life to dead souls, imparting His own life to them, and living in them—that we shall enter into the glory of our work, receiving the very life of God from Him, and passing it on to men.

As to the strength for the work. Paul says of his work as a mere master builder, that it was "according to the grace of God which was given me." For divine work nothing but divine power suffices. The power by which God works must work in us. That power is His Holy, Spirit. Study the second chapter of this epistle, and the third of the second, and see how absolute was Paul's acknowledgment of his own impotence, and his dependence on the teaching and power of the Holy Spirit. As this great truth begins to live in the hearts of God's workers, that God's work can only be done by God's power in us, we shall feel that our first need every day is to have the presence of God's Spirit renewed within us. The power of the Holy Spirit is the power of love. God is love. All He works for the salvation of men is love. It is love alone that truly conquers and wins the heart. In all God's fellow-workers love is the power that reaches the hearts of men. Christ conquered and conquers still by the love of the cross. Let that mind be in you, O worker, which was in Christ Jesus, the spirit of a love that sacrifices itself to the death, of a humble, patient, gentle love, and you will be made meet to be God's fellow-worker.

As to the relation we are to hold to God. In executing the plans of some great building the master builder has only one care; to carry out to the minutest detail the thoughts of the architect who designed it. He acts in constant consultation with him, and is guided in all by his will. His instructions to those under him have all reference to the one thing—the embodiment, in visible shape, of what the master mind has conceived. The one great characteristic of fellow-workers with God ought to be that of absolute surrender to His will, unceasing dependence on His teaching, exact obedience to His wishes. God has revealed His plan in His Word. He has told us that His Spirit alone can enable us to enter into His plans, and fully master His purpose with the way he desires to have it carried out. The clearer our insight into the divine glory of God's work of saving souls, into the utter insufficiency of our natural powers to do the work, into the provision that has been made by which the divine love can animate us, the more we shall feel that a childlike teachableness, a continual looking upward and waiting on God, is ever to be the chief mark of one who is His fellow-laborer. Out of the sense of humility, helplessness, and nothingness there will grow a holy confidence and courage that knows that our weakness need not hinder us, that Christ's strength is made perfect in weakness, that God himself is working out His purpose through us. And of all the blessings of the Christian life, the most wonderful will be that we are allowed to be God's fellow-workers!

REFLECTION

1. God's fellow-worker! How easy to use the word, and even to apprehend some of the great truths it contains! How little we live in the power and the glory of what it actually involves!

2. Fellow-workers with God! Everything depends upon knowing, in His holiness and love, the God with whom we are associated as partners.

3. He who has chosen us, that in and through us He might do His great work, will fit us for His use.

4. Let our purpose be of adoring worship, deep dependence, great waiting, and full obedience.

DAY 25

ACCORDING TO THE WORKING OF HIS POWER

"Whom we preach, warning every man, and teaching every man, that we may present every man perfect in Christ Jesus; whereunto I also labor, striving according to His working, which worketh in me mightily"
(Colossians 1:29).

"The mystery of Christ, whereof I was made a minister, according to the gift of that grace of God which was given me according to the working of His power"
(Ephesians 3:7).

In the words of Paul to the Philippians, which we have already considered, in which he called upon them and encouraged them to work, because it was God who worked in them, we found one of the richest and comprehensive statements of the great truth that it is only by God's working in us that we can do true work. In our texts for this chapter we have Paul's testimony as to his own experience. His whole ministry was to be according to the grace that was given him according to the working of God's power. And of his labor he says that it was a striving according to the power of Him who worked mightily in him.

We find here the same principle we found in our Lord—the Father doing the works in Him. Let every worker who reads this pause, and say, "If the ever-blessed Son, if the Apostle Paul, could only do their work according to the working of His power who worked in them mightily, how much more do I need this working of God in me, to fit me for doing His work aright." This is one of the deepest spiritual truths of God's Word. Let us look to the Holy Spirit within us to give it such a hold of our inmost life, that it may become the deepest inspiration of all our work. I can only do true work as I yield myself to God to work in me.

We know the ground on which this truth rests: "There is none good but God"; "There is none holy but the Lord"; "Power belongeth unto God." All goodness and holiness and power are only to be found in God, and where He gives them. And He can only give them in the creature, not as something He parts with, but by His own actual presence and dwelling and working. And so God can only work in His people in as far as He is allowed to have complete possession of the heart and life. As our will and life and love are yielded up in dependence and faith, and God is waited on to keep possession and to abide, even as Christ waited on Him, God can work in us.

This is true of all our spiritual life, but especially of our work for God. The work of saving souls is God's own work, none but He can do it. The gift of His Son is the proof of how great and precious He counts the work, and how His heart is set upon it. His love never for one moment ceases working for the salvation of men. And when He calls His children to be partners in His work, He shares with them the joy and the glory of the work of saving and blessing men. He promises to work His work through them, inspiring and energizing them by His power working in them. To him who can say with Paul; "I labor, striving according to His power who worketh in me mightily" (Colossians 1:29), his whole relation to God becomes the counterpart and the continuation of Christ's, a blessed, unceasing, momentary, and most absolute dependence on the Father for every word He spoke and every work He did.

Christ is our pattern. Christ's life is our law and works in us. Christ lived in Paul his life of dependence on God. Why should any of us hesitate to believe that the grace given to Paul of laboring and striving "according to the working of the power" will be given to us too. Let every worker learn to say, as the power that worked in Christ worked in Paul too, that power works no less in me. There is no possible way of working God's work aright, but by God working it in us.

How I wish that I could take every worker who reads this by the hand, and say, "Come, my brother! Let us quiet our minds, and hush every thought in God's presence, as I whisper in your ears the wonderful secret: God is working in you. All the work you have to do for Him, God will work in you. Take time and think it over. It is a deep spiritual truth which the mind cannot grasp nor the heart realize. Accept it as a divine truth from Heaven. Believe that this word is a seed out of which can grow the very spiritual blessing of which it speaks. And in the faith of the Holy Spirit's making it live within you, say ever again: God worketh in me. All the work I have to work for Him, God will work in me.

The faith of this truth, and the desire to have it made true in you, will constrain you to live very humbly and closely with God. You will see how work for God must be the most spiritual thing in a spiritual life. And you will ever bow in holy stillness. God is working; God will work in me. I will work for Him according to the power which works mightily in me.

REFLECTION

1. The gift of the grace of God (Ephesians 2:7, 3:7), the power that worketh in us (Ephesians 3:20), the strengthening with might by the Spirit (Ephesians 3:16)—the three expressions all contain the same thought of God's working all in us.

2. The Holy Spirit is the power of God. Seek to be filled with the Spirit, to have your whole life led by Him, and you will become fit for God's working mightily in you.

3. "Ye shall receive the power of the Holy Spirit coming on you." Through the Spirit dwelling in us God can work in us mightily.

4. What holy fear, what humble watchfulness and dependence, what entire surrender and obedience become us if we believe in God's working in us.

DAY 26

LABORING MORE ABUNDANTLY

"But by the grace of God I am what I am: and His grace which was bestowed on me was not in vain; but I labored more abundantly than they all: yet not I, but the grace of God which was with me" (1 Corinthians 15:10).

*"And He hath said unto me, My grace is sufficient for
thee: for My power is made perfect in weakness.... In
nothing was I behind the chiefest of the apostles, though
I am nothing" (2 Corinthians 12:9,11).*

In both of these passages Paul speaks of how he had
abounded in the work of the Lord. "In nothing was I behind
the chiefest of the apostles." "I labored more abundantly,
than they all." In both he tells how entirely it was all of God,
who worked in him, and not of himself. In the first he says,
"Not I, but the grace of God which was with me." And then
in the second, showing how this grace is Christ's strength
working in us, while we are nothing, he tells us, "He said unto
me: My grace is sufficient for thee; My power is made perfect
in weakness." May God give us "the Spirit of revelation,
enlightened eyes of the heart," to see this wonderful vision,
a man who knows himself to be nothing, glorying in his
weakness, that the power of Christ may rest on him, and
work through him, and who so labors more abundantly than
all. What does this teach us as workers for God?

God's work can only be done in God's strength. It is only
by God's power, that is, by God himself working in us, that
we can do effective work. Throughout this little book this
truth has been frequently repeated. It is easy to accept of it. It
is far from easy to see its full meaning, to give it the mastery
over our whole being, to live it out. This will need stillness of
soul, and meditation, strong faith and fervent prayer. As it is
God alone who can work in us, it is equally God who alone
can reveal himself as the God who works in us. Wait on Him,
and the truth that ever appears to be beyond thy reach will be
opened up to thee, through the knowledge of who and what
God is. When God reveals himself as "God who worketh all
in all," thou wilt learn to believe and work "according to the
power of Him who worketh in thee mightily."

209

God's strength can only work in weakness. It is only when we truly say, "Not I!" That we can fully say, but the grace of God with me. The man who said, "In nothing behind the chiefest of the apostles!" Had first learned to say, though I am nothing. He could say, "I take pleasure in weaknesses, for when I am weak then am I strong." This is the true relation between the Creator and the creature, between the Divine Father and His child, between God and His servant. Christian worker! Learn the lesson of thine own weakness, as the indispensable condition of God's power working in thee. Do believe that to take time and in God's presence to realize thy weakness and nothingness is the sure way to be clothed with God's strength. Accept every experience by which God teaches thee thy weakness as His grace preparing thee to receive His strength. Take pleasure in weaknesses!

God's strength comes in our fellowship with Christ and His service. Paul says, "I will glory in my weakness, that the strength of Christ may rest upon me." "I take pleasure in weaknesses for Christ's sake." And he tells how it was when he had besought the Lord that the messenger of Satan might depart from him, that He answered, "My grace is sufficient for thee." "Christ is the wisdom and the power of God." We do not receive the wisdom to know, or the power to do God's will as something that we can possess and use at our discretion. It is in the personal attachment to Christ, in a life of continual communication with Him, that His power rests on us. It is in taking pleasure in weaknesses for Christ's sake that Christ's strength is known.

God's strength is given to faith, and the work that is done in faith. It needs a living faith to take pleasure in weaknesses, and in weakness to do our work, knowing that God is working in us. Without seeing or feeling anything, to go on in the confidence of a hidden power working in us.

This is the highest exercise of a life of faith. To do God's own work in saving souls, in persevering prayer and labor; amid outwardly unfavorable circumstances and appearances still to labor more abundantly—this only faith can do. Let us be strong in faith, giving glory to God. God will show himself strong towards him whose heart is perfect with Him.

My brother! Be willing to yield yourself to the very utmost to God, that His power may rest upon you, may work in you. Do let God work through you. Offer yourself to Him for His work as the one object of your life. Count upon His working all in you, to fit you for His service, to strengthen and bless you in it. Let the faith and love of your Lord Jesus, whose strength is going to be made perfect in your weakness, lead you to live even as He did, to do the Father's will and finish His work.

REFLECTION

1. Let every minister seek the full personal experience of Christ's strength made perfect in His weakness. This alone will fit him to teach believers the secret of their strength.

2. Our Lord says, "My grace, My strength." It is as, in close personal fellowship and love, we abide in Christ and have Christ abiding in us, that His grace and strength can work.

3. It is a heart wholly given up to God, to His will and love that will know his power working in our weakness.

DAY 27

A DOER THAT WORKS SHALL BE
BLESSED IN DOING

"Be ye doers of the word, and not hearers only, deluding
your own selves. He that looketh into the perfect law,
the law of liberty, and so continueth, being not a hearer
that forgetteth, but a doer that worketh, this man shall be
blessed in doing" (James 1:22, 25).

"God created us not to contemplate but to act. He created us in His own image, and in Him there is no thought without simultaneous action." True action is born of contemplation. True contemplation, as a means to an end, always begets action. If sin had not entered there would never have been a separation between knowing and doing. In nothing is the power of sin more clearly seen than this, that even in the believer there is such a gap between intellect and conduct. It is possible to delight in hearing, to be diligent in increasing our knowledge of God's word, to admire and approve the truth, even to be willing to do it, and yet to fail entirely in the actual performance. Hence the warning of James is not to delude ourselves with being hearers and not doers. Hence his pronouncing the doer who works blessing in his doing.

Blessed in doing. The words are a summary of the teaching of our Lord Jesus at the close of the Sermon on the Mount: "He that doeth the will of My Father shall enter the Kingdom of Heaven." "Every one that heareth My words, and doeth them, shall be likened unto a wise man." To the woman who spoke of the blessedness of her who was his mother: "Yea rather, blessed are they that hear the word of

212

God and keep it." To the disciples in the last night; "If ye know these things, happy are ye if ye do them." It is one of the greatest dangers in religion that we rest content with the pleasure and approval, which a beautiful representation of a truth calls forth, without the immediate performance of what it demands. It is only when conviction has been translated into conduct that we have proof that the truth is mastering us.

A doer that works shall be blessed in doing. The doer is blessed. The doing is the victory that overcomes every obstacle it brings out and confirms the very image of God, the Great Worker. It removes every barrier to the enjoyment of all the blessing God has prepared. We are ever inclined to seek our blessedness in what God gives, in privilege and enjoyment. Christ placed it in what we do, because it is only in doing that we really prove and know and possess the life God has bestowed. When one said, "Blessed is he that shall eat bread in the kingdom of God," our Lord answered with the parable of the supper, "Blessed is he that forsakes all to come to the supper." The doer is blessed. As surely as it is only in doing that the painter or musician, the man of science or commerce, the discoverer or the conqueror find their blessedness, so, and much more, is it only in keeping the commandments and in doing the will of God that the believer enters fully into the truth and blessedness of deliverance from sin and fellowship with God. Doing is the very essence of blessedness, the highest manifestation, and therefore the fullest enjoyment of the life of God.

A doer that works shall be blessed in doing. This was the blessedness of Abraham, of whom we read: "Thou seest that faith wrought with his works, and by works was faith made perfect" (James 2:22). He had no works without faith; there was faith working with them and in them all. And he had no faith without works. Through them his faith was exercised and strengthened and perfected. As his faith, so his blessedness was perfected in doing. It is in doing that the doer that works is blessed. The true insight into this, as a divine revelation of the true nature of good works, in perfect harmony with all our experience in the world, will make us take every command, and every truth, and every opportunity to abound in good works as an integral part of the blessedness of the salvation Christ has brought us. Joy and work, work and joy, will become synonymous: we shall no longer be hearers but doers.

Let us put this truth into immediate practice. Let us live for others, to love and serve them. Let not the fact of our being unused to labors of love, or the sense of ignorance and unfitness, keep us back. Only begin. If you think you are not able to labor for souls, begin with the bodies. Only begin, and go on, and abound. Believe the word, "It is more blessed to give than to receive." Pray for and depend on the promised grace. Give yourself to a ministry of love; in the very nature of things, in the example of Christ, in the promise of God you have the assurance. If you know these things, happy are ye if ye do them. Blessed is the doer!

REFLECTION

1. Delight in work insures success. Doing God's work makes you share in the spirit and likeness of Christ and strengthens Christian character. Consider how much we have good intentions that are not acted upon.

2. Fear that we do not possess the power to perform good works is often a cause for the neglect of them. What can we do to overcome to such fear?

DAY 28

THE WORK OF SOUL-SAVING

"My brethren, if any of you do err from the truth, and one convert him, let him know that he which converteth a sinner from the error of his ways shall save a soul from death, and shall cover a multitude of sins"
(James 5:19-20).

We sometimes hesitate to speak of men being converted and saved by men. Scripture here twice uses the expression of one man converting another, and once of his saving him. Let us not hesitate to accept it as part of our work, of our high prerogative as the sons of God, to convert and to save men. "For it is God who worketh in us."

"Shall save a soul from death." Every workman studies the material in which he works: the carpenter the wood, the goldsmith the gold. "Our works are wrought in God." In our good works we deal with souls. Even when we can at first do no more than reach and help their bodies, our aim is the soul. For these Christ came to die. For these God has appointed us to watch and labor. Let us study these. What care a huntsman or a fisherman takes to know the habits of the spoil he seeks. Let us remember that it needs Divine wisdom and training and skill to become winners of souls. The only way to get that training and skill is to begin to work. Christ himself will teach each one who waits on Him.

In that training the Church with its ministers has a part to take. The daily experience of ordinary life and teaching prove how often there exist in a man unsuspected powers, which must be called out by training before they are known to be there. When a man thus becomes conscious and

215

master of the power there is in himself he is, as it were, a new creature; the power and enjoyment of life is doubled. Every believer has hidden within himself the power of saving souls. The Kingdom of Heaven is within us as a seed, and every one of the gifts and graces of the spirit are each also a hidden seed. The highest aim of the ministry is to awaken the consciousness of this hidden seed of power to save souls. A depressing sense of ignorance or impotence keeps many back. James writes: "Let him know, that he which converteth the sinner from the error of his way shall save a soul from death" (James 5:20). Every believer needs to be taught to know and use the wondrous blessed power with which he has been endowed. When God said to Abraham, "I will bless thee, then shall all the nations of the earth be blessed," He called him to a faith not only in the blessing that would come to him from above, but in the power of blessing he would be in the world. It is a wonderful moment in the life of a child of God when he sees that the second blessing is as sure as the first.

"He shall save a soul." Our Lord bears the name of Jesus, Savior. He is the embodiment of God's saving love. Saving souls is His own great work, is His work alone. As our faith in Him grows to know and receive all there is in Him, as He lives in us, and dwells in our heart and disposition, saving souls will become the great work to which our life will be given. We shall be the willing and intelligent instruments through whom He will do His mighty work.

"If any err, and one convert him, he which converteth a sinner shall save a soul." The words suggest personal work. We chiefly think of large gatherings to whom the Gospel is preached. The thought here is of one who has erred and is sought after. We increasingly do our work through associations and organizations. "If one convert him, he saveth a soul." It is the love and labor of some individual believer that has won the erring one back. It is this we need in the Church of Christ. Every believer who truly follows Jesus Christ looking out for those who are erring from the way, loving them, and laboring to help them back. Not one of us may say, "Am I my brother's keeper?" We are in the world only and solely that as the members of Christ's body we may continue and carry out His saving work. As saving souls was and is His work, His joy, His glory, let it be ours, let it be mine, too. Let me give myself personally to watch over individuals, and seek to save them one by one.

"Know that he which converteth a sinner shall save a soul." "If ye know these things, happy are ye if you do them." Let me translate these Scripture truths into action. Let me give these thoughts shape and substance in daily life. Let me prove their power over me, and my faith in them, by work. Is there not more than one Christian around me wandering from the way, needing loving help and not unwilling to receive it? Are there not some whom I could take by the hand, and encourage to begin again? Are there not many who have never been in the right way, for some of whom Christ Jesus would use me, if I were truly at His disposal?

If I feel afraid—oh! Let me believe that the love of God as a seed dwells within me, not only calling but enabling me actually to do the work. Let me yield myself to the Holy Spirit to fill my heart with that love, and fit me for its service. Jesus the Savior lives to save. He dwells in me; He will do His saving work through me. "Know that he which converteth a sinner shall save a soul from death, and cover a multitude of sins."

REFLECTION

1. More love to souls, born out of fervent love to the Lord Jesus—is not this our great need?

2. Let us pray for love, and begin to love, in the faith that as we exercise the little we have more will be given.

3. Lord! Open our eyes to see Thee doing Thy great work of saving men, and waiting to give Thy love and strength into the heart of every willing one. Make each one of Thy redeemed a soul-winner.

DAY 29

PRAYING AND WORKING

"If any man see his brother sin a sin which is not unto death, he shall ask, and God will give him life for them that sin not unto death" (1 John 5:16).

"Let us consider one another to provoke unto love and good works" these words in Hebrews express what lies at the very root of a life of good works—the thoughtful loving care we have for each other, that not one may fall away. As it says in Galatians: "Brethren, if a man be overtaken in a fault, ye which are spiritual, restore such an one in the spirit of meekness" (Galatians 6:1). Or as Jude writes, apparently of Christians who were in danger of falling away, "Some save, snatching them out of the fire; and on some have mercy with fear." As Christ's doing good to men's bodies ever aimed at winning their souls, all our ministry of love must be subordinated to that which is God's great purpose and longing—the salvation unto life eternal.

218

In this labor of love praying and working must ever go together. At times prayer may reach those whom the words cannot reach. At times prayer may chiefly be needed for us, to obtain the wisdom and courage for the words. At times it may be specially called forth for the soul by the very lack of fruit from our words. As a rule, praying and working must be inseparable—the praying to obtain from God what we need for the soul. The working to bring to it what God has given us. The words of John here are most suggestive as to the power of prayer in our labor of love. It leads us to think of prayer as a personal work, with a very definite object and a certainty of answer.

Let prayer be a personal effort. If any man sees his brother, he shall ask. We are so accustomed to act through societies and associations that we are in danger of losing sight of the duty resting upon each of us to watch over those around him. Every member of my body is ready to serve any other member. Every believer is to care for the fellow-believers who are within his reach, in his church, his house, or social circle. The sin of each is a loss and a hurt to the body of Christ. Let your eyes be open to the sins of your brethren around you, not to speak evil or judge or helplessly complain, but to love and help and care and pray. Ask God to see your brother's sin, in its sinfulness, its danger to himself, its grief to Christ, its loss to the body; but also as within reach of God's compassion and deliverance. Shutting our eyes to the sin of our brethren around us is not true love. See it, and take it to God, and make it part of your work for God to pray for your brother and seek new life for him.

Let prayer be definite. If any man sees his brother sinning let him ask. We need prayer from a person for a person. Scripture and God's spirit teach us to pray for all society, for the Church with which we are associated, for nations, and for special spheres of work.

Prayer is most needful and blessed. But somehow more is needed—to take of those with whom we come into contact, one by one, and make them the subjects of our intercession. The larger supplications must have their place, but it is difficult with regard to them to know when our prayers are answered. But there is nothing will bring God so near, will test and strengthen our faith, and make us know we are fellow workers with God, as when we receive an answer to our prayers for individuals. It will quicken in us the new and blessed consciousness that we indeed have power with God. Let every worker seek to exercise this grace of taking up and praying for individual souls.

Count upon an answer. He shall ask, and God will give him (the one who prays) life for them that sin. The words follow on those in which John had spoken about the confidence we have of being heard, if we ask anything according to His will. There is often complaint made of not knowing God's will. But here there is no difficulty. "He willeth that all men should be saved." If we rest our faith on this will of God, we shall grow strong and grasp the promise. "He shall ask, and God will give him life for them that sin." The Holy Spirit will lead us, if we yield ourselves to be led by Him, to the souls God would have us take as our special care, and for which the grace of faith and persevering prayer will be given us. Let the wonderful promise, "God will give to him who asks life for them who sin," stir us and encourage us to our priestly ministry of personal and definite intercession, as one of the most blessed among the good works in which we can serve God and man.

Praying and working are inseparable. Let all who work learn to pray well. Let all who pray learn to work well.

REFLECTION

1. To pray confidently, and, if need be, perseveringly, for an individual, needs a close walk with God, and the faith that we can prevail with Him.

2. In all our work for God, prayer must take a much larger place. If God is to work all; if our posture is to be that of entire dependence, waiting for Him to work in us; if it takes time to persevere and to receive in ourselves what God gives us for others; there needs to be a work and a laboring in prayer.

3. Oh that God would open our eyes to the glory of this work of saving souls, as the one thing God lives for, as the one thing He wants to work in us.

4. Let us pray for the love and power of God to come on us, and for the blessed work of soul-winning.

DAY 30

I KNOW THY WORKS

"To the angel of the church in Ephesus ... in Thyatira ... in Sardis ... in Philadelphia ... in Laodicea write: I know thy works" (Revelation 2:1,2,8,9,12,13,18,19; 3:1,2,7,8,14,15).

"I know thy works." These are the words of Him who walks in the midst of the seven golden candlesticks, and whose eyes are like a flame of fire. As He looks upon the churches, the first thing He sees and judges them of is the

221

works. The works are the revelation of the life and character. If we are willing to bring our works into His holy presence, His words can teach us what our work ought to be.

To Ephesus He says: "I know thy works, and thy labor and thy patience, and how thou canst not bear them which are evil ... and hast patience, and for My name's sake hast labored and hath not fainted. Nevertheless, I have somewhat against thee, because thou hast left thy first love ... repent, and do the first works" (Revelation 2:2-5). There was here much to praise amidst toil, and patience, and zeal that had never grown weary. But there was one thing lacking—the tenderness of their first love.

In His work for us Christ gave us before and above everything His love, the personal tender affection of His heart. In our work for Him He asks us nothing less. There is such a danger of work being carried on, and our even bearing much for Christ's sake, while the freshness of our love has passed away. And that is what Christ seeks. And that is what gives power. And that is what nothing can compensate for. Christ looks for the warm loving heart, the personal affection which ever keeps Him the center of our love and joy.

Christian workers, see that all your work be the work of love, of tender personal devotion to Christ Jesus.

To Thyatira He says: "I know thy works, and charity, and service, and faith, and thy patience, and thy works; and the last to be more than the first. Notwithstanding I have a few things against thee, because thou sufferest that woman Jezebel, who calleth herself a prophetess, to teach and seduce My servants." Here again the works are enumerated and praised, and the last had even been more than the first. But then there is one failure. A false toleration of what led to impurity and idolatry. And then He adds of His judgments, "the churches shall know that I am He which searches the reins and hearts, and I will give to each one of you according to your works."

Along with much of good works there may be some one form of error or evil tolerated which endangers the whole church. In Ephesus there was zeal for orthodoxy, but a lack of love. Here in Thyatira love and faith, but a lack of faithfulness against error. If good works are to please our Lord, if our whole life must be in harmony with them, in entire separation from the world and its allurements, we must seek to be what He promised to make us, established in every good word and work. Our work will decide our estimate in His judgment.

To Sardis: "I know thy works, that thou hast a name, that thou livest, and art dead. Be watchful and strengthen the things which remain, that are ready to die: for I have not found thy works perfect before God."

There may be all the forms of godliness without the power, and many activities of religious organization without the life. There may be many works, and yet He may say, I have found no work of thine fulfilled before My God, none that can stand the test and be really acceptable to God as a spiritual sacrifice. In Ephesus it was works lacking in love, in Thyatira works lacking in purity, in Sardis works lacking in life.

To Philadelphia: "I know thy works: behold I have set before thee an open door, and no man can shut it: for thou hast a little strength, and hast kept My word and hast not denied My name.... Because thou hast kept the word or My patience, I also will keep thee."

On earth Jesus had said: "He that hath My commandments and keepeth them, he it is that loveth Me: and he that loveth Me shall be loved of My Father" (John 14:21). Philadelphia, the church for which there is no reproof, had this mark: its chief work and the law of all its work, was that it kept Christ's word, not in an orthodox creed only, but in practical obedience. Let nothing less be the mark and spirit of all our work—keeping of the word of Christ. Full, loving conformity to His will be rewarded.

To Laodicea: "I know thy works, that thou art neither cold nor hot.... Because thou sayest, I am rich and increased with goods, and have need of nothing." There is not a church without its works, its religious activities.

And yet the two great marks of Laodicean religion, lukewarmness, and its natural accompaniment, self-complacence, may rob them of their worth. It not only, like Ephesus, teaches us the need of a fresh and fervent love, but also the need of that poverty of spirit, that conscious weakness out of which the absolute dependence on Christ's strength for all our work will grow, and which will no longer leave Christ standing at the door, but enthrone Him in the heart.

"I know thy works." He who tested the works of the seven churches still lives and watches over us. He is ready in His love to discover what is lacking, to give timely warning and help, and to teach us the path in which our works can be fulfilled before His God. Let us learn from Ephesus the lesson of fervent love to Christ, from Thyatira that of purity and separation from all evil, from Sardis that of the need of true life to give worth to work, from Philadelphia that of keeping His word, and from Laodicea that of the poverty of spirit which possesses the Kingdom of Heaven, and gives

Christ the throne of all! Workers! Let us live and work in Christ's presence. He will teach and correct and help us, and one day give the full reward of all our works because they were His own works in us.

REFLECTION

1. In many passages in Revelation the Lord speaks of us being "judged according to our works." In Revelation 20:12 we read, "And I saw the dead, small and great, stand before God; and the books were opened: and another book was opened which was the Book of Life: and the dead were judged out of those things which were written in the books, according to their works." What does it mean to be "judged according to our works?"

2. Works done without a spirit of love are not worthy of the Lord.

3. By what power can we, as God's people, do anything pleasing to Him?

DAY 31

THAT GOD MAY BE GLORIFIED

"If any man speak, let him speak as the oracles of God; if any man minister, let him do it as to the ability which God giveth: that God in all things may be glorified through Jesus Christ, to whom be praise and dominion for ever and ever. Amen" (1 Peter 4:11).

Work is not done for its own sake. Its value consists in the object it attains. The purpose of him who commands or performs the work gives it its real worth. And the clearer a man's insight into the purpose, the better fitted will he be to

225

take charge of the higher callings of the work. In the erection of some splendid building, the purpose of the worker may simply be as a hired hand to earn his wages. The trained stone cutter has a higher object. He thinks of the beauty and perfection of the work he does. The master mason has a wider range of thought. His aim is that all the masonry shall be true and good. The contractor for the whole building has an even higher aim—that the whole building shall perfectly correspond to the plan he has to carry out. The architect has had a still higher purpose—that the great principles of art and beauty might find their full expression in material shape. With the owner we find the final end—the use to which the grand structure is to be put when he, say, presents the building as a gift for the benefit of his townsmen. All who have worked upon the building honestly have done so with some true purpose. The deeper the insight and the keener the interest in the ultimate design, the more important the share in the work, and the greater joy there is in carrying it out.

Peter tells us what our aim ought to be in all Christian service: "that in all things God may be glorified through Jesus Christ." In the work of God, a work not to be done for wages but for love, the humblest laborer is admitted to a share in God's plans, and to an insight into the great purpose which God is working out. That purpose is nothing less than that God may be glorified. This is the one purpose of God, the great worker in heaven, the source and master of all work—that the glory of His love and power and blessing may be shown. This is the one purpose of Christ, the great worker on earth in human nature, the example and leader of all our work. This is the great purpose of the Holy Spirit, the power that works in us, or, as Peter says here, "ability which God giveth." As this becomes our deliberate, intelligent purpose, our work will rise to its true level, and lift us into living fellowship with God.

"That in all things God may be glorified." What does this mean? The glory of God is that He alone is the Living One, who has life in himself. Yet not for himself alone, but, because His life is love, for His people as much as for himself. The glory of God is that He is the alone and ever-flowing fountain of all life and goodness and happiness, and that His creatures can have all this only as He gives it and works it in them. His working all in all is His glory. And the only glory His creature, His child, can give Him is to receive all He is willing to give, yielding to Him to let Him work, and then acknowledging that He has done it. Thus God himself shows forth His glory in our willing surrender to Him, and in our joyful acknowledgment that He does all we glorify Him. And so our life and work is glorified, as it has one purpose with all God's own work, "God in all things may be glorified through Jesus Christ, to whom be praise and dominion for ever and ever. Amen."

See here now the spirit that ennobles and consecrates Christian service according to Peter: "He that serveth (in ministering to the saints or the needy), let him serve as of the ability which God giveth." Let me cultivate a deep conviction that God's work, down into the details of daily life, can only be done in God's strength, "by the power of the Spirit working in us." Let me believe firmly and unceasingly that the Holy Spirit does dwell in me, as the power from on high, for all work to be done for on high. Let me in my Christian work fear nothing so much, as working in my own human will and strength, and so losing the one thing needful in my work, God working in me. Let me rejoice in the weakness that renders me so absolutely dependent upon such a God, and wait in prayer for His power to take full possession.

"Let him serve as of the ability which God giveth, that God in all things may be glorified through Jesus Christ." The more you depend on God alone for your strength, the more will He be glorified. The more you seek to make God's purpose your purpose, the more will you be led to give way to His working and His strength and love. Oh! That every—even the feeblest—worker might see what a nobility it gives to work, what a new glory to life, what a new urgency and joy in laboring for souls, when the one purpose has mastered us—that in all things God may be glorified through Jesus Christ.

REFLECTION

1. The glory of God as Creator was seen in His making man in His own image. The glory of God as Redeemer is seen in the work He carries on for saving men, and bringing them to himself.

2. This glory is the glory of His holy love, casting sin out of the heart, and dwelling there.

3. The only glory we can bring to God is to yield ourselves to His redeeming love to take possession of us, to fill us with love to others, and so through us to show forth His glory.

4. Let this be the one end of our lives: To glorify God in living to work for Him, "as of the ability which God giveth," and winning souls to know and live for His glory.

5. Lord! Teach us to serve in the ability which God giveth, that God in all things may be glorified through Jesus Christ, whose is the glory for ever and ever. Amen.

BE
PERFECT

PREFACE AND PRAYER

If any one takes up this little volume with the idea of finding a theory of perfection expounded or vindicated, he will be greatly disappointed. My purpose is a very clear and different one. What I wish to do is to go with my reader through the Word of God, noting the principal passages in which the word "Perfect" occurs, and seeking in each case from the context to find what the impression is the word was meant to convey. It is only when we have yielded ourselves simply and prayerfully to allow the words of Scripture to have their full force, that we are on the right track for combining the different aspects of truth into one harmonious whole.

Among the thoughts which have specially been brought home to me in these meditations and in which I trust I may secure the assent of my reader, the following are the chief:

1. There is a perfection of which Scripture speaks as possible and attainable. There is great diversity of opinion as to how the term is to be defined. But there can be only one opinion as to the fact that God asks and expects His children to be perfect with Him. He promises it as His own work, and that Scripture speaks of some as having been perfect before Him, and having served Him with a perfect

heart. Scripture speaks of a perfection that is at once our duty and our hope.

2. To know what this perfection is we must begin by accepting the command, and obeying it with our whole heart. Our natural tendency is the very opposite. We want to discuss and define what perfection is, to understand how the command can be reconciled with our assured conviction that no man is perfect, to provide for all the dangers we are sure are to be found in the path of perfection.

This is not God's way. Jesus said, "If any man will do, he will know." The same principle holds good in all human attainment. It is only he who has accepted the command, "Be perfect," in adoring submission and obedience, who can hope to know what the perfection is that God asks and gives. Until the Church is seen prostrate before God, seeking this blessing as her highest good, it will be no wonder if the very word "Perfection," instead of being an attraction and a joy, is a cause of apprehension and anxiety, of division and offence. May God increase the number of those who, in childlike humility, take the word from His own lips, as a living seed, in the assurance that it will bring forth much fruit.

3. Perfection is no arbitrary demand. In the very nature of things God can ask nothing less. And this is true whether we think of Him or of ourselves.

If we think of Him, who as God has created the universe for himself and for His glory, who seeks and alone is able to fill it with His happiness and love, we see how impossible it is for God to allow anything else to share man's heart with himself. God must be all and have all. As Lawgiver and Judge, He dare not be content with anything less than absolute legal perfection. As Redeemer and Father it equally becomes Him to claim nothing less than a real childlike perfection. God must have it all.

If we think of ourselves, the call to perfection is no less imperative. God is such an infinite, spiritual good, and the soul is so incapable of receiving or knowing or enjoying Him except as it gives itself wholly to Him, that for our own sakes God's love can demand of us nothing less than a perfect heart.

4. Perfection, as the highest aim of what God in His great power would do for us, is something so divine, spiritual, and heavenly, that it is only the soul that yields itself very tenderly to the leading of the Holy Spirit that can hope to know its blessedness.

God has worked into every human heart a deep desire for perfection. That desire is manifested in the admiration, which all men have for excellence in the different objects or pursuits to which they attach value. In the believer who yields himself wholly to God, this desire fastens itself upon God's wonderful promises, and inspires a prayer like that of Robert Murray M'Cheyne; "Lord, make me as holy as a pardoned sinner can be made."

The more we learn to desire this full conformity to God's will, for the consciousness that we are always pleasing to Him, we will see that all this must come as a gift direct from heaven. This gift is the full working in us of the life of God, the inbreathing of the Holy Spirit of Jesus in those who are wholly yielded to His indwelling and rule. Trusting ever less to men's thoughts and teachings, we will retire often into the secret of God's presence, in the assurance that the more we see God's face, and hear the secret voice that comes direct from Him, "BE PERFECT," the more will the Holy Spirit dwelling within us unfold the heavenly fullness and power of the words, and make them, as God's words, bring and give and create the very thing He speaks.

In the hope that these simple meditations may help some of God's children to go on to perfection, I commit them and myself to the Blessed Father's teaching and keeping.

Andrew Murray

Ever blessed Father! You have sent me a message by Your Beloved Son that I am to be perfect as You are perfect. Coming from You, O You incomprehensible and most glorious God, it means more than man can grasp. Coming to You, I ask that You will teach me what it means, create in me what it claims, give me what it promises.

My Father! I accept the word in the obedience of faith. I will yield my life to its rule. I will hide it in my heart as a living seed, in the assurance that there, deeper than thought or feeling, Your Holy Spirit can make it strike root and grow up.

And as I go through Your Word, to meditate on what it says of the path of the perfect, teach me, O my Father, to bring every thought of mine captive to the obedience of Christ, and to wait for that teaching of Your Holy Spirit which is so sure to the upright in heart. In Him, with whom You have sent me the message, give me the answer to this prayer also.

Amen

WAITING ON GOD

DAY 1

A PERFECT HEART MAKES A PERFECT MAN

*"Noah was a righteous man, and perfect in his generation,
and Noah walked with God" (Genesis 6:9).*

*"And the Lord said unto Satan, Have you considered My
servant Job, that there is none like him in the earth,
a perfect and an upright man, one that fears God and
shuns evil?" (Job 1: 8).*

*"The heart of David was perfect with the Lord his God"
(1 Kings 11:4,15:3).*

*"Asa's heart was perfect with the Lord all his days"
(1 Kings 15:14).*

We have grouped together four men, of all of whom
Holy Scripture testifies that they were perfect men,
or that their heart was perfect with God. Of each of them
Scripture testifies, too, that they were not perfect in the sense
of absolute sinlessness. We know how Noah fell. We know
how Job had to humble himself before God. We know how
sadly David sinned. And of Asa we read that there came a
time when he did foolishly, and relied on the Syrians and not

235

on the Lord his God; when in his disease he sought not to the Lord, but to the physicians. And yet the heart of these men was perfect with the Lord their God.

To understand this, there is one thing we must remember. The meaning of the word "perfect" must in each case be decided by that particular stage in God's education of His people in which it is used. What a father or a teacher counts perfection in a child of ten years, is very different from what he would call so in one of twenty. As to the disposition or spirit, the perfection would be the same. In its contents, as the proofs by which it was to be judged of, there would be a wide difference. We shall see later on how in the Old Testament nothing was really made perfect; how Christ has come to reveal, and work out, and impart the true perfection; how the perfection, as revealed in the New Testament, is something infinitely higher, more spiritual and efficacious, than under the old economy. And yet at root they are one. God looks at the heart. A heart that is perfect with Him is an object of complacency and approval. A wholehearted consecration to His will and fellowship, a life that takes as its motto, "Wholly for God," has in all ages, even where the Spirit had not yet been given to dwell in the heart, been accepted by Him as the mark of the perfect man.

The lesson that these Scripture testimonies suggest to us is a very simple, but a very searching one. In God's record of the lives of His servants there are some of whom it is written: His heart was perfect with the Lord his God. Is this, let each reader ask, what God sees and says of me? Does my life, in the sight of God, bear the mark of intense, wholehearted consecration to God's will and service? Of a burning desire to be as perfect as it is possible for grace to make me? Let us yield ourselves to the searching light of this question. Let us believe that with this word "perfect," God means something very real and true. Let us not evade its force, or hide ourselves from its condemning power, by the vain subterfuge that we do not fully know what it means. We must first accept it, and give up our lives to it, before we can understand it. It cannot be insisted upon too strongly that, whether in the Church at large and its teaching, or in the life of the individual believer, there can be no hope of comprehending what perfection is except as we count all things loss to be apprehended of it, to live for it, to accept it, to possess it.

But so much we can understand. What I do with a perfect heart I do with love and delight, with a willing mind and all my strength. It implies a determined purpose, and a concentration of effort, that makes everything subordinate to the one object of my choice. This is what God asks, what His saints have given, and what we must give.

Again I say to every one who wishes to join me in following through the Word of God its revelation of His will concerning perfection, yield yourself to the searching question: Can God say of me as of Noah and Job, of David and Asa, that my heart is perfect with the Lord my God? Have I given myself up to say that there must be nothing, nothing whatever, to share my heart with God and His will? Is a heart perfect with the Lord my God the object of my desire, my prayer, and my hope? Whether it has been so or not, let it be so today. Make the promise of God's word your own: "The God of peace himself perfect you." The God, who is of power to do above all we ask or think, will open up to you the blessed prospect of a life of which He shall say: "His heart was perfect with the Lord his God."

REFLECTION
1. Giving completely of ourselves, our goals, our plans, our future to God is the path to perfection.

2. As we see the recorded lives of many servants of God, we read of many whose was perfect with the Lord God. Is this what God sees in me?

3. Does my life bear the mark of intense, wholehearted consecration to God's will and service? Do I have a burning desire to be as perfect as it is possible for grace to make me?

DAY 2

WALK BEFORE ME, AND BE PERFECT

"And when Abram was ninety-nine years old, the Lord appeared to Abram, and said to him, I am Almighty God: walk before Me, and be perfect. And I will make My covenant between Me and you, and will multiply you exceedingly. And Abram fell on his face: and God talked with him" (Genesis 17:1-3).

"You shall be perfect with the Lord your God" (Deuteronomy 18:13).

"Let your heart be perfect with the Lord your God to walk in His statutes" (1 Kings 8:61).

It was now twenty-four years since God had called Abram to go out from his father's home, and that he had obeyed. All that time he had been a learner in the school of faith. The time was approaching for him to inherit the promise, and God comes to establish His covenant with him. In view of this, God meets him with this threefold word: I am Almighty God; walk before Me; be perfect.

Be perfect. The connection in which we find the word will help us to understand its meaning. God reveals himself as God Almighty. Abram's faith had long been tried. It was about to achieve one of its greatest triumphs. Faith was to be changed to vision in the birth of Isaac. God invites Abram more than ever to remember, and to rest upon, His omnipotence. He is Almighty God. All things are possible to Him. He holds rule over all. All His power is working for those who trust Him. And all He asks of His servant is that he be perfect with Him, and give Him his whole heart, his perfect confidence. God Almighty with all His power is wholly for you. Be wholly for God. The knowledge and faith of what God is lies at the root of what we are to be. "I am Almighty God; be perfect." As I know Him whose power fills heaven and earth, I see that this is the one thing needed—to be perfect with Him, wholly and entirely given up to Him. Wholly for God is the keynote of perfection.

Walk before Me, and be perfect. It is in the life fellowship with God, in His realized presence and favor, that it becomes possible to be perfect with Him. Walk before Me. Abraham had been doing this. God's word called him to a clearer and more conscious apprehension of this as his life calling. It is easy for us to study what Scripture says of perfection, to form our ideas of it, and argue for them. But let us remember that it is only as we are walking closely with God, seeking and in some measure attaining, uninterrupted communion with Him, that the divine command will come to us in its divine power, and unfold to us its divine meaning. Walk before Me, and be perfect. God's realized presence is the school and the secret of perfection. It is only he who studies what perfection is in the full light of God's presence to whom its hidden glory will be opened up.

That realized presence is the great blessing of the redemption in Jesus Christ. The veil has been rent, the way into the true sanctuary and the presence of God has been opened. We have access with boldness into the holiest of all. God, who has proved himself God Almighty in raising Jesus from the dead and setting Him, and us in Him, at His right hand, speaks now to us: I am God Almighty. Walk before Me, and be perfect.

That command came not only to Abraham. Moses gave it to the whole people of Israel: "You shall be perfect with the Lord your God" (Deuteronomy 18:13). It is for all Abraham's children, for all the Israel of God, and for every believer. Oh! Think not that you can obey, you must first understand and define what perfection means. No, God's way is the very opposite of this. Abraham went out, not knowing where he went. You are called to go on to perfection. Go out, not knowing where you are going. It is a land God will show you. Let your heart be filled with His glory: I am God Almighty. Let your life be spent in His presence: walk before Me. As His power and His presence rest upon you and fill you, your heart will, before you know, be drawn up, and strengthened to accept and rejoice in and fulfill the command: be perfect. As surely as the opening bud has but to abide in the light of the sun to attain perfection, will the soul that walks in the light of God be perfect too. As the God, who is ALL, shines upon it, it cannot but rejoice to give Him all.

REFLECTION

1. There are many who think they cannot rightly obey until they can first understand what perfection means. But this is not God's way. It is those who step out and go forward, like Abraham, without know where it would lead, who receive the perfecting work from the Lord.

DAY 3

PERFECT WITH THE LORD YOUR GOD

"You shall be perfect with the Lord your God"
(Deuteronomy 18:13).

To be perfect before God is not only the calling and the privilege of a man like Abraham, it is equally the duty of all his children. The command is given to all Israel, for each of God's people to receive and obey: "You shall be perfect with the Lord your God." It comes to each child of God. No one professing to be a Christian may turn aside from it, or refuse it obedience, without endangering his salvation. It is not a command like, "You shall not kill," or, "You shall not steal," having reference to a limited sphere in our life, but is a principle that lies at the very root of all true religion. If our service of God is to be acceptable, it must not be with a divided, but a whole, a perfect heart.

The chief hindrance in the way of obedience to this command lies in our misapprehension of what religion is. Man was created simply to live for God, to show forth His glory, by allowing God to show how completely He could reveal His likeness and blessedness in man. God lives for man, longing in the greatness of His love to communicate His goodness and His love. It was to this life, lost by sin, Christ came to redeem us back. The selfishness of the human heart looks upon salvation as simply the escape from hell, with so much of holiness as is needed to make our happiness secure. Christ meant us to be restored to the state from which we had fallen—the whole heart, the whole will, the whole life given up to the glory and service of God. To be wholly given up to God, to be perfect with the Lord our God, lies at the very root, is the very essence of true religion. The enthusiastic devotion of the whole heart to God is what is asked of us.

When once this misconception has been removed, and the truth begins to dawn upon the soul, a second hindrance is generally met with in the question of unbelief, how can these things be? Instead of first accepting God's command, and then waiting in the path of obedience for the teaching of the Spirit, men are at once ready with their own interpretation of the word, and confidently affirm, "it cannot be." They forget that the whole object of the gospel and the glory of Christ's redemption is, that it makes possible what is beyond man's thoughts or powers. It reveals God, not as a Lawgiver and Judge, exacting the last penny, but as a Father, who in grace deals with each one according to his capacity, and accepts the devotion and the intention of the heart.

We understand this of an earthly father. A child of ten is doing some little service for the father, or helping him in his work. The work of the child is very defective, and yet the cause of joy and hope to the father, because he sees in it the proof of the child's attachment and obedience, as well as the pledge of what that spirit will do for the child when his intelligence and his strength have been increased. The child has served the father with a perfect heart, though the perfect heart does not at once imply perfect work. Even so the Father in heaven accepts as a perfect heart the simple childlike purpose that makes His fear and service its one object. The Christian may be deeply humbled at the involuntary uprisings of the evil nature, but God's Spirit teaches him to say, "It is no more I, but sin that dwells in me." He may be sorely grieved by the consciousness of shortcoming and failure, but he hears the voice of Jesus, "The spirit is willing, but the flesh is weak." Even as Christ counted the love and obedience of His faithless disciples as such, and accepted it as the condition on which He had promised them the Spirit, the Christian can receive the witness of the Spirit that the Father sees and accepts in him the perfect heart, even where there is not yet the perfect performance.

"Thou shalt be perfect with the Lord thy God" (Deuteronomy 18:13). Oh! Let us beware of making the Word of God of no effect by our traditions. Let us believe the message, "You are not under the law, but under grace." Let us realize what grace is in its pitying tenderness, "As a father pities his children, so the Lord pities them that fear Him." And what, in its mighty power working in us both to will and to do, "The God of all grace shall Himself perfect you." If we hold fast our integrity, our confidence, and the rejoicing of hope steadfast unto the end, being perfect in heart will lead us on to be perfect in the way, and we will realize that Christ fulfils this too in us, "You shall be perfect with the Lord your God."

REFLECTION

1. The blessed work of Christ was not just to save us from the punishment of hell, but to restore us, by His grace, to the perfect relationship originally intended at creation.

2. "To be wholly given up to God, to be perfect with the Lord our God, lies at the very root, is the very essence of true religion." Are we giving all up to God?

DAY 4

I HAVE WALKED BEFORE YOU
WITH A PERFECT HEART

*"Then Hezekiah prayed unto the Lord, saying, 'I beg You,
O Lord, remember now how I have walked before You in
truth, and with a perfect heart, and have done that which
is good in Your sight.' And the word of the Lord came to
Isaiah, saying, 'Tell Hezekiah, this is what the Lord says,
I have heard your prayer, and seen your tears; I will heal
you'" (2Kings 20:2-5).*

What a childlike simplicity of communication with God. When the Son was about to die, He spoke, "I have glorified You on earth, I have finished the work which You gave Me to do. And now, O Father, You glorify Me." He pleaded His life and work as the ground for expecting an answer to His prayer. And so Hezekiah, the servant of God, also pleaded, not as a matter of merit, but in the confidence that "God is not unrighteous to forget our work of faith and labor of love," that God should remember how he had walked before Him with a perfect heart.

The words first of all suggest to us this thought, that the man who walks before God with a perfect heart can know it—it may be a matter of consciousness. Let us look at the testimony Scripture gives of him, "He did that which was right in the sight of the Lord, according to all that David his father did" (2 Kings 18: 3-6). Then follow the different elements of this life that was right in God's sight. "He trusted in the Lord God of Israel. He held to the Lord. He departed not from following Him. He kept His commandments, which the Lord commanded Moses. And the Lord was with him." His life was one of trust and love, of steadfastness

and obedience. And the Lord was with him. He was one of
the saints of whom we read, "By faith they obtained a good
report." They had the witness that they were righteous, that
they were pleasing to God.

Let us seek to have this blessed consciousness. Paul had
it when he wrote, "Our glorying is, the testimony of our
conscience, that in holiness and sincerity of God, not in fleshly
wisdom, but in the grace of God, we behaved ourselves"
(2 Corinthians 1:12). John had it when he said, "Beloved,
if our heart condemn us not, we have boldness toward
God; and whatever we ask we receive, because we keep His
commandments, and do the things that are pleasing in His
sight" (1 John 3: 21,22). If we are to have perfect peace and
confidence, if we are to walk in the holy boldness and the
blessed glorying of which Scripture speaks, we must know
that our heart is perfect with God.

Hezekiah's prayer suggests a second lesson—that the
consciousness of a perfect heart gives wonderful power in
prayer. Read over again the words of his prayer, and notice
how distinctly this walk with a perfect heart is his plea. Read
over again the words just quoted from John, and see how
clearly he says that "because we keep His commandments
we receive what we ask." It is a heart that does not condemn
us, that knows that it is perfect toward God that gives us
boldness.

There is most probably not a single reader of these lines
who cannot testify how painfully at some time or other the
consciousness of the heart not being perfect with God has
hindered confidence and prayer. And mistaken views as to
what the perfect heart means, and as to the danger of self-
righteousness in praying Hezekiah's prayer, have in very many
cases banished all idea of its ever being possible to attain to

that boldness and confident assurance of an answer to prayer which John connects with a heart that does not condemn us. Oh! That we would give up all our prejudices and learn to take God's Word as it stands as the only rule of our faith, the only measure of our expectations. Our daily prayers would be a new reminder that God asks of the perfect heart; a new occasion of childlike confession as to our walking or not walking with a perfect heart before God; a new motive to make nothing less the standard of our intercourse with our Father in heaven. How could our boldness in God's presence be ever clearer and our consciousness of His acceptance be ever brighter. How could the humbling thought of our nothingness be quickened, and our assurance of His strength in our weakness, and His answer to our prayer, become the joy of our life.

Oh! The comfort, amid all consciousness of imperfection of attainment, of being able to say, in childlike simplicity, "Remember, O Lord, how I have walked before Thee in truth and with a perfect heart" (Isaiah 38:3).

REFLECTION

1. If our conscience is uneasy we cannot be perfect in our prayers.

2. If we are to have perfect peace and confidence, we must know that our heart is perfect with God.

DAY 5

LORD, GIVE ME A PERFECT HEART

"Give to Solomon my son a perfect heart, to keep Thy commandments, Thy testimonies, and Thy statutes"
(1 Chronicles 29:19).

"Let my heart be perfect in Thy testimonies"
(Psalm 119:80).

In his parting commission to Solomon, David had laid it upon him to serve God with a perfect heart, because He is God who searches the hearts. It is nothing less than the heart, the whole heart, a perfect heart that God wants. Very shortly afterwards, in his dedication prayer after the giving of all the material for the temple, he turns again to this as the one thing needful, and asks it for his son as a gift from God. "Give my son Solomon a perfect heart." The perfect heart is a gift from God, given and received under the laws, which rule all His giving, as a hidden seed to be accepted and acted on in faith. The command, "Be perfect," comes and claims immediate and full submission. Where this submission is yielded, the need of a divine power to make the heart fit for perfection becomes the motive for urgent and earnest prayer. The word of command, received and hid in a good and honest heart, becomes itself the seed of a divine power. God works His grace in us by stirring us to work. So the desire to listen to God's command, and to serve Him with a perfect heart, is a beginning that God looks to, and that He will himself strengthen and perfect. The gift of a perfect heart is thus obtained in the way of the obedience of faith. Begin at once to serve God with a perfect heart, and the perfect heart will be given to you.

The perfect heart is a gift from God, to be asked for and obtained by prayer. No one will pray for it earnestly, perseveringly, believingly, until he accepts God's word fully that it is a positive command and an immediate duty to be perfect. Where this has been done, the consciousness will soon grow strong of the utter impossibility of attempting obedience in human strength. And the faith will grow that the word of command was simply meant to draw the soul to Him who gives what He asks.

The perfect heart is a gift to be obtained in prayer. David asked the Lord to give it to his son Solomon, even as he had prayed for himself long before, "Let my heart be perfect in Your testimonies." Let all of us who desire for this blessing follow his example. Let us make it a matter of definite, earnest prayer. Let each son and daughter of God say to the Father, "Give Your child a perfect heart." Let us in the course of our meditations in this little book turn each word of command, or teaching, or promise into prayer—pointed, personal prayer that asks and claims, that accepts and proves the gift of a perfect heart. And when the seed begins to take root, and the spirit gives the consciousness that the first beginnings of the perfect heart have been bestowed in the wholehearted purpose to live for God alone, let us hold on in prayer for the perfect heart in all its completeness. A heart perfect in its purpose towards God is only the initial stage. Then there comes the putting on of one grace after another, going from strength to strength on to perfection—the putting on, in ever-growing distinctness of likeness, the Lord Jesus, with every trait of His holy image. All this is to be sought and found in prayer. It is those who know most of what it is to be perfect in purpose who will pray most to be perfect in practice too.

In the words of Hezekiah, we see that there are two elements in the perfect heart: the relation to God, and to His commandments. "I have walked before Thee with a perfect heart, and have done that which is good in Thy sight." David speaks of the second of these in his prayer, "a perfect heart to keep Thy commandments." The two always go together: walking before God, in the awareness of His presence, will ensure walking in His commandments.

"Every good gift and every perfect gift is from above, and comes from the Father of lights" (James 1:17), including the gift of a perfect heart. "But let us ask in faith, nothing wavering" (James 1:6). Let us be sure that in the believing, adoring worship of God there will be given to the soul that is set upon having it, nothing less than what God Himself means with a perfect heart. Let us pray the prayer boldly, "Lord, give Thy child a perfect heart. Let my heart be perfect in Thy testimonies."

REFLECTION

1. Let us ask of God, in faith in prayer, for the gift of a perfect heart.

2. To be perfect in purpose is necessary before one can be perfect in practice.

DAY 6

GOD'S STRENGTH FOR THE PERFECT HEART

"Were not the Ethiopians and the Lubims a huge host?
Yet, because thou didst rely on the Lord, He delivered
them into thine hand. For the eyes of the Lord run to and
fro throughout the whole earth, to show Himself strong in
behalf of them whose heart is perfect toward Him"
(2 Chronicles 16:8,9).

We have here the same three thoughts we had in God's words to Abraham. There, it was the command to be perfect in connection with the faith in God's power and a walk in His Presence. Here, we have the perfect heart spoken of as the condition of the experience of God's power, and as that which His eyes seek and approve in those who walk in His presence. The words teach us the great lesson of the value of the perfect heart in His sight. It is the one thing He desires. "His eyes run to and fro through the whole earth" to find such. The Father seeks such to worship Him. And when He finds them, then He shows himself strong in their behalf. It is the one thing that marks the soul as having the capacity of receiving and showing God's glory—His strength.

The context proves that the chief mark of the perfect heart is trust in God. "Because you relied on the Lord, He delivered them into your hand. For the eyes of the Lord run to and fro to show himself strong in behalf of them whose heart is perfect toward Him." The essence of faith is that it gives God His place and glory as God. It allows Him free scope to work, relying on Him alone. It lets God be God. In such faith or reliance the heart proves itself perfect toward God, with no other object of confidence or desire. It depends only upon Him. As the eyes of God go to and fro throughout the world, wherever He discovers such a man, He delights to prove himself strong to him, to work for him or in him, as the case may be, according to the riches of the glory of His power.

What precious lessons these words teach us for the Christian life. To have God reveal His strength in us, to have Him make us strong for life or work, for doing or for suffering, our heart must be perfect with Him. Let us not shrink from accepting the truth. Let no preconceived opinion as to the impossibility of perfection keep us from allowing the Word of God to have its full effect upon us. He shows himself strong to those whose heart is perfect towards Him. Before we attempt to define exactly, let us first receive the truth that there is such a thing as what God calls a perfect heart, and say it shall be ours. Let us rest contented with nothing short of knowing that the eyes of the Lord have seen that we are wholehearted with Him. Let us not be afraid to say, "With my whole heart, I have sought Thee."

We saw how the chief mark of this perfect heart is reliance upon God. God looks for men who trust Him fully. In them He will show His power. God is a Being of infinite and incomprehensible glory and power. Our mind can form no right conception of what He can do for us. Even when we have His word and promises, our human thoughts of what He means are always defective. By nothing do we dishonor God more than by limiting Him. By nothing do we limit Him more than by allowing our human ideas of what He purposes to be the measure of our expectations. The reliance of a heart perfect towards Him is simply to yield to Him as God. It rests upon Him, it allows Him, as God, to do in His own way what He has promised. The heart is perfect towards Him in meeting Him with a perfect faith for all that He is and does as God. Faith expects from God what is beyond all expectation.

The Father seeks such. Oh! With what joy He finds them. How He delights in them as His eyes, running to and fro throughout the world, rests upon them to show himself their strong and mighty Helper! Let us walk before this God with a perfect heart, relying upon Him yet to work in us above all that we can ask or think. The one great need of the spiritual life is to know how entirely it is dependent upon God working in us, and what the exceeding greatness of His power is in us who believe. As the soul knows this, and with a perfect heart yields to this Almighty God to let Him do His work within, oh, how strong He will show himself in its behalf.

REFLECTION

1. The primary mark of the perfect heart is absolute trust in God. God looks for those who trust Him fully. Are we trusting the Lord completely in all things? Are we open to receiving His power?

2. Let us not dishonor God by limiting Him with our human ideas of what He can do.

DAY 7

WITH THE PERFECT
GOD SHOWS HIMSELF PERFECT

*"I was also upright before Him, and I kept myself
from mine iniquity."*
"With a perfect man, Thou wilt show thyself perfect."
"As with God, His way is perfect."
"He is a shield to all those that trust in Him."
*"It is God who girdeth me with strength and
maketh my way perfect"*
(Psalms 18:23,25,30,32).

" **A** s with God, His way is perfect." In all He does and all He is, God is the perfection of goodness and beauty. In nature and grace, in heaven and on earth, in the greatest and the least, everything that is in God and of God, down to the very hem of His garment, is infinite perfection. If men who study and admire the perfection of His works, if saints who love and seek the perfection of His service and fellowship, but understood it, they would see that here alone perfection can be truly known and found in God himself. As for God the highest we can say of Him, though we can hardly comprehend it is that His way is perfect.

"He makes my way perfect." Of God's perfection this is the chief excellence—that He does not keep it for himself. Heaven and earth are full of His glory. God is Love; who lives, not for himself, but in the energy of an infinite life. He makes His people, as far as they can possibly receive it, partakers of His perfection. It is His delight to perfect all around Him. And especially the soul of man that rises up to Him. Between His servant and himself, God would have perfect harmony. The Father wants the child to be like himself. The more I learn

253

in adoring worship to say, "As for God, His way is perfect," the sooner I will have faith and grace with the Psalmist to say, "He makes my way perfect."

As we receive the heavenly truth of these words into our inmost being and assimilate it, we shall not wonder that the same man also said, "I was also perfect with Him, and kept myself from my iniquity." "The God that arms me with strength, and makes my way perfect," His alone is the power and the honor and the glory of what He has created. This makes the confession, "I was also perfect with Him," so far from being presumption or self-righteousness, nothing but an ascription of praise to Him to whom it is due.

And then follow the words in which the perfection of God and that of man are seen in their wonderful relationship and harmony. "With the perfect man, Thou wilt show Thyself perfect." As little as there can be a ray of the light of day, however dull and clouded it be, but what speaks of the sun, so little can there be any perfection except what is of God. In its feeblest beginnings in a soul, in its darkest and almost hopeless struggles, it is all God's perfection wrestling with man to break through and get possession. As long as man refuses to consent, God cannot make His perfection known, for God must be to us what we are to Him. "With the warped, You show Yourself twisted." But where man's will consents, and his heart chooses this perfection and this perfect God as its portion, God meets the soul with ever larger manifestation of how perfect He is towards His own. "With the perfect man Thou wilt show Thyself perfect."

Christian! Walk before God with a perfect heart, and you will experience how perfect the heart, and the love, and the will of God to bless, is towards you. Of a heart perfectly yielded to Him, God will take perfect possession.

Walk before God in a perfect way. It is God who makes my way perfect—and your eyes and heart will be opened to see, in adoring wonder, how perfect God's way is with you and for you. Do take hold of this word as the law of God's revelation of Himself: "With the perfect man, Thou wilt show Thyself perfect." To a soul perfectly devoted to Him, God will wonderfully reveal Himself. Turn with your whole heart and life, your whole trust and obedience, towards God—walk before Him with a perfect heart—and He will show Himself perfect to you, the God whose way is perfect and makes your way perfect, the God who perfects you in every good thing. Meet God and say, "With my whole heart I have sought Thee." He will answer you with, "Yes, I will rejoice over you to do you good, with my whole heart and with my whole soul." Oh! Say it in faith, and hope, and joy, "With the perfect man Thou wilt show Thyself perfect."

REFLECTION

1. Of a heart perfectly yielded to Him, God will take perfect possession.

2. God makes His people, as far as they can possibly receive it, partakers of His perfection

DAY 8

PERFECT IN HEART LEADS TO PERFECT IN THE WAY

"Blessed are they that are perfect in the way, who walk in the law of the Lord. Blessed are they that keep His testimonies, that seek Him with the whole heart"
(Psalms 119: 1,2).

"Let my heart be perfect in Thy testimonies"
(Psalms 119: 80).

"I will behave myself wisely in a perfect way. Oh!
When wilt Thou come to me? I will walk within my house
with a perfect heart" (Psalms 101: 2.

We have seen what Scripture says of the perfect heart. Here it speaks of the perfect walk. "Blessed are the perfect in the way, who walk in the law of the Lord." These are the opening words of the beautiful psalm, in which there is given to us the picture, from the witness of personal experience, of the wonderful blessedness of a life in the law and the will of God. As he looks back upon the past, the Psalmist does not hesitate to claim that he has kept that law: "I have kept Thy testimonies"; "I have conformed to Thy law"; "I did not desert Thy standards"; "I have not strayed from Thy judgments"; "I have done judgment and justice"; "I have not swerved from Thy testimonies"; "I have kept Thy commandments"; "My soul has conformed to Thy declarations." Can it be that there are some who can look up to God and, in simplicity of soul, say, "How blessed are the perfect in the way?"

What is meant by "perfect in the way" becomes plain as we study the psalm. Perfection includes two elements. The one is the perfection of heart, the earnestness of purpose, with which a man gives himself up to seek God and His will. The other, the perfection of obedience, in which a man seeks, not only to do some, but all the commandments of his God, and rests content with nothing less than the New Testament privilege of "standing perfect in all the will of God." Of both, the Psalmist speaks with great confidence. Hear how he testifies of the former in words such as these: "Blessed are they that seek Him with the whole heart"; "With my whole heart I have sought Thee"; "With my whole heart, I will conform to Thy law;"; "I will keep Thy standards with my whole heart"; "Thy standards are my delight"; "O, how I love Thy standards!" "Consider how I love Thy standards"; "I love them exceedingly." This is indeed the perfect heart of which we have already heard. The whole psalm is a prayer, and an appeal to God himself to consider and see how His servant in wholehearted simplicity has chosen God and His standard as his only portion.

We have more than once said that in this wholeheartedness, in the perfect heart, we have the root of all perfection. But it is only the root and beginning. There is another element that must not be lacking. God is to be found in His will. Those who would truly find and fully enjoy God, must meet Him in all His will. This is not always understood. A man may have his heart intent on serving God perfectly, and yet may be unconscious how very imperfect his knowledge of God's will is. The very earnestness of his purpose, and his consciousness of integrity towards God, may deceive him. As far as he knows, he does God's will. But he forgets how much there is of that blessed will that he does not yet know. He can learn a very blessed lesson from the writer of our psalm.

Hear how he speaks: "I have refrained my feet from every evil way"; "I hate every false way"; "I esteem all Thy standards concerning all things to be right." It is this surrender to a life of entire and perfect obedience that explains at once the need he felt of divine teaching, and the confidence with which he pleaded for it and expected it: "Let my heart be perfect in Thy testimonies." The soul that longs for nothing less than to be perfect in the way, and in deep consciousness of its need of a divine teaching pleads for it, will not be disappointed.

In our next meditation we pass on to the New Testament. In the Old Testament we have the time of preparation, the awakening of the spirit of holy expectancy, waiting God's fulfillment of His promises. In the Old Testament the perfect heart was the receptacle, emptied and cleansed for God's filling. In the New Testament we will find Christ perfected forevermore, perfecting us, and fitting us to walk perfect in Him. In the New Testament the word that looks at the human side, perfect in heart, disappears, to give place to that which reveals the divine filling that awaits the prepared vessel: Perfect Love; God's love perfected in us.

"Blessed are the perfect in the way!" We have heard the testimony of an Old Testament saint, and is it not written of New Testament times, "He that is feeble shall be as David"? Surely now, in the fullness of time, when Jesus our High Priest in the power of an endless life saves completely, and the Holy Spirit has come out of God's heaven to dwell within us and be our life, surely now there need not be one word of the psalm that is not meant to be literal truth in the mouth of every believer. Let us read it once more. Speaking it word for word before God, as the writer did, we too shall begin to sing, "Blessed are the perfect in the way, that seek Him with their whole heart."

"I will behave myself wisely in a perfect way. Oh! When wilt Thou come unto me! I will walk within my house with a perfect heart" (Psalms 101:2).

REFLECTION
1. What are the two elements of "perfection" the Lord is referring to in Psalms 119: 1,2? How do these two elements work together towards "perfection" in the child of God?

DAY 9

PERFECT AS THE FATHER

"Be ye therefore perfect, even as your Father which is in heaven is perfect" (Matthew 5:48).

Perfect before God, perfect with God, perfect towards God. These are the expressions we find in the Old Testament. They all indicate a relationship—the choice or purpose of the heart set upon God, the wholehearted desire to trust and obey Him. The first word of the New Testament at once lifts us to a very different level, and opens to us what Christ has brought for us. Not only perfect towards God, but perfect as God. This is the wonderful prospect it holds out to us. It reveals the infinite fullness of meaning the word "perfect" has in God's mind. It gives us at once the only standard we are to aim at and to judge by. It casts down all hopes of perfection as a human attainment; but awakens hope in Him who, as God, has the power, as Father has the will, to make us like himself.

A young child may be the perfect image of his father. There may be a great difference in age, in stature, in power, and yet the resemblance may be so striking that every one notices it. And so a child of God, though infinitely less, may yet bear the image of the Father so markedly, and may have such a striking likeness to his Father, that in his creaturely life he will "be perfect," as the Father is in His Divine life. This is possible! It is what Jesus here commands. It is what each one should aim at. "Perfect as your Father in heaven is perfect," must become one of the first articles of our creed, one of the guiding lights of our Christian life.

Wherein this perfection of the Father consists is evident from the context. "Love your enemies, that ye may be children of your Father which is in heaven; for He maketh His sun to rise on the evil and the good (Matthew 5:44,45); Be therefore perfect, as your Father in heaven is perfect." Or as it is in Luke 6:36: "Be ye therefore merciful, as your Father is merciful." The perfection of God is His love—His will to communicate His own blessedness to all around Him. His compassion and mercy are the glory of His being. He created us in His image and after His likeness, to find our glory in a life of love and mercy and beneficence. It is in love we are to be perfect, even as our Father is perfect.

The thought that comes up at once, and that ever returns again, is this: But is it possible? And if so, how? Certainly not as a fruit of man's efforts. But the words themselves contain the answer, "perfect as your Father is perfect." It is because the little child has received his life from his father, and because the father watches over his training and development, that there can be such a striking and ever-increasing resemblance between him in his feebleness and his father in his strength. It is because the sons of God are partakers of the Divine nature, have God's life, and spirit, and love within them, that the command is reasonable, and its obedience in ever-increasing measure possible—Be perfect, as your Father is. The perfection is our Father's, but we have its seed in us, and He delights to give the increase. The words that first appear to cast us down in utter helplessness now become our hope and strength. Be perfect, as your Father is perfect. Claim your child's heritage. Give up yourself to be wholly a child of God. Yield yourself to the Father to do in you all He is able.

And then, remember too, who it is that gives this message from the Father. It is the Son, who himself was, by the Father, perfected through suffering. He learned obedience and was made perfect, and who has perfected us forever. The message, "Be perfect," comes to us from Him, our elder brother, as a promise of infinite hope. What Jesus asks of us, the Father gives. What Jesus speaks, He does. To "present every man perfect in Christ Jesus" is the one aim of Christ and His gospel. Let us accept the command from Him, in yielding ourselves to obey it. Let us yield ourselves to Him. Let our expectation be from Him in whom we have been perfected. Through faith in Him we receive the Holy Ghost, by whom the love of God is shed abroad in our hearts. Through faith in Him, that love becomes in us a fountain of love springing up without ceasing. In union with Him, the love of God is perfected in us, and we are perfected in love. Let us not fear to accept and obey the command, "Be perfect, as your Father is perfect."

REFLECTION

1. God's compassion and mercy are the glory of His being, yet the perfection of God is His love. Consider how we are called to be in His likeness, and find our "perfection" in living a life of love, mercy and compassion.

2. Indeed, the thought arises in our heart and mind, "Is perfection possible?" Can it ever be the fruit of man's own efforts? The perfection is God's, but we have its seed in us, and He delights to give us the increase. It is our heritage in Christ. May we not fear to accept and obey the command, "Be perfect, as your Father is perfect."

DAY 10

PERFECTED AS THE MASTER

*"Be ye therefore merciful, as your Father also is merciful
... The disciple is not above his master: but every one who
is perfected will be as his master" (Luke 6:36,40).*

In his report of part of the Sermon on the Mount, Luke
records that Jesus does not say, "Be perfect," but, "Be
merciful," as your Father is. He then introduces the word
perfect immediately after that; not, however, in connection
with the Father, but the Son, as the Master of His disciples.
The change is most instructive. It leads us to look to Jesus,
as He dwelt in the flesh, as our model. It might be said that
our circumstances and powers are so different from those of
God that it is impossible to apply the standard of His infinite
perfection in our little world. But here comes the Son, in the
likeness of sinful flesh, tempted in all things like as we are,
and offers himself as our master and leader. He lives with
us that we may live with Him. He lives like us that we may
live like Him.

The divine standard is embodied and made visible, is
brought within our reach, in the human model. Growing
into His likeness, who is the image of the Father, we shall
bear the likeness of the Father too: becoming like Him, the
firstborn among many brethren, we shall become perfect as
the Father is. "The disciple is not above his master: but every
one who is perfected shall be as his master."

"The disciple is not above his master." The thought of
the disciple being as the master sometimes has reference to
outward humiliation. Like the master he will be despised and
persecuted (Matthew 10:24,25; John 15:20), and sometimes

to inward humility, the willingness to be a servant (Luke 22:27, John 13:16). Both in his external life and his inner disposition the perfected disciple knows nothing higher than to be as his master.

To take Jesus as Master, with the distinct desire and aim to be and live and act like Him is true Christianity. This is something far more than accepting Him as a Savior and Helper. Far more even than acknowledging Him as Lord and Master.

A servant may obey the commands of his master most faithfully, while he has little thought of rising up into the master's likeness and spirit. This alone is full discipleship, to long in everything to be as like the master as possible, to count His life as the true expression of all that is perfect, and to aim at nothing less than the perfection of being perfect as He was. "Everyone who is perfected shall be like his master."

The words suggest to us very distinctly that in discipleship there is more than one stage. Just as in the Old Testament it is said only of some that they served the Lord with a perfect heart, while of others we read that their heart was not perfect with the Lord (1 Kings 11:4, 15:3; 2 Chronicles 25:2), so even now there are great differences between disciples. Some there are to whom the thought of aiming at the perfect likeness of the master has never come. They only look to Christ as a Savior. And some there are whose heart indeed longs for full conformity to their Lord, "to be as the master," but who have never understood, though they have read the words, that there is such a thing as "a perfect heart" and a life "perfected in love."

But there are those, too, to whom it has been given to accept these words in their divine meaning and truth, and who do know in blessed experience what it is to say with Hezekiah, "I have walked before Thee with a perfect heart," and with John, "as He is, even so are we in this world."

As we go on in our study of what Scripture says of perfection, let us hold fast the principle we have learned here. Likeness to Jesus in His humiliation and humility: the choice, like Him, of the form of a servant, the spirit that does not exercise lordship and would not be ministered unto, but girds itself to minister and to give its life for others, this is the secret of true perfection. "The disciple is not above his master, but every one who is perfected shall be as his master." With the perfect love of God as our standard, with that love revealed in Christ's humanity and humility as our model and guide, with the Holy Spirit to strengthen us with might, that this Christ may live in us, we shall learn to know what it is that every one who is perfected shall be as his master.

REFLECTION

1. Perfection in this world is not possible, except through the power of the indwelling Spirit, by faith in Jesus Christ, who lived like us that we might live like Him.

2. Through Christ, the divine standard of perfection is embodied and made visible, and brought within our reach, that we might bear the likeness of the Father.

3. Both in his external life and his inner disposition the "perfected" disciple knows nothing higher than to be like his master.

DAY 11

THE PERFECT SELLING ALL TO FOLLOW CHRIST

"Jesus said unto him, 'If thou wilt be perfect, go and sell that thou hast, and give to the poor, and thou shalt have treasure in heaven; and come and follow Me'"
(Matthew 19:21).

To the rich young ruler poverty was to be the path to perfection. "The disciple is not above his Master, but every one who is perfected shall be as his Master." Poverty was part of the Master's perfection, part of that mysterious discipline of self-denial and suffering through which it became God to perfect Him. While He was on earth, poverty was to be the mark of all those who would be always with, and wholly as, the Master.

What does this mean? Jesus was Lord of all. He might have lived here on earth in circumstances of comfort and with moderate possessions. He might have taught us how to own, and to use, and to sanctify property. He might in this have become like us, walking in the path in which most men have to walk. But He chose poverty. He chose the life of self-sacrifice and direct dependence on God, with its humiliation, its trials and temptations. He was to exhibit elements of that highest perfection.

In the disciples whom He chose to be with Him, poverty was to be the mark of their fellowship with Him, the training school for perfect conformity to His image, the secret of power for victory over the world, for the full possession of the heavenly treasure, and the full exhibition of the heavenly spirit. And even in him, who, when the humiliation was past, had his calling from the throne, in Paul, poverty was still the chosen and much-prized vehicle of perfect fellowship with his Lord.

What does this mean? The command, "Be perfect," comes to the rich as well as the poor. Scripture has nowhere spoken of the possession of property as a sin. While it warns against the danger riches bring, and denounces their abuse, it has nowhere promulgated a law forbidding riches. And yet it speaks of poverty as having a very high place in the life of perfection.

To understand this we must remember that perfection is a relative term. We are not under a law, with its external commands as to duty and conduct that takes no account of diversity of character or circumstance. In the perfect law of liberty in which we are called to live, there is room for infinite variety in the manifestation of our devotion to God and Christ. According to the diversity of gifts, and circumstances, and calling, the same spirit may be seen in apparently conflicting paths of life. There is a perfection, which is sought in the right possession and use of earthly goods as the Master's steward. There is also a perfection, which seeks even in external things to be as the Master himself was, and in poverty to bear its witness to the reality and sufficiency of heavenly things.

In the early ages of the Church this truth, that poverty is for some the path of perfection, exercised a mighty and a blessed influence. Men felt that poverty, as one of the traits of the holy life of Jesus and His apostles, was sacred and blessed. As the inner life of the Church grew feeble, the spiritual truth was lost in external observances, and the fellowship of the poverty of Jesus was scarce to be seen. In its protest against the self-righteousness and the superficiality of the Romish system, the Protestant Church has not yet been able to give to poverty the place it ought to have either in the portraiture of the Master's image or the disciple's study of perfect conformity to Him.

And yet it is a truth many are seeking after. If our Lord found poverty the best school for His own strengthening in the art of perfection, and the surest way to rise above the world and win men's hearts for the Unseen, it surely need not surprise us if those who feel drawn to seek the closest possible conformity to their Lord even in external things, and who long for the highest possible power in witnessing for the Invisible, should be irresistibly drawn to count this word as spoken to them too: "If you desire to be perfect, sell everything, and follow Me."

When this call is not felt, there is a larger lesson of universal application. No perfection without the sacrifice of all. To be perfected here on earth Christ gave up all. To become like Him, to be perfected as the Master, means giving up all. The world and self must be renounced. "If you desire to be perfect, sell all, and give to the poor; and come, follow Me."

REFLECTION

1. In the early days of Christianity, poverty was the chosen mark of fellowship with Christ, the secret to victory over this world, and possession of the heavenly treasure. Is conformity to this world keeping you from being perfect in Christ?

DAY 12

THE PERFECT MAN IS A SPIRITUAL MAN

"Howbeit we speak wisdom among the perfect"
(1 Corinthians 2:60).

"And I, brethren, could not speak to you as unto spiritual,
but as unto carnal, even as unto babes in Christ. For
whereas there is among you envying and strife, and
divisions, are ye not carnal, and walk as men?"
(1 Corinthians 3:1,3).

Among the Corinthians there were mighty and abundant operations of the Holy Spirit. Paul could say to them, "That in everything ye are enriched in Him ... so that you come behind in no gift" (1 Corinthians 1:5,7). And yet in the sanctifying grace of the Holy Spirit there was much that was wanting. He had to say, "There are contentions among you (vs. 11). I beseech you that there be no divisions among you, but that you may be perfected together in the same mind." The spirit of humility, and gentleness, and unity was wanting; without these they could not be perfected, either individually or as a body. They needed the injunction, "Above all these things put on love, which is the bond of perfection" (Colossians 3:14).

The Corinthians were carnal. The gifts of the Spirit were among them in power, but the gracious, renewing, sweetening, sanctifying likeness of Jesus was lacking much. The wisdom Paul preached was a heavenly, spiritual wisdom. God's wisdom was a mystery, even the hidden wisdom, which needed a spiritual, heavenly mind to apprehend it. "We speak wisdom among the perfect"; he could not speak to them "as unto spiritual, but as unto carnal." Spiritual things must be spiritually discerned. The wisdom among the perfect could not be received by those who were carnal, but by the spiritual. The perfect of whom Paul speaks are the spiritual.

And who are the spiritual? Those in whom not only the gifts, but the graces of the Spirit have obtained supremacy and are made manifest. God's love is His perfection (Matthew 5:40-46); Christ's humility is His perfection. The self-sacrificing love of Christ, His humility, and meekness, and gentleness, manifested in daily life, are the most perfect fruit of the Spirit, the true proof that a man is spiritual. A man may have great zeal in God's service, he may be used to influence many for good, and yet, when weighed in the balance of love, be found sadly wanting. In the heat of controversy, or under unjust criticism, haste of temper, slowness to forgive and forget, quick words, and sharp judgments often reveal an easily wounded sensitivity, which proves how little the Spirit of Christ has full possession or real mastery. The spiritual man is the man who is clothed with the spirit of the suffering, crucified Jesus.

And it is only the spiritual man who can understand "the wisdom among the perfect," "even the mystery which now has been manifested to the holy ones, to whom God was pleased to make known what is the riches of the glory of this mystery, which is Christ in you." A Christian teacher may be a man of wonderful sagacity and insight, may have the power of opening the truth, of mightily stimulating and helping others, and may yet have so much of the carnal that the deeper mystery of Christ in us remains hidden. It is only as we yield ourselves wholly to the power of God's Holy Spirit, as the question of being made free from all that is carnal, of attaining the utmost possible likeness to Jesus in His humiliation, of being filled with the Spirit, rules heart and life, that the Christian, be he scholar or teacher, can fully enter into the wisdom among the perfect.

To know the mind of God we must have the mind of Christ. And the mind of Christ is that He emptied and humbled himself, and became obedient to death. His humility was His capacity and fitness for rising to the throne of God. This mind must be in us if the hidden wisdom of God is to be revealed to us in its power. This is the mark of the spiritual, the perfect man.

May God increase the number of the perfect. And to that end the number of those who know to speak wisdom among the perfect, even God's wisdom in a mystery. As the distinction between the carnal and the spiritual, the babes and the perfect, comes to recognition in the Church, the connection between a spiritual life and spiritual insight will become clearer, and the call to perfection will gain new force and meaning. And it will once again be counted just cause of reproof and of shame not to be among the perfect.

REFLECTION

1. Perfection in a biblical, spiritual sense is not to be confused with sinlessness or absence from error, but it is a maturity of the faith and practice in the Christian life that transcends mere religion and good works. "Lord, make me as perfectly holy as a redeemed sinner can be."

DAY 13

PERFECT HOLINESS

"Having therefore these promises, beloved, let us cleanse ourselves from all filthiness of flesh and spirit, perfecting holiness in the fear of God" (2 Corinthians 7:1).

These words give us an insight into one of the chief aspects of perfection and an answer to the question: "How is it we are to be perfect?" We must be perfect in holiness. We must be perfectly holy. Such is the exposition of the Father's message, "Be perfect."

We know what holiness is. God alone is holy, and holiness is that which God communicates of himself. Separation and cleansing and consecration are not holiness, but only the preliminary steps on the way to it. The temple was holy because God dwelt in it. Not that which is given to God is holy, but that which God accepts and appropriates, that which He takes possession of, takes up into His own fellowship and use—that is holy. "I am the Lord who makes you holy," was God's promise to His people of old, on which the command was based, "Be holy." God's taking them for His own made them a holy people. Their entering into this holiness of God, yielding themselves to His will, and fellowship, and service, was what the command, "Be holy," called them to.

Even so it is with us Christians. We are made holy in Christ, as saints or holy ones. The call comes to us to follow after holiness, to perfect holiness, to yield ourselves to the God who is ready to sanctify us wholly. It is the knowledge of what God has done in making us His holy ones, and has promised to do in sanctifying us wholly, that will give us courage to perfect holiness.

271

"Having therefore these promises, beloved, let us perfect holiness." Which promises? They had just been mentioned: "I will dwell in them; I will be their God; I will receive you; I will be to you a Father" (see 2 Corinthians 6:16). It was God's accepting the temple and dwelling there himself that made it holy. It is God's dwelling in us that makes us holy. This gives us not only the motive, but the courage and the power to perfect holiness, to yield ourselves for Him to possess perfectly and entirely. It is God's being a Father to us, begetting His own life, His own Son within us, forming Christ in us, until the Son and the Father make their abode in us, that will give us confidence to believe that it is possible to perfect holiness, and will reveal to us the secret of its attainment. "Having therefore these promises, beloved"— that is, knowing them, living on them, claiming and obtaining them—let us "perfect holiness."

This faith is the secret power of the growth of the inner life of perfect holiness. But there are hindrances that check and prevent this growth. These must be watched against and removed. "Having these promises, let us cleanse ourselves from all filthiness of flesh and spirit, perfecting holiness in the fear of the Lord." Every defilement, outward or inward, in conduct or inclination, in the physical or the spiritual life, must be cleansed and cast away. Cleansing in the blood, cleansing by the word, cleansing by the pruning knife or the fire—in any way or by any means—but we must be cleansed. In the fear of the Lord every sin must be cut off and cast out. Everything doubtful or defiling must be put away. Soul, body and spirit must be preserved entire and blameless. In cleansing ourselves from all defilement we will perfect holiness. The spirit of holiness will fill God's temple with His holy presence and power.

Beloved, having these promises, let us perfect holiness. Perfectly holy! Perfect in holiness let us yield ourselves to these thoughts, to these wishes, to these promises, of our God. Beginning with the perfect childlike heart, pressing on in the perfect way, clinging to a perfect Savior, living in fellowship with a God whose way and work is perfect, let us not be afraid to come to God with His own command as our prayer: Perfect holiness, O my Lord! He knows what He means by it, and we will know if we follow on to know. Lord, I am called to perfect holiness. I come to You for it. Make me as perfectly holy as a redeemed sinner can be on earth.

Let this be the spirit of our daily prayer. I would walk before God with a perfect heart—perfect in Christ Jesus, in the path of perfect holiness. I would this day come as near perfection as grace can make it possible for me. "Perfecting holiness" shall, in the power of His Spirit, be my aim.

REFLECTION

1. What are the hindrances to perfection? Everything doubtful or defiling must be removed. Soul, body and spirit must be completely preserved and blameless.

2. What made the temple of old holy was God dwelling there. What makes us holy is God dwelling in our hearts, giving us the motive, courage and power to perfect holiness.

DAY 14

WE PRAY FOR YOUR PERFECTING: BE PERFECTED

"This we also pray for, even your perfecting.... Finally, brethren, farewell. Be perfected, be comforted, be of the same mind, live in peace; and the God of love and peace will be with you" (2 Corinthians 13:9,11).

The word here translated "perfect" means to bring a thing into its right condition, so that it is as it should be. It is used of mending nets, restoring them to their right state, or of equipping a ship: fitting it with all it needs. It implies two things: the removal of all that is still wrong, and the supply of all that is still lacking.

Within two verses Paul uses the word twice. First, as the expression of the one thing, which he asks of God for them, the summary of all grace and blessing: "This we pray for, even your perfecting." That you be perfectly free from all that is wrong and carnal, and that you should perfectly possess and exhibit all that God would have you be. We pray for your perfecting. Next as the summing up in a farewell word of what He would have them aim at. "Finally, brethren, farewell. Be perfected." And then follow three other verbs, which show how this one, which takes the lead, has reference to the Christian's daily life, and is meant to point to what is to be his daily aim and experience. "Be perfected, be comforted, be of the same mind, live in peace." Just as the comfort of the Spirit, and the unity of love, and the life of peace are, if the God of love and peace is to be with us, our duty and our privilege every hour, so too, the being perfected. The close of the two epistles gathers up all its teaching in this one injunction. Farewell! Be perfected.

The two texts together show us what the prayer and the preaching of every minister of the gospel ought to be; what his heart, above everything, ought to be set on. We justly look upon Paul as a model whom every minister ought to copy—let every Gospel minister copy him in this, so that his people may know as he goes in and out among them. His heart breathes heavenward for them this one wish: Your perfecting! And may feel that all his teaching has this one aim: Be perfected!

If ministers are to seek this above everything in their charge of the Church of God, they need themselves to feel deeply and to expose faithfully the low standard that prevails in the Church. Some have said that they have seen perfectionism slay its thousands. All must admit that imperfectionism has slain its tens of thousands. Multitudes are soothing themselves in a life of worldliness and sin with the thought that since no one is perfect, imperfection cannot be so dangerous. Numbers of true Christians are making no progress because they have never known that we can serve God with a perfect heart, that the perfect heart is the secret of a perfect way, of a work going on unto perfection. God's call to us to be perfect, to perfect holiness in His fear, to live perfect in Christ Jesus, to stand perfect in all the will of God, must be preached, until the faith begins to live again in the Church that all teaching is to be summed up in the words, and each day of our life to be spent under their inspiration: Be perfected!

When once ministers know themselves and are known as the messengers of this God-willed perfection, they will feel the need of nothing less than the teaching of the Holy Spirit to guide men in this path. They will see and preach that religion must indeed be a surrender of all to God. Becoming as conformed to His will, living as entirely to His glory, being as perfectly devoted to His service, as grace can enable us to be, and no less, will be the only rule of duty and measure of expectation. The message, "Be perfected," will demand the whole heart, the whole life, the whole strength. As the soul learns each day to say, "Father! I desire to be perfect in heart with You today, I desire to walk before You and be perfect," the need and the meaning of abiding in Christ will be better understood. Christ himself with His power and love will have new preciousness, and God will prove what He can do for souls, and for a Church wholly given up to Him.

O you ministers of Christ, you messengers of His salvation, say to the Churches over which the Holy Spirit has made you overseers: This also we pray for—even your perfecting! Finally, brethren, be perfected!

REFLECTION

1. Multitudes are comforting themselves in a life of worldliness and sin with the thought that since no one is perfect, imperfection cannot be so dangerous.

2. Many true Christians are not making progress because they have never known that we can serve God with a perfect heart, and that the perfect heart is the secret of a perfect way.

DAY 15

NOT PERFECTED, YET PERFECT

"Not that I have already obtained, or am already perfected; but I press on....One thing I do, I press on towards the goal. Let us therefore, as many as be perfect, be thus minded" (Philippians 3:12-15).

In perfection there are degrees. We have perfect, more perfect, and most perfect. We have perfect waiting to be perfected. So it was with our Lord Jesus. In Hebrews we read three times of Him that He was perfected or made perfect. Of sinful imperfection there was not the faintest shadow in Him. At each moment of His life He was perfect—just what He should be. And yet He needed, and it became God to perfect Him through suffering and the obedience He learned in it. As He conquered temptation, and maintained His allegiance to God, and amid strong crying and tears gave up His will to God's will, His human nature was perfected, and He became High Priest, "the Son perfected forevermore." Jesus during His life on earth was perfect, but not yet perfected.

The perfected disciple shall be as his Master. What is true of Him is true, in our measure, of us too. Paul wrote to the Corinthians of speaking wisdom among the perfect—a wisdom carnal Christians could not understand. Here in our text he classes himself with the perfect, and expects and enjoins them to be of the same mind with himself. He sees no difficulty either in speaking of himself and others as perfect, or in regarding the perfect as needing to be yet further and fully perfected.

And what is this perfection, which has yet to be perfected? And who are these perfect ones? The man who has made the highest perfection his choice, and who has given his whole heart and life to attain to it, is counted by God as a perfect man. "The kingdom of heaven is like a seed." Where God sees in the heart the single purpose to be all that God wills, He sees the divine seed of all perfection. And as He counts faith for righteousness, so He counts this wholehearted purpose to be perfect as incipient perfection. The man with a perfect heart is accepted by God, amid all imperfection of attainment, as a perfect man. Paul could look upon the

Church and unhesitatingly say, "As many of us as be perfect, let us be thus minded."

We know how among the Corinthians he describes two classes. One is the large majority, carnal and content to live in strife. The other is the spiritual, the perfect. In the Church of our day it is to be feared that the great majority of believers have no conception of their calling to be perfect. They have not the slightest idea that it is their duty not only to be religious, but to be as eminently religious, as full of grace and holiness, as it is possible for God to make them. Even where there is some measure of earnest purpose in the pursuit of holiness, there is such a want of faith in the earnestness of God's purpose when He speaks, "Be perfect," and in the sufficiency of His grace to meet the demand, that the appeal meets with no response. In no real sense do they understand or accept Paul's invitation: "Let us, as many as be perfect, be thus minded."

But, thank God! It is not so with everyone. There is an ever-increasing number who cannot forget that God means what He says when He says, "Be perfect," and who regard themselves as under the most solemn obligation to obey the command. The words of Christ, "Be perfect," are to them a revelation of what Christ is come to give and to work—a promise of the blessing to which His teaching and leading will bring them. They have joined the band of like-minded ones whom Paul would associate with himself. They seek God with their whole heart and serve Him with a perfect heart. Their one aim in life is to be made perfect, even as the Master.

My reader! As in the presence of God, who has said to you, "Be perfect!" and of Christ Jesus, who gave himself that you might obey this command of your God, I charge you that you do not refuse the call of God's servant, but enroll yourself among those who accept it; "Let us, as many as be perfect, be thus minded." Fear not to take your place before God with Paul among the perfect in heart. So far will it be from causing self-complacency, that you will learn from him how the perfect has yet to be perfected, and how the one mark of the perfect is that he counts all things loss as he presses on unto the prize of the high calling of God in Jesus Christ.

REFLECTION

1. So, who are the perfect? Consider those who have made perfection their highest aim, and who have given their whole heart and life to attain to it. It is they who are counted by God as perfect.

2. Where God sees a heart with a determined purpose to be all that He wills, He sees the divine seed of all perfection. As He counts faith for righteousness, so He counts this wholehearted purpose to be perfect.

DAY 16

PERFECT, AND YET TO BE PERFECTED

"Not as though I had already attained, either were already perfect, but I press on.... This one thing I do ... I press on toward the mark for the prize. Let us therefore, as many as be perfect, be thus minded. Brethren, be ye imitators together of me" (Philippians 3:12-17).

The mark of the perfect, as set before us in Paul and all who are thus minded, is the passionate desire to be yet made perfect. This looks like a paradox. And yet what we see in our Master proves the truth of what we say; that the consciousness of being perfect is in entire harmony with the

279

readiness to sacrifice life itself for the sake of being made perfect. So it was with Christ. So it was with Paul. And so it will be with us, as we open our hearts fully and give God's word room and time to do their work. Many think that the more imperfect one is the more he will feel his need of perfection. All experience, in every department of life, teaches us the very opposite. It is those who are nearest perfection that most know their need of being yet perfected, and are most ready to make any sacrifice to attain to it. To count everything loss for perfection in practice, is the surest proof that perfection in principle has possession of the heart. The more honestly and earnestly the believer claims that he seeks God with a perfect heart, the more ready will he be with Paul to say: "Not that I have already obtained, or am already perfected."

We see from this passage that Paul longed to be made perfect? Read the Word with care, and without prejudice or preconceived ideas, and I think you will see that he gives here no indication of it being sin or sinful imperfection from which he was seeking to be perfectly free. Whatever his writings teach elsewhere, the thought is not in his mind here. The perfected disciple is as his Master. Paul is speaking here of his life and lifework, and feels that it is not perfected until he has reached the goal and obtained the prize. To this he is pressing on. He that runs in a race may, as far as he has gone, have done everything perfectly. All may pronounce his course perfect as far as it has gone. Still it has to be perfected. The contrast is not with failure or shortcoming, but with what is as yet unfinished, and waiting for its full end. And so Paul uses expressions, which tell us that what he already had of Christ was only a part. He did know Christ, he had gained Christ, he was found in Him, he had apprehended in wonderful measure that for which Christ had apprehended him. And yet of all these things—of knowing Christ, of gaining Him, of being found in Him, of apprehending that for which he was apprehended—he speaks regarding what he was striving after with all his might: "If by any means I may attain to the resurrection of the dead"; "I press on to the goal, unto the mark." It is of all this he says, "Not that I am already made perfect. Let as many as are perfect be thus minded."

Paul had known Christ for many years, but he knew there were in Him riches and treasures greater than he had yet known, and nothing could satisfy him but the full and final and eternal possession of what the resurrection would bring him. For this he counted all things but loss; for this he forgot the things that were behind; for this he pressed on to the goal, unto the prize. He teaches us the spirit of true perfection. A man who knows he is perfect with God, a man who knows he must yet be perfected, a man who knows that he has counted all things loss to attain this final perfection, such is the perfect man.

Christian, learn here the price of perfection, as well as the mark of the perfect ones. The Master gave His life to be made perfect forever. Paul did the same. It is a solemn thing to profess the pursuit of perfection. The price of the "pearl of great price" is high. All things must be counted loss. I have urged you to put down your names on the list of the perfect; to ask the Master to put it down and give you the blessed witness of the Spirit to a perfect heart. I urge you now, if, like Paul, you claim to be perfect, single and wholehearted in your surrender to God, to live the life of the perfect, with all things loss for Jesus as its watchword and its strength, and its one desire to possess Him wholly, to be possessed of Him, and to be made perfect even as He was.

O our Father! Be pleased to open the eyes of Your children, that they may see what the perfection of heart is that You now ask of them, and what the perfection in Christ is that You desire for them to seek at any cost.

REFLECTION

1. Those who are closest to perfection are those most ready to sacrifice for it. How much are we willing to give all for the sake of Christ?

2. We must learn the price of perfection—that we must count all things loss for Christ.

DAY 17

PERFECT IN CHRIST

"Christ in you, the hope of glory: whom we proclaim, admonishing every man, and teaching every man in all wisdom; that we may present every man perfect in Christ: whereunto I labor also, striving according to His working which works in me mightily" (Colossians 1:27-29).

In our inquiry into the teaching of the Word as to perfection, we have here a new word opening up to us the hope, giving us the assurance, of what we have seen to be our duty. It links all that we have seen of God's call and claim, with all that we know of Christ in His grace and power. Perfect in Christ. Here is the open gateway into the perfect life. He to whom it is given to see fully what it means, finds through it an abundant entrance into the life of Christian perfection.

There are three aspects in which we need to look at the truth of our being perfect in Christ. There is, first, our perfection in Christ, as it is prepared for us in Him, our Head. As the second Adam, Christ came and wrought out a new nature for all the members of His body. This nature is His own life, perfected through suffering and obedience. In thus being perfected himself, He perfected forever them that are sanctified. His perfection, His perfect life, is ours. And that not only judicially, or by imputation, but as an actual spiritual reality, in virtue of our real and living union with Him. Paul says in the same epistle, "You are complete, made full in Him"; all that you are to be is already fulfilled, and so you are fulfilled in Him—circumcised in Him, buried with Him, raised with Him, quickened together with Him. All Christ's members are in Him, and fulfilled in Him.

Then there is our perfection in Christ, as imparted to us by the Holy Spirit in uniting us to Him. The life that is implanted in us at the new birth, planted into the midst of a mass of sin and flesh, is a perfect life. As the seed contains in itself the whole life of the tree, so the seed of God within us is the perfect life of Christ, with its power to grow, and fill our life, and bring forth fruit to perfection.

And then there is also our perfection in Christ, as wrought in us by the Holy Spirit, appropriated by us in the obedience of faith, and made manifest in our life and conduct. As our faith grasps and feeds upon the truth in the two former aspects, and yields itself to God to have that perfect life master and pervade the whole of our daily life in its ordinary actions, perfect in Christ will become each moment a present practical reality and experience. All that the Word has taught of the perfect heart, and the perfect way, of being perfect as the Father, and perfect as the Master, shines with new meaning and with the light of a new life. Christ, the living Christ, is our Perfection. He lives each day and hour to impart it. The measureless love of Jesus, and the power of the endless life in which His life works, become the measure of our expectation. In the life in which we now live in the flesh, with its daily duties in relationship with men and money, with care and temptation, we are to give the proof that Perfect in Christ is no mere ideal, but in the power of Almighty God, simple and literal truth.

It is in the last of these three aspects that Paul has used the expression in our text. He speaks of admonishing every man, and teaching every man, in all wisdom, that he may present every man perfect in Christ Jesus. It is to perfection in daily life and walk that the admonishing and teaching have reference. In principle, Christians are made perfect in Christ. In practice they are to become perfect. The aim of the Gospel ministry of Paul among believers was to present everyone perfect in Christ Jesus, to teach them how they might put on the Lord Jesus, have His life cover them and have His life in them.

What a task! What a hopeless task to the minister, as he looks upon the state of the Church! What a task of infinite hopefulness, if he does his work as Paul did, "Whereunto," nothing less than presenting every man perfect in Christ; "Whereunto I also labor, striving according to His working which works in me mightily." The aim is high, but the power is divine. Let the minister, in full purpose of heart, make Paul's aim his own—to present every man perfect in Christ Jesus. He may count upon Paul's strength: "His working which works in me mightily."

REFLECTION

1. There are three things we must examine regarding the truth of our being perfect in Christ. First, is the perfect work of Christ imputed to us—our inheritance in righteousness because of our faith in the eternal Head. Second, is perfection through suffering and obedience—Christ's perfection

becomes ours. Third, is perfection in Christ, imparted by the
Holy Spirit—made manifest in our life and conduct.

DAY 18

PERFECT IN ALL THE WILL OF GOD

*"Epaphras, who is one of you, a servant of Christ, saluteth
you, always laboring fervently for you in prayers, that ye
may stand perfect and complete in all the will of God"*
(Colossians 4:12).

In this, as in some of the other epistles, there is set before
us the life of the believer as he lives it in heaven in Christ,
and then as he lives it here on earth with men. The teaching
of Scripture is intensely spiritual and supernatural, but, at
the same time, intensely human and practical. This comes out
very beautifully in the two expressions of our epistle. Paul
told the Colossians what he labored for. He now tells them
what another minister, Epaphras, prayed on their behalf.
Paul's striving was in his labor that they might be perfect in
Christ Jesus. The striving of Epaphras was in the prayer that
they might be perfect in all the will of God.

First we have "Perfect in Christ Jesus." The thought is so
unearthly and divine that its full meaning eludes our grasp.
It lifts us up to life in Christ and heaven. Then we have
"Perfect in all the will of God." This word brings us down
to earth and daily life, placing all under the rule of God's
will, and calling us in every action and disposition to live in
the will of God.

"That ye may stand perfect and complete in all the will
of God." "The perfection of the creature consists in nothing

but willing the will of the Creator." The will of God is the expression of the divine perfection. Nature has its beauty and glory in being the expression of the divine will. The angels have their place and bliss in heaven in doing God's will. The Son of God was perfected in learning obedience, in giving himself up unto the will of God. His redemption has but one object, to bring man into that only place of rest and blessedness—the will of God. The prayer of Epaphras shows how truly he had entered into the spirit of his Master. He prays for his people, that they may stand in the will of God, and that in all the will of God, there would be nothing in their life in which they were not in God's will. Perfect in the will of God, at each moment, with a perfect heart walking in a perfect way. Perfect in the will of God is ever his one thought of what ought to be asked and could be found in prayer.

Paul prayed for the Colossians, "that they might be filled with the knowledge of God's will in all wisdom and spiritual understanding." These two servants of God were of one mind, that young converts must be reminded that their knowledge of God's will is very defective, that they need to pray for a divine teaching to know that will, and that their one aim should be to stand perfect in all that will.

Let all seekers after perfection, let all who would be like-minded with Paul, note well the lesson. In the joy of a consecration sealed by the Holy Spirit, in the consciousness of a wholehearted purpose, and of serving God with a perfect heart, the believer is often tempted to forget how much there may be in which he does not yet see God's will. There may be grave defects in his character, serious shortcomings from the law of perfect love in his conduct, which others can observe. The consciousness of acting up to the full light of what we know to be right is a most blessed thing, one of the marks of the perfect heart. But it must ever be accompanied with the remembrance of how much there may be that has not yet been revealed to us. This sense of ignorance as to much of God's will, this conviction that there is still much in us that needs to be changed, and sanctified, and perfected, will make us very humble and tender, very watchful and hopeful in prayer. So far from interfering with our consciousness that we serve God with a perfect heart, it will give it new strength, while it cultivates that humility which is the greatest beauty of perfection. Without it, the appeal to the consciousness of our uprightness becomes superficial and dangerous, and the doctrine of perfection becomes a stumbling block and a snare.

Perfect in all the will of God. Let this be our unceasing aim and prayer. Striking its roots deep in the humility, which comes from the conviction of how much there is yet to be revealed to us. May we be strengthened by the consciousness that we have given ourselves to serve Him with a perfect heart; full of the glad purpose to be content with nothing less than standing perfect in all the will of God; rejoicing in the confidence of what God will do for those who are before Him perfect in Christ Jesus. Let our faith claim the full blessing. God will reveal to us how perfect in Christ Jesus, and perfect in all the will of God, are one in His thought, and may be so in our experience.

Paul prayed for the Colossians "without ceasing," that they might be filled with the knowledge of God's will. Epaphras was "always striving in his prayers" for them, that they might stand perfect in all the will of God. It is by prayer, by unceasing striving in prayer, that this grace must be sought for the Church. It is before the throne, in the presence of God, that the life of perfection must be found and lived. It is by the operation of the mighty quickening power of God himself, waited for and received in prayer, that believers can indeed stand perfect in all the will of God. God give us grace so to seek and so to find it.

REFLECTION

1. It is the daily casting our all before the throne of God in humble submission that the life of perfection can be found and lived. It is by the operation of the mighty quickening power of God, through the Holy Spirit, waited for and received in prayer, that believers can indeed stand perfect in all the will of God.

2. The will of God is the expression of the divine perfection.

DAY 19

CHRIST MADE PERFECT THROUGH SUFFERING

"It became Him to make the Leader of their salvation perfect through sufferings" (Hebrews 2:10).

"Though He was a Son, yet He learned obedience by the things which He suffered; and having been perfected, He became, for all them that obey Him, the Author of eternal salvation" (Hebrews 5:8,9).

"But the word of the oath appointeth a Son, perfected forevermore" (Hebrews 7:28).

We have here three passages in which we are taught that Jesus Christ himself, though He was the Son of God, had to be perfected. The first tells us that it was as the Leader of our salvation that He was perfected. It was God's work to perfect Him. And there was a need for it—"it became God" to do it, and that it was through suffering the work was accomplished. The second speaks to the power of suffering unto perfection. In it He learned obedience to God's will, and being thus perfected, He became the author of eternal salvation to all who obey Him. The third, that the Son, perfected forevermore, was appointed High Priest in the heavens.

The words open to us the inmost secret of Christian perfection. The Christian has no other perfection than the perfection of Christ. The deeper his insight into the character of his Lord, as having been made perfect by being brought into perfect union with God's will through suffering and obedience, the more clearly will he apprehend wherein that redemption which Christ came to bring really consists, and what the path is to its full enjoyment.

In Christ there was nothing of sinful defect or shortcoming. He was from His birth the perfect One. And yet He needed to be perfected. There was something in His human nature which needed to grow, to be strengthened and developed, and which could only thus be perfected. He had to follow on, as the will of God opened up to Him, and in the midst of temptation and suffering to learn and prove what it was at any cost to do that will alone. It is this Christ who is our leader and forerunner, our High Priest and Redeemer.

And it is as this perfection of His, this being made perfect through obedience to God's will, is revealed to us, that we will know fully what the redemption is that He brings.

We learn to take Him as our example. Like Him we say, "I am come, not to do my own will, but the will of Him that sent me." We accept the will of God as the one thing we have to live for and to live in. In every circumstance and trial we see and bow to the will of God. We meet every providential appointment, in every ordinary duty of daily life, as God's will. We pray to be filled with the knowledge of His will, that we may enter into it in its fullness, that we may stand complete in all the will of God. Whether we suffer or obey God's will, we seek to be perfected as the Master was.

We not only take Christ as our example and law in the path of perfection, but as the promise and pledge of what we are to be. All that Christ was and did as substitute, representative, Head and Savior, is for us. All He does is in the power of the endless life. This perfection of His is the perfection of His life, His way of living. This life of His, perfected in obedience, is now ours. He gives us His own Spirit to breathe, to work it in us. "He is the Vine, we are the branches." The very mind and disposition that was in Him on earth is communicated to us.

Yet it is not only Christ in heaven who imparts to us somewhat of His Spirit. He comes to dwell in our heart as the Christ who was made perfect through learning obedience. It is in this character that He reigns in heaven. "He became obedient unto death ... therefore God highly exalted Him" (Philippians 2:8,9). It is in this character that He dwells and rules in the heart. The real character, the essential attribute of the life Christ lived on earth, and which He maintains in us is a will perfect with God, and ready at any cost to be perfected in all His will. It is this character He imparts to His own: the perfection with which He was perfected in learning obedience. As those who are perfect in Christ, who are perfect of heart towards God, and are pressing on to be made perfect, let us live in the will of God, our one desire to be even as He was, to do God's will, to stand perfect in all the will of God.

REFLECTION

1. With perfection comes a clearer understanding of our redemption in Christ, and what that path is to a more complete enjoyment of Him.

2. There is no other perfection than that which comes from Christ.

DAY 20

LET US PRESS ON TO PERFECTION

"But solid food is for the perfect, even those who by reason of use have their senses exercised to discern good and evil. For this reason, let us cease to speak of the first principles of Christ, and press on unto perfection" *(Hebrews 5:14; 6:1).*

The writer had criticized the Hebrews for being dull of hearing, for having made no progress in the Christian life, and for still being as little children who needed milk. They could not bear solid food, the deeper and more spiritual teaching in regard to the heavenly state of life into which Christ had entered, and into which He gives admission to those who are ready for it. Such our writer calls the perfect, mature or full-grown men of the house of God. We must not connect the idea of mature or full-grown with time. In the Christian life it is not as in nature: a believer of three years old may be counted among the mature or perfect, while one of twenty years' standing may be but a babe, unskilled in the word of righteousness. Nor must we connect it with power of intellect or maturity of judgment. These may be found without that insight into spiritual truth, and that longing after the highest attainable perfection in character and fellowship with God, of which the writer is speaking.

We are told what the distinguishing characteristic of the perfect is "even those who by reason of use have their senses exercised to discern good and evil." It is the desire after holiness, the tender conscience that longs above everything to discern good and evil, the heart that seeks only, and always, and fully to know and do the will of God, that marks the perfect. The man who has set his heart upon being holy, and in the pursuit after the highest moral and spiritual perfection exercises his senses in everything to discern good and evil, is counted the perfect man.

The epistle has spoken of the two stages of the Christian life. It now calls upon the Hebrews to be no longer babes, no longer to remain content with the first principles, the mere elements of the doctrine of Christ. With the exhortation, "Let us press on to perfection"; it invites them to come and learn how Jesus is a Priest in the power of an endless life, who can save completely. He is the Mediator of a better covenant, lifting us into a better life by writing the law in our heart, and how the Holiest of all has been set open for us to enter in, and there to serve the living God. "Let us go on to perfection" is the landmark pointing all to that heavenly life in God's presence which can be lived even here on earth, to which the full knowledge of Jesus as our heavenly High Priest leads us.

"Let us press on to perfection." It is not the first time we have the word in the epistle. We read of God's perfecting Christ through suffering. Perfection is that perfect union with God's will, that blessed meekness and surrender to God's will, which the Father wrought in Christ through His suffering. We read of Christ's learning obedience, and so being made perfect. This is the true maturity or perfection, the true wisdom among the perfect, the knowing and doing God's will. We read of strong food for the perfect, who by reason of practice, have their senses exercised to discern good and evil. Here again perfection is, even as with Christ, the disposition, the character that is formed when a man makes conformity to God's will, fellowship with God in His holiness, the one aim of His life, to which everything else, even life itself, is to be sacrificed.

It is to this that Jesus, our High Priest, and the further teaching of the epistle, would lead us on. The knowledge of the mysteries of God, and of the highest spiritual truth, cannot profit us, because we have no inward capacity for receiving them, unless our inmost life is given up to receive as ours the perfection with which Jesus was perfected. When this disposition is found, the Holy Spirit will reveal to us how Christ has perfected forever, in the power of an endless life, those who are sanctified. He has prepared a life, a disposition, with which He clothes them. And we will understand that, "Let us go on to perfection," just means this, "Let us go on to know Christ perfectly, to live entirely by His heavenly life now that He is perfected, to follow wholly His earthly life, and the path in which He reached perfection." Union with Christ in heaven will mean likeness to Christ on earth in that lamb-like meekness and humility in which He suffered, in that Son-like obedience through which He entered into glory.

REFLECTION

1. The babe in Christ needs to continue to feed on the "milk" of the Word, but, "The solid food is for the perfect," which is a reference to the mature Christian.

2. It is the perfect man who sets his feet upon a path of holiness and seeks a greater understanding of the character and will of God, then lives wholly by it.

3. We can never attain perfection through the law, but through Jesus alone.

DAY 21

NO PERFECTION BY THE LAW

*"Now, if there was perfection through the Levitical
priesthood (for under it the people had received the law),
what further need that another priest should arise after
the order of Melchisedek? ... who has been made, not
after the law of a carnal commandment, but after the
power of an endless life.... For there is a disannulling of
a former commandment, because of its weakness and
unprofitableness, for the law made nothing perfect"*
(Hebrews 7:11-19).

*"Gifts and sacrifices are offered, which cannot, as
touching the conscience, make the worshiper perfect"*
(Hebrews 9:9).

*"For the law, having a shadow of the good things to come,
can never make perfect them that draw nigh"*
(Hebrews 10:1).

"That apart from us they should not be made perfect"
(Hebrews 11:40).

Of the epistles of the New Testament there is none in
which the word "perfect" is used so often as that to
the Hebrews. There is none that will help us more to see
what Christian perfection is, and the way to its attainment.
The word is used three times of our Lord Jesus, and His
being made perfect. It is also used twice of our subjective

perfection, five times of the perfection of which the law was the shadow, but which could not be until Jesus came. It speaks three times of Christ's work in perfecting us, and once of the work of God in perfecting us. These five thoughts will each give us a subject of meditation. Of the first two we have spoken already.

A careful perusal of the verses placed above, will show that the writer thought it of great importance to make it clear that the Law could perfect no person or thing. It was all the more of consequence to press this, both because of the close connection in which the Law stood to the true perfection, as its promise and preparation, and of the natural tendency of the human heart to seek perfection by the Law. It was not only the Hebrews who greatly needed this teaching. Among Christians in our days the greatest hindrance in accepting the perfection the gospel asks and offers, is that they make the Law its standard, and then our impotence to fulfill the Law, the excuse for not attaining or even seeking it. They have never understood that the Law is but a preparation for something better, and that when that which is perfect is come, that which is in part is done away.

The Law demands, the Law calls to effort, the Law means self. It puts self upon doing its utmost. But it makes nothing perfect, neither the conscience nor the worshiper. This is what Christ came to bring. The very perfection that the law could not give He does give. The epistle tells us that He was made a Priest, not as Aaron, after the Law and in connection with the service of a carnal commandment, which had to be disannulled because of its weakness and unprofitableness, but after the power of an endless life. What Christ, as Priest, has wrought and now works, is all in the power of an inward birth, of a new life, of the eternal life. What is born into me, what is as a spirit and life within me, has its own power of growth and action. Christ's being made perfect himself through suffering and obedience; His having perfected us by that sacrifice by which He was perfected himself; and His communication of that perfection to us, is all in the power of an endless life. It works in us as a life power. In no other way could we become partakers of it.

Perfection is not through the Law. Let us listen to the blessed lesson. Let us take the warning. The Law is so closely connected with perfection, was so long its only representative and forerunner that we can hardly realize that the Law makes nothing perfect. Let us take the encouragement that what the law could not do, God, sending His Son, has done. The Son, perfected for evermore, has perfected us forever. It is in Jesus we have our perfection. It is in living union with Him, it is when He is within us, not only as a seed or a little child, but formed within us, dwelling within us, that we shall know how far He can make us perfect. It is faith that leads us in the path of perfection. It is the faith that sees, that receives, that lives in Jesus the Perfect One that will bear us on to the perfection God would have.

DAY 22

CHRIST HAS PERFECTED US

"But Christ, through the greater and more perfect tabernacle, through His own blood, entered once for all into the holy place" (Hebrews 9:11,12).

"By one offering He has perfected forever them that are sanctified" (Hebrews 10:14).

In Christ's work, as set before us in the epistle to the Hebrews, there are two parts. In contrast with the worldly sanctuary, He is the minister of the true tabernacle. The Holiest of all is now open to us. Christ has opened the way through a more perfect tabernacle into the presence of God. He has prepared and opened up for us a place of perfect fellowship with God, of access, in a life of faith, which means a life in full union with Christ, into God's immediate presence.

There must be harmony between the place of worship and the worshiper. As He has prepared the perfect sanctuary, the Holiest of all, for us, He has prepared us for it too. "By one offering He has perfected forever them that are sanctified." For the sanctuary the sanctified ones; for the Holiest of all a holy priesthood; for the perfect tabernacle the perfected worshiper.

"By one sacrifice He has perfected forever them that are sanctified." The word perfected cannot mean here anything different from what it meant in the three passages where it has been previously used of Him (Hebrews 2:11, 5:9, 7:28). They all point to that which constituted the real value, the innermost nature, of His sacrifice. He was himself perfected for our sakes, so that He might perfect us with the same perfection with which God had perfected Him. What is this perfection with which God perfected Him through suffering, in which He was perfected through obedience, in which as the Son, perfected forevermore, He was made our High Priest?

The answer is to be found in what the object was of Christ's redeeming work. The perfection of man as created consisted in this, that he had a will with power to will as God willed, and so to enter into inner union with the divine life and holiness and glory. His fall was a turning from the will of God to do the will of self. And so this self and self-will became the source and the curse of sin. The work of Christ was to bring man back to that will of God in which alone is life and blessedness. Therefore it became God, it was proper and needful if He was to be the Leader of our salvation, that God should make Him perfect through suffering. In His own person He was to conquer sin, to develop and bring to perfection a real human life, sacrificing everything that men hold dear, willing to give up even life itself, in surrender to God's will. He proved that it is the meat, the very life of man's spirit, to do God's will. This was the perfection with which Christ was perfected as our High Priest, who brings us back to God. This was the meaning and the value of His sacrifice, that "one sacrifice" by which "He has perfected forever them that are sanctified." In the same sacrifice in which He was perfected, He perfected us. As the second Adam, He made us partakers of His own perfection. Just as Adam in his death corrupted us and our nature forevermore, so Christ, in His death, in which He was perfected, perfected us and our nature for evermore. He has created for us a new perfect nature, a new life. With Him we died to sin, in Him we live for God.

And how do we become partakers of this perfection with which Christ has perfected us? First of all the conscience is perfected so that we have no more conscience of sin and enter boldly into the Holiest, the Presence of God. The consciousness of a perfect redemption possesses and fills the soul. And then, as we abide in this, God himself perfects us in every good thing, to do His will, working in us that which is pleasing in His sight, through Jesus Christ. Through Christ, the High Priest in the power of the endless life, there comes to us in a constant stream from on high, the power of the heavenly life. So that day by day we may present ourselves perfect in Christ Jesus.

A soul that seeks to dwell in the divine perfection of which the epistle speaks holds fellowship with Him who in such intense human reality was perfected through suffering and obedience. In faith he turns to Him who has perfected us, and now holds our perfection in himself to be communicated as a life in us day by day, for us to practice and put it into exercise in walking in His footsteps; may count most surely that He himself will lead it into the promised inheritance.

REFLECTION

1. Christ was perfected through two things: His suffering and His obedience to the will of the Father. How are we walking in the steps of our Savior?

2. Was man, through Adam, created perfect? If so, how could he fall into sin? Did he have the power to resist sin and perfectly obey the will of God?

3. The redeeming work of Christ was to bring man back to that perfect relationship with the Father.

DAY 23

GOD PERFECT YOU IN EVERY GOOD THING

"Now the God of peace, who brought again from the dead the great shepherd of the sheep, through the blood of the everlasting covenant, make you perfect in every good work to do His will, working in you that which is well pleasing in His sight, through Jesus Christ; to whom be the glory for ever and ever. Amen" (Hebrews 13:20,21).

These two verses contain a summary of the whole Epistle in the form of a prayer. In the former of the two we have the substance of what was taught in the first or doctrinal half—what God has done for us in the redemption in Christ Jesus. In the second of the two verses we have a revelation and a promise of what this God of redemption will do for us. We see how God's one aim and desire is to make us perfect. We have said before, the word "perfect" here implies the removal of all that is wrong, and the supply of all that is lacking. This is what God waits to do in us. "God make you perfect in every good thing."

We need a large faith to claim this promise. So that our faith may be full and strong, we are reminded of what God has done for us. This is the assurance of what He will yet do in us. Let us look to Him as the God of peace, who has made peace in the entire putting away of sin, who now proclaims peace, who gives perfect peace. Let us look to Jesus Christ, the Great Shepherd of the sheep, our High Priest and King, who loves to care for and keep us. Let us remember the blood of the eternal covenant, in the power of which God raised Him and He entered heaven. His blood is God's pledge that the covenant with its promises will be fulfilled in our hearts. Let us think of God's bringing Him again from the dead, that our faith and hope might be in God. The power that raised Jesus is the power that works in us. Yes, let us look, and worship, and adore this God of peace, who has done it all, who raised Christ through the blood of the covenant that we might know and trust Him.

And let us believe the message that tells us that the God of peace will perfect you in every good thing. The God who perfected Christ will perfect you too. The God who has worked out such a perfect salvation for us, will perfect it in us. The more we gaze upon Him who has done such wondrous things for us, will we trust Him for this wondrous thing He promises to do in us, to perfect us in every good thing. What God did in Christ is the measure of what He will do in us to make us perfect. The same omnipotence that worked in Christ to perfect Him, waits for our faith to trust its working in us day by day to perfect us in the doing of God's will. And on our part, the surrender to be made perfect will be the measure of our capacity to experience what God has done in Christ.

And now hear what this perfection is which this God promises to work in us. It is truly divine, as divine as the work of redemption. May the God of peace, who brought Christ from the dead, perfect you. It is intensely practical, in every good thing, to do His will. It is universal, with nothing excluded from its operation, in every good thing. It is truly human and personal: God perfects us, so that we do His will. It is inward: God working in us that which is pleasing in His sight. And it is most blessed, giving us the consciousness that our life pleases Him, because it is His own work. He works in us that which is pleasing in His sight.

"God perfect you to do His will" is the conclusion of the whole epistle. "To do His will" is the blessedness of the angels in heaven. For this the Son became man. By this He was perfected, and through his work and will, "We are sanctified." It is "To do His will" that God perfects us, and works in us that which is pleasing in His sight.

Believer, let God's aim be your aim also. Say to God that you do desire this above everything. Give yourself, at once, entirely, absolutely, to this, and say with the Son, "I come to do Your will, O my God." This will give you an insight into the meaning, and the need, and the preciousness of the promise, "God perfect you to do His will." This will fix your heart upon God in the wondrous light of the truth. He who perfected Christ is perfecting me too. This will give you confidence, in the fullness of faith, to claim this God as your God, the God who perfects in every good thing.

The perfecting of the believer by God, restoring him to his right condition to fit him for doing His will, may be instantaneous. A valuable piece of machinery may be out of order. The owner has spent time and trouble, but in vain, to put it right. The maker comes and it takes him only a moment to see and remove the hindrance. And so the soul that has for years wearied itself in the effort to do God's will, may often in one moment be delivered from some misapprehension as to what God demands or promises, and find itself restored, perfected for every good thing. And what was done in a moment becomes the secret of the continuous life, as faith each day claims the God that perfects, to do that which is well pleasing in His sight.

Yes, the soul that dares say to God that it yields itself in everything to do His will, and through all the humiliation which comes from the sense of emptiness and impotence, abides by its vow in simple trust, will be made strong to rise and to appropriate and experience in full measure what God has offered in this precious word: "The God of peace perfect you, in every good thing, to do His will, working in you that which is pleasing in His sight, through Jesus Christ."

And it will sing with new meaning, and in fullness of joy, the song of adoring love: "To Him be glory for ever and ever. Amen."

REFLECTION
1. It is God's will to make us perfect. By perfect He intends to remove the wrong and supply what is missing. Are we claiming this promise and hope through the power of the Holy Spirit?

2. The power that raised Christ from the dead is the same that works in us!

DAY 24

PERFECT PATIENCE MAKES A PERFECT MAN

"And let patience have its perfect work, that you may be perfect and entire, lacking in nothing" (James 1:4).

Perfection is a seed. The life, given in regeneration, is a perfect life. Through ignorance and unbelief the soul may never get beyond knowing that it has life, and remain unconscious of what a wonderful, perfect life it has.

Perfection is a seed. It is a blessed hour when the soul awakens to know this, and with a perfect heart yields itself to appropriate all that God has given. The perfection of the perfect heart, a heart wholly yielded to seek God with all its strength, is again a seed, with infinite power of growth and increase.

Perfection is a growth. As the Christian awakens to the consciousness of what God asks and gives, and maintains the vow of a wholehearted surrender, he grows in his sense of need and his trust in the promise of a divine life and strength, until all the promises of grace come to a focus in the one assurance, "The God of all grace will himself perfect you." Faith, which was the fruit of previous growth, becomes the new seed of further growth. Perfection now develops into something riper and mellower. The overshadowing presence of Him who perfects, rests continually on the spirit, and the whole character bears the impression of heavenliness and fellowship with the Unseen. The soul makes way for God, and gives Him time to do His work. The God of Peace, perfecting in every good thing, gets entire possession. The soul rests in the rest of God.

This is not the work of a day. Perfection is a growth. "You have need of patience, that having done the will of God, you may inherit the promise." "Be imitators of them who through faith and patience inherit the promises." Man is the creature of time, and is under the law of development. In the Kingdom of Heaven it is as in nature: from the seed first the blade, then the ear, then the full corn in the ear. There is nothing at times that appears more mysterious to the believer than the slowness of God. It is as if our prayers are not heard, as if His promises are not fulfilled, as if our faith is vain. And all the time God is hastening on His work with all speed. He will avenge His own elect speedily, though He bear long with them.

"Let patience have its perfect work." We are so often impatient with ourselves, not content to trust God to do His work, and so hindering just when we want to hurry on His work. We are impatient with God; instead of the adoring trust of Him, the God of peace, who is perfecting us, we fret ourselves because we do not see what we had thought out for ourselves. "Rest in the Lord, and wait patiently for Him," is the law of faith, not only in times of well-being, but especially in the path of perfection. Faith is the law of the Christian life to an extent that very few realize. The assurance that rests in the unseen power that is working out its holy purpose will never be disappointed. As it has been said of an elderly saint, she was sure that, however long any soul might have to continue in the path of humiliation, with self-emptying, the end, with all who were faithful, would one day be a filling to overflowing of all their inward being with the presence of the Holy One.

"Let patience have its perfect work." This is the command. To those who obey it, the potential offered is certain, "that you may be perfect and entire, lacking in nothing." How words are heaped up to make us appreciate what the aim and expectation of the believer ought to be! Perfect, something finished that satisfies its purpose; entire, that in which every part is in its place; and lacking in nothing, just all that the Father expects. Such is the Christian character as God's Spirit sets it before us. There is a perfection, which the Christian is to regard as his duty and his life. Where patience has its perfect work it will bring forth what the husbandman longs for, fruit unto perfection. God's work in man is the man. If God's teaching by patience has a perfect work in you, you are perfect.

But where there is to be this perfect fruit, there must first be the perfect seed. And that seed is the perfect heart. Without this, whence could patience have its perfect work? With this, every trial, every difficulty, every failure even, is accepted as God's training school, and God is trusted as the Faithful One, who is perfecting His own work. Let there be first the perfect heart—that will lead to perfect patience, and that again to the fully perfected man.

Jesus Christ was himself not perfected in one day. It took time; in Him patience had its perfect work. True faith recognizes the need of time, and rests in God. And time to us means days and years. Let us learn each day to renew the vow; "This day I intend to live for God as perfectly as His grace will enable me. This day I intend, in the patience of hope, to trust the God of all grace, who himself is perfecting me. This day I intend to be perfect and entire, lacking nothing." With such a vow renewed day by day, with faith in Christ who has perfected us, and God who is perfecting us, patience will do its perfect work. And we will be perfect and entire, lacking nothing.

REFLECTION

1. If God's teaching by patience has a perfect work in you, then you are perfect.

2. Describe the "seed of perfection," and how does it grow? What is the fruit of perfection?

DAY 25

THE PERFECT TONGUE MARKS THE PERFECT MAN

"In many things we all stumble. If anyone does not stumble in word, the same is a perfect man, able to bridle the whole body also" (James 3:2).

There can be no perfection in art or science without attention to little things. One of the truest marks of genius is the power, in presence of the highest ideal, to attend to even the least details. No chain is stronger than its feeblest link. The weakest point in the character of a Christian is the measure of his nearness to perfection. It is in the little things of daily life that perfection is attained and proved.

The tongue is a little member. A word of the tongue is, oh, such a little thing in the eyes of many. And yet we are told by our blessed Lord that, "By thy words thou shalt be justified" (Matthew 12:37). When the Son of man comes in the glory of His Father to repay to every man according to his deeds, every word will be taken into account. In the light of the great day of God, if anyone stumbles not in word, the same is a perfect man. This is the full-grown man, who has attained maturity, who has reached unto the measure of the stature of the fullness of Christ.

But is it possible for any man to be thus perfect, and not to stumble in a single word? Has not James just said, "In many things we all stumble"? Just think of all the foolish words one hears among Christians, the sharp words, the hasty, thoughtless, unloving words, the words that are only half honest and not spoken from the heart. Think of all the sins of the tongue against the law of perfect love and perfect truth, and we must admit the terrible force of James' statement: "In many things we all stumble." When he adds, "If any stumble not in word, the same is a perfect man," can he really mean that God expects that we should live so, and that we must seek and expect it too?

Let us think. With what objective does he use these words? In the beginning of his epistle he had spoken of patience having its perfect work that we may be perfect and entire, lacking in nothing. There, entire perfection, with nothing lacking, is set before us as a definite promise to those who let patience have its perfect work. His epistle is written, as all the epistles are, under the painful impression of how far ordinary Christian experience is from such perfection, but in the faith that it is not a hopeless task to teach God's people that they ought to be, that they can be, perfect and entire, lacking in nothing. Where he begins to speak of the tongue, the two sides of the truth again rise up before him. The ordinary experience he expresses in the general statement: "In many things we all stumble." The will of God and the power of grace he sets forth in the blessed and not impossible ideal of all who seek to be perfect and entire: "If any man stumble not in word, the same is a perfect man."

307

James speaks of it in all simplicity as a condition as actual as the other condition of everyone stumbling.

The question is again asked: But is it really a possible ideal? Does God expect it of us? Is grace promised for it? Let us call in Peter as a witness, and listen to what God's Spirit says through him, as to that terrible necessity of always stumbling which some hold fast, as to the blessed possibility of being kept from stumbling. "Give the more diligence," he writes, "to make thy calling and election sure; for if ye do these things, ye shall never fall" (2 Peter 1:10). "Never"—that includes, not even in word. Let us hear what Jude says, "Now unto Him that is able to keep you from falling and to present you faultless before the presence of His glory with exceeding joy, to the only wise God our savior, be glory, majesty, dominion, and power both now and forever. Amen" (Jude 1:25). It is the soul that knows and without ceasing trusts God as a God who guards from stumbling, as a God who watches and keeps us every moment through Jesus Christ, that will without ceasing sing this song of praise.

The three texts on "stumbling" are the only ones in the New Testament in which the word occurs in reference to the Christian life. The text in James is heard quoted a hundred times for every time the texts in Peter and Jude are cited. And Christ has said, "According to your faith be it unto you." If our faith feeds only and always on, "In many things we all stumble," no wonder that we do stumble. If with that "stumble" we take the "stumble not" that follows, "If any man stumble not in word, the same is a perfect man," and the "not stumble" of Peter and Jude, the faith that embraces the promise will obtain it. God's power will translate it into our experience, and our life will be a living Epistle into which God's words have been transcribed. Out of the abundance of the heart the mouth speaks. Out of a heart that is perfect towards God, in which the love of God is shed abroad, in which Christ dwells, the tongue will bring forth words of truth and uprightness, of love and gentleness, full of beauty and of blessing. God wills it, God works it, let us claim it.

REFLECTION

1. Is it possible to be perfect in word?

2. It is in the little things of daily life that perfection is attained and proved.

DAY 26

GOD WILL HIMSELF PERFECT YOU

"The God of all grace, who called you unto His eternal glory in Christ, after you have suffered awhile, will Himself perfect, establish, and strengthen you. To Him be the dominion forever and ever. Amen" (1 Peter 5:10,11).

Through suffering to glory—this is the keynote of the first epistle of Peter. The word "suffer" occurs sixteen times, the word "glory" fourteen times. In its closing words the readers are reminded of all its teaching, as he writes to them, "The God of all grace, who has called you to His eternal glory, after you have suffered a little while." In no epistle of the New Testament are the two aspects of Christ's death—that He suffered for us, and that we are to suffer with Him and like Him—so clearly and closely linked together. Fellowship with Christ, likeness to Christ, manifested in suffering, is the point of view from which Peter would have us look on life as the path to glory. To be a partaker of the sufferings and the glory of Christ is the Christian's privilege. He was perfected through suffering by God: the same God perfects us for suffering and glorifying Him in it.

"God will himself perfect you!" In God alone is perfection. In Him is all perfection. And all perfection comes from Him. When we consider the wondrous perfection there is in the sun, in the laws it obeys, and in the blessings it dispenses, and remember that it owes all to the will of the Creator, we acknowledge that its perfection is from God. And so, through the whole of nature, to the tiniest insect that floats in the sunbeam, and the humblest little flower that basks in its light, everything owes its beauty to God alone. All His works praise Him. His work is perfect.

And have we not here in nature the open secret of Christian perfection? It is God who must perfect us! "God will himself perfect you." What is revealed in nature, is the pledge of what is secured to us in grace. "It suited Him, for whom are all things, and of whom are all things, in leading many unto glory, to make the Leader of their salvation perfect through suffering." It was appropriate that God should show that He is the God who works out perfection amid the weakness and suffering of a human life. This is what constitutes the very essence of salvation, to be perfected by God; to yield oneself to the God, for whom, and of whom are all things, himself to perfect us.

God has planted deep in the heart of man the desire for perfection. Is it not this that stirs the spirit of the artist and the poet, of the discoverer and the artificer? Is it not the nearest possible approach to this that wakens admiration and enthusiasm? And is it only in grace that all thought and all joy of present perfection is to be banished? Certainly not, if God's word be true. The promise is sure and bright for this our earthly life; "God will himself perfect you."

310

Joined with the words, "establish, and strengthen you," the "himself perfect you," can refer to nothing but the present daily life. God shall himself put you into the right position, and in that position then establish and strengthen you, so as to fit you perfectly for the life you have to live, and the work you have to do.

We find it so hard to believe this, because we do not know what it means. "You are not under the Law, but under grace." The Law demands what we cannot give or do. Grace never asks what it does not give; and so the Father never asks what we cannot do. He who raised Jesus from the dead is always ready, in that same resurrection power, to perfect us to do His will. Let us believe, and be still, until our soul is filled with the blessed truth, and we know that it will be done to us.

O my soul, learn to know this God, and claim Him, in this His character, as yours: "God will himself perfect you!" Worship and adore Him here, until your faith is filled with the assurance, "My God himself is perfecting me." Regard yourself as the clay in the hands of the Great Artist, spending all His thought and time and love to make you perfect. Yield yourself in voluntary, loving obedience to His will and His Spirit. Yield yourself in full confidence into His very hands, and let the word ring through your whole being, God shall himself perfect you, perfectly fit you for all He intends you to be or do. Let every perfect bud or flower you see whisper its message; "Only let God work, only wait upon God. God shall himself perfect you."

Believer! Have you desired this? Oh claim it now. Or rather, claim now in every deed this God as your God. Just as the writer to the Hebrews, and Peter in this epistle, gather up all their varied teaching into this one central promise, "God shall himself perfect you," so there may come in the life of the believer a moment when he gathers up all his desires and efforts, all his knowledge of God's truth, and all his faith in God's promises, concentrates them in one simple act of surrender and trust, and, yielding himself wholly to do His will, dares to claim God as the God that perfects him. And his life becomes one doxology of adoring love. To Him be the dominion for ever and ever. Amen.

REFLECTION

1. God has planted deep in the heart of His people the desire for perfection. Is this not what stirs in your soul?

2. He who raised Jesus from the dead is always ready, in that same resurrection power, to perfect us to do His will.

3. Is it your desire to be perfected by God, whatever the cost?

DAY 27

PERFECT LOVE IS KEEPING CHRIST'S WORD

"Whosoever keeps His words, in him truly has the love of God been perfected" (John 2:5).

Tauler says of the Apostle John: "In three ways, dear children, did the beloved Lord attract to himself the heart of John. First, did the Lord Jesus call him out of the world to make him an apostle. Next, did He grant to him to rest upon His loving breast. Thirdly, and this was the greatest and most perfect nearness, when on the holy day of Pentecost He gave to him the Holy Ghost, and opened to him the door through which he should pass into the heavenly places. Thus, children, does the Lord first call you from the world and make you to be the messengers of God. And next, He draws you close to Himself, that you may learn to know His holy gentleness and lowliness, and His deep and burning love, and His perfect unshrinking obedience. And yet this is not all. Many have been drawn thus far, and are satisfied to go no further. And yet they are far from the perfect nearness, which the heart of Jesus desires. John was at one moment on the breast of the Lord Jesus, and then he forsook Him and fled. If you have been brought so far as to rest on the breast of Christ, it is well. But yet there was to John a nearness still to come, one moment of which would be worth a hundred years of all that had gone before. The Holy Ghost was given to him—the door was opened. There is a nearness in which we lose ourselves, and God is all in all. This may come to us in one swift moment, or we may wait for it with longing hearts, and learn to know it at last. It was of this that the apostle Paul spoke when he said that the thing, which the heart has not conceived, God has now revealed to us by His Holy Spirit. The soul is drawn within the inner chamber, and there are the wonders and the riches revealed." (*Three Friends of God*, by Mrs. Bevan.)

To understand a writer it is often needful to know his character and history. When John wrote the epistle, he had for fifty years been living in that inmost nearness of which Tauler speaks, in the inner chamber within the veil. While on earth Jesus had found in him a congenial spirit, receptive of His highest spiritual teaching, one to whom He felt drawn in special love. Fifty years of communing with the Son in the glory of the Father, and experiencing the power of the Holy Spirit to make the eternal life, the heavenly life of Jesus in fellowship with the Father, an everyday reality. No wonder that when John testifies of it as a life of perfect love, the Church that is not living on this level can only speak of it as an ideal, in this life unattainable. To one who thinks of what

John was and knew of his Lord, and what a Church under his teaching would be, the words are simply descriptive of characters he saw around him; men to whom he could write, "Beloved, if our hearts condemn us not, we have boldness toward God ... because we keep His commandments, and do the things that are pleasing in His sight." "Whosoever keepeth His word, in him verily is the love of God perfected" (1 John 2:5).

John is the disciple whom Jesus loved! The words Jesus spoke about the love of God had a special attraction for him. The love with which Jesus loved him exercised its mighty influence. The Holy Spirit that came from the heart of the glorified Jesus intensified and spiritualized it all. And John became the apostle of love, who, gazing into the very depths of the divine glory and being, found there that *God is love.* With this word "love" as the sum of his theology, he links to the word he found in the Old Testament and in the writings of his brother apostles, the word "Perfect," and tells us that this is perfection, this the highest type of Christian character, the highest attainment of the Christian life—for a man to have God's love perfected in him.

The condition and the mark of this being perfected in love Jesus had taught him, saying, "If a man loves me, he will keep my word, and my Father will love him; and we will come unto him, and make our abode with him" (John 14:23). Keeping His word is the link between the love of the disciple and the love of the Father, leading to that wondrous union in which the Father's love draws Him to come and dwell in the loving heart. "If ye keep my commandments," Jesus said, "ye shall abide in my love; even as I have kept my Father's commandments, and abide in His love" (John 15:10). And John confirms from his own experience what the Master spoke, "Whosoever keeps His word, in him has the love of God been perfected."

Thank God! This is a life to be found on earth. God's love can be perfected in us. Let not what we see in the Church around us make us doubt God's word. When John spoke of perfect love, and Paul of the love of God shed abroad in our hearts by the Holy Ghost, they testified from personal experience of what they had received in direct communication from the throne of glory. The words were to them the expression of a life of which we have little conception. To us they convey no more truth than our low experience can put into them. Oh! That our hearts might be roused to believe in their heavenly, supernatural, fullness of meaning, and not to rest until we know that the love that passes knowledge, the love that God is, the love of Christ, dwells within us as a fountain springing up unto everlasting life. The prospect that the love of God is perfected in us is sure to everyone who will allow the love of God in Christ to have the mastery, and to prove what God can do for them that love Him.

REFLECTION

1. There are indeed many who cannot see the possibility of perfection, but speak of it only as an unattainable ideal or concept. But the apostle John says by keeping His Word the love of God is perfected in us (1 John 2:5). And how do we keep His Word? If we abide in Him and walk as He walked, and embrace the love of God. Without love there is no perfection.

2. Perfection is the highest form of Christian character, the highest attainment of the Christian life, which can only take place when God's love is perfected in him.

DAY 28

PERFECT LOVE IS LOVING THE BRETHREN

*"Beloved! If God so loved us, we ought also to
love one another. No man has beheld God at any time.
If we love one another, God abides in us, and His love is
perfected in us" (1 John 4:11,12).*

The first mark of a soul in whom the love of God is to be perfected is keeping His word. The path of obedience, the loving obedience of the perfect heart, the obedience of a life wholly given up to God's will, is the path the Son opened up into the presence and the love of the Father. It is the only path that leads into perfect love.

The commandments of Christ are all included in the one word "Love," because "Love is the fulfilling of the law." "A new commandment I have given you, that ye love one another, even as I have loved you." This is Christ's word: He that keeps this word, keeps all the commandments. Love to the brethren is the second mark of a soul seeking to enter the life of perfect love.

In the very nature of things it cannot be otherwise. Love seeks not her own; love loses itself in going out to live in others. Love is the death of self; where self still lives there can be no thought of perfect love. Love is the very being and glory of God. It is His nature and property as God to give of His own life to all His creatures, to communicate His own goodness and blessedness. The gift of His Son is the gift of himself to be the life and joy of man. When that love of God enters the heart it imparts its own nature—the desire to give itself to the very death for others. When the heart wholly yields itself to be transformed into this nature and likeness, then Love takes possession; there the love of God is perfected.

The question is often asked whether it be the love of God to us, or our love to God, that is meant by perfect love. The word includes both, because it implies a great deal more. The love of God is One, as God is One—His life, His very being. Where that love descends and enters, it retains its nature. It is ever the divine life and love within us. God's love to us, and our love to God and Christ, our love to the brethren and to all men—all these are but aspects of one and the same love. Just as there is one Holy Spirit in God and in us, so it is one divine love, the love of the Spirit that dwells in God and in us.

To know this is a wonderful help to faith. It teaches us that to love God, or the brethren, or our enemies, is not a thing our efforts can attain. We can only do it, because the divine love is dwelling in us; only as far as we yield ourselves to the divine love as a living power within, as a life that has been born into us, and that the Holy Spirit strengthens into action. Our part is first of all to rest, to cease from effort, to know that He is in us, and to give way to the love that dwells and works in us in a power that is from above.

How well John remembered the night when Jesus spoke so wonderfully of love in His parting words! How impossible it appeared to the disciples indeed to love as He had loved! How much there had been among them of pride, and envy, and selfishness; anything but love like His! How it had broken out among them that very night at the supper table! They never could love like the Master—it was impossible.

But what a change was wrought when the Risen One breathed on them, and said, "Receive the Holy Ghost!" And

317

how that change was consummated when the Holy Spirit came down from heaven, and out of that wonderful Love which there flowed in holy interchange between the Father and the Son, when they met again in the glory, shed abroad in their hearts *the love of God*! In the love of the day of Pentecost, the perfect love celebrated its first great triumph in the hearts of men.

The love of God still reigns. The Spirit of God still waits to take possession of hearts where He has hitherto had too scanty room. He had been in the disciples all the time, but they had not known of what manner of spirit they were. He had come upon them on that evening when the Risen One breathed upon them. But it was on Pentecost He filled them so that love divine prevailed and overflowed, and they were perfected in love. Let every effort we make to love, and every experience of how feeble our love is, lead us and draw us on to Jesus on the throne. In Him the love of God is revealed and glorified, and rendered accessible to us. Let us believe that the love of God can come down as a fire that will consume and destroy self, and make love to one another, fervent perfect love, the one mark of discipleship. Let us believe that this love of God, Perfect Love, can be shed abroad in our hearts, in measure to us hitherto unknown, by the Holy Ghost given to us. Our tongues and lives, our homes and churches will then prove to sinful, perishing fellowmen that there still are children of God in whom the love of God is perfected.

Even as is the whole Christian life, so love too has its two stages. There is love seeking, struggling, and doing its best to obey, and ever failing. And there is love finding, resting, rejoicing, and ever triumphing. This takes place when self and its efforts have been given into the grave of Jesus, and His life and love have taken their place. When the birth of heavenly love in the soul has come in the power of the heavenly life, loving is natural and easy. Christ dwells in the heart, now we are rooted and grounded in love, and know the love that transcends knowledge.

REFLECTION

1. Love to the brethren is a mark of the soul seeking to enter the life of perfect love. Perfect love seeks to live for others. Where self reigns there is no perfect love.

2. Are we giving of ourselves sacrificially for the good of others? How are we exercising the holy call to "bear one another's burdens"?

DAY 29

PERFECT LOVE: GOD ABIDING IN US

"No man has seen God at any time: if we love one another, God abides in us, and His love is perfected in us. By this we know that we abide in Him, and He in us, because He has given us of His Spirit" (1 John 4:12,13).

"No man has seen God at any time." The vision of God we may not yet have. The all-consuming, all-absorbing fire of its glory, bringing death to all that is of nature, is not consistent with this our earthly state. But there is given to us in its stead an equivalent that can prepare and train us for the beatific vision, and also satisfy the soul with all that it can contain of God. We cannot behold God, but we can have God abiding in us and His love perfected in us. Though the brightness of God's glory is not now to be seen, the presence of what is the very essence of that glory—His love—may now be known. God's love perfected in us, God himself abiding in us is the Heaven we can have on Earth.

319

And what is the way to this blessedness? "God abides in us, and His love is perfected in us, if we love one another." We may not see God; but we see our brother, and, lo, in him we have an object that will repay us for the loss of the vision of God. An object that will awaken and call forth the divine love within us; will exercise and strengthen and develop it; will open the way for the divine love to do its beloved work through us, and so to perfect us in love; will awaken the divine complacency and draw it down to come and take up its abode within us. In my brother I have an object on which God bids me prove all my love to him. In loving him, however unlovely he may be, love proves that self no longer lives; that it is a flame of that fire which consumed the Lamb of God; that it is God's love being perfected in us; that it is God himself living and loving within us.

"If we love one another, God abides in us. By this we know that we abide in Him, and He in us, because He has given us of His Spirit." The wondrous knowledge that God abides in us, and His love is perfected in us, is no result of reflection, a deduction from what we see in ourselves. No, divine things, divine love, and divine indwelling are only seen in a divine light. "By this we know them, because He has given us of His Spirit." John remembers how little the disciples understood or experienced of the words of Jesus until that never-to-be forgotten day when, in the light of the fire that came from heaven, all became luminous and real. It is the Holy Spirit alone, not in His ordinary gracious workings, such as the disciples also had before that day, but in His special bestowment direct from the throne of the exalted Jesus, to make Him personally and permanently present to the soul that will rest content with nothing less. It is the Holy Spirit alone by whom we know that God dwells in us, and we in Him, and that His love is perfected in us.

It is in the Christian life now, even as it was then. It is the special work of the Holy Spirit to reveal the indwelling God and to perfect us in love. By slow steps we have to master now one side of truth and then another—to practice now one grace and then the very opposite. For a time our whole heart goes out in the aim to know and do His will. Then, again, it is as if there is but one thing to do—to love, and we feel as if in our own home, in all our dealings with men, in our outlook in the Church and the world, we need but to practice love. After a time we feel how we fail, and we turn to the word that calls us to faith, to cease from self and to trust in Him who works both to will and to do. Here once more we fall short, and we feel that this alone can meet our need—a share in the Pentecostal gift—the Spirit given in power as never before. Let none faint nor be discouraged. Let us seek to obey, and to love, and to trust with a perfect heart. Wherever we have attained let us be faithful. So let us press on to perfection. Let us confidently expect that this portion also of the word will be made our own: "If we love one another, God abides in us, and the love of God is perfected in us. By this we know it, because He has given us of His Spirit."

It is only in the path of love—love in practical exercise seeking to be perfect love—that this wondrous blessing can be found; God abiding in us, and we in Him. And it is only by the Holy Ghost that we can know that we have it—God abiding in us, and His love perfected in us. God is love. How sure it is that He longs to abide with us! God is love, who sends forth the Spirit of His Son to fill the hearts that are open to Him. How sure it is that we can be perfected in love. A perfect heart can count upon being filled with a perfect love. Let nothing less than perfect love be our aim that we may have God abiding in us, and His love perfected in us. We shall know it by the Spirit, which He has given us.

REFLECTION

1. It is in the practical exercise of love that we seek perfect love, but it is only by God abiding in us through the power of the Holy Spirit that we can know we have it. Are we seeking to have God's love perfected in us?

DAY 30

PERFECT LOVE: AS HE IS, EVEN SO ARE WE

"Herein is love made perfect in us, that we may have boldness in the day of judgment: because as He is, even so are we in this world" (1 John 4:17).

Let us look back on the steps in the life of perfected love that have been set before us thus far. The divine love entering the heart manifests itself first in loving obedience to Christ. Of that obedience, love to the brethren in active exercise becomes the chief mark and manifestation. In this obedient love and loving obedience, the principle of fellowship with God, God abiding in us, is developed and strengthened. Of this fellowship the Holy Spirit gives the evidence and abiding consciousness. Such is the path in which love is perfected. Obedience to Christ; love to the brethren; the indwelling of God in us, and us in Him; the communication and revelation of all this by the Holy Spirit: all these are correlated ideas, which imply and condition each other. Together they make up the blessed life of perfect love.

The perfect heart began by seeking God wholly and alone. It found Him in the perfect way, of obedient love to the Lord, ministering and loving to the brethren. So it came in Christ to the Father, and fellowship with Him. So it was prepared and opened for that special illumination of the Spirit, which revealed God's indwelling—the Father taking up His abode. What was at first only a little seed—the perfect heart—has grown up and borne fruit. The perfect heart is now a heart in which the love of God is perfected. Love has taken full possession, and reigns throughout the whole being.

Has the apostle now anything more that he can say of perfect love? Yes, he speaks of two things. He tells us what is its highest blessing: "Herein is love made perfect in us, that we may have boldness in the day of judgment." And what is its deepest ground or reason? "Because as He is, even so are we in the world." The former of these two thoughts we find again in the next verse. Let us here consider the latter.

"Because as He is, even so are we in the world." It is in Christ we are perfect. It is with the same perfection with which Christ was perfected himself that He made us perfect, that God now perfects us. Our relationship with Christ implies perfect unity of life and spirit, of disposition and character. John gathers up all the elements of the perfect love he has mentioned, and in view of the day of judgment, and the boldness perfect love will give us, combines them into this one, "Because as He is, even so are we in the world."

"As He is, so are we." In chapter 2 he said, "He that says he abides in Him, ought himself also to walk even as He walked." Likeness to Christ in His walk of obedience on earth is the mark of perfect love.

In chapter 3 we read, "Everyone that has this hope set on Him (the hope of being like Him, when we will see Him as He is), perfects himself, even as He is pure." Likeness to Christ in His heavenly purity is the mark of perfect love.

In chapter 3 we read further, "Hereby know we love, because He laid down His life for us; and we ought to lay down our lives for the brethren." Likeness to Christ in His love to us is the mark of perfect love.

In the last night Jesus prayed, "That they may be one, even as we are one; I in them, and You in Me, that they may be made perfect in one." Likeness to Christ in His fellowship with the Father, God in us and we in Him, is the mark of perfect love. God gave Christ to save us, by becoming our life, by taking us up into union with himself. God could have no higher aim, could bestow no higher blessing than that He should see Christ in us, that we may have boldness in the day of judgment. Herein is love made perfect, "because as He is, even so are we in the world."

"That we may have boldness in the day of judgment," God has committed judgment unto the Son, as the perfected Son of man. His judgment will be a spiritual one. He himself will be its standard and likeness to Him is the fitness to pass in and reign with Him. Perfect love is perfect union and perfect likeness. We have boldness even in the day of judgment, because as He is, even so are we in this world. O ye seekers after perfection! It is to be found only in Christ. In Him is God's love revealed. In Him and His life you enter into it, and it enters into you. In Him love takes possession, and transforms you into His likeness. In Him God comes to make His abode in you. In Him love is perfected. The prayer is fulfilled, "That the love wherewith Ye love Me may be in them, and I in them." The love of God is perfected in us and we are perfected in love. We have boldness in the day of judgment, because as He is, even so are we.

The love of God, as a fire from the altar before the throne, as the presence of the God of love himself living in us, makes itself felt in its heavenly power, so that the world may know that God has loved us, as He loved His Son. The love that flows from God to Christ rests on us also, and makes us one with Him. As He is, in heaven, even so are we, in the world, living in the Father and in His love.

REFLECTION

1. The perfect heart begins by seeking God wholly and completely. Consider your own heart. Consider that it is only in Christ we are made perfect.

2. Our relationship with Christ implies perfect unity of life and spirit, of disposition and character.

3. Likeness to Christ is the mark of perfect love.

DAY 31

PERFECT LOVE: CASTING OUT FEAR

"There is no fear in love; but perfect love casts out fear: because fear has punishment. And he that fears is not made perfect in love" (1 John 4:18).

Bengel says that in the religious life there are four steps: "Serving God without fear or love; with fear without love; with fear and love; with love without fear." And Augustine says: "Fear prepares the way for love; where there is no fear, there is no opening for love to enter. Fear is the medicine, but love the healing. Fear leads to love; when love is perfected fear is done. Perfect love casts out fear. Herein is love perfected, that we may have boldness in the day of judgment. Because as He is, even so are we in this world."

The day of judgment! What a day that will be! Many have no fear of that day, because they trust that they have been justified. They imagine that the same grace, which justified the ungodly will give the passage into heaven. This is not what Scripture teaches. The reality of our having obtained forgiveness will be tested in that day by our having bestowed forgiveness on others. Our fitness for entering the Kingdom, will be by the way in which we have served Jesus in the ministry of love to the sick and the hungry (Matthew 25). This has no part in our justification, but in the judgment it will be the all-important element (Revelation 20:12, 22:12). If we are to see Him as He is, and to be like Him, we must have been purified as He is pure. It is perfect love, it is to be in this world even as He is, that casts out fear, and gives us boldness in the day of judgment. He that fears is not made perfect in love.

The day of judgment! What a day! What a blessed thing to have boldness in that day! To meet the burning, fiery furnace of God's holiness, to be ready to be judged by our conformity to Christ's likeness and image, and to have no fear. What blessedness! It is this that makes what Scripture reveals of perfection and of love perfected in us of such immediate and vital interest to each one of us.

We have come to the close of our meditations on what Scripture teaches of the perfection attainable in this life. We began with the perfect heart, the heart wholly set upon God, as the mark of the man whom God counts a perfect man. We saw the perfect man walking in a perfect way, "walking in all the commandments and ordinances of the Lord blameless." We found with the New Testament the standard at once infinitely raised. Perfect as the Father, is the child's standard. Perfected as the Master, is the disciple's model. Perfect in all the will of God, is the Christian's aim and hope. And then to meet this high demand, the word came to us: perfect in Christ, perfected by Christ, God himself perfecting us in every good thing. And now John, the beloved disciple, has summed up all the teaching of the word with his perfect love. Keeping Christ's word, loving the brethren, abiding in God, filled with the Spirit, being even as Christ is, we can live perfected in love. With a heart that does not condemn us, we have boldness before God, because we keep His commandments, and do the things that are pleasing in His sight. With God's love perfected in us we have boldness in the day of judgment.

Beloved fellow Christian! To have the love of God perfected in us and to be perfected in love—perfect love: these are all a divine possibility, a divine reality, and the ripened fruit of the perfect life. We know now the tree on which this fruit grows. Its root is a heart perfect with God, walking before Him and being perfect. Let us be perfect in our surrender to Him in obedience and trust. Let deep dependence on Him, let faith in Him, let a patient waiting, having our expectation from Him alone, be the spirit of our daily life. It is God himself who must give it. Let us count upon Him for nothing less than to be perfected in love and to have God abiding in us. This is what He longs to do for us.

The tree that grows on this root is a life in union with Christ, aiming at perfect conformity to Him. Perfect in Christ, perfected by Christ, perfected by God like Christ and through Christ. Then when these words, pregnant with the will and love of God and the mystery of redemption, become the daily life of the soul, the perfect heart rules the life, and the believer learns to stand perfect in all the will of God. The tree brings forth fruit abundantly.

Even unto perfection. Obedience and brotherly love, fellowship with God and likeness to Christ, and the unhindered flow and rule of the Holy Spirit, will lead the soul into a life of perfect love. The God of love gets His heart's desire. The love of God celebrates its triumph. The days of heaven are begun on earth. The soul is perfected in love.

"Finally, brethren, farewell! Be perfected." Be perfect with God. Let nothing less be your aim. God will show himself perfect with you. He will perfectly reveal himself and perfectly possess you. Believe this! God will himself perfect you day by day, with each new morning you may claim it. Live in surrender to His work, and accept it. And fear not, nor be discouraged. God himself will grant it to you to know what it is. God dwells in us, and His love is perfected in us.

REFLECTION

1. The reality of our having obtained forgiveness will be tested in that day by our having bestowed forgiveness on others.

2. Our fitness for entering the Kingdom, will be by the way in which we have served Jesus in the ministry of love to the sick and the hungry (Matthew 25). This has no part in our justification, but in the judgment it will be the all-important element (Revelation 20:12, 22:12).

3. Let us be perfect in our surrender to Him in obedience and trust. Let deep dependence on Him, let faith in Him, let a patient waiting, having our expectation from Him alone, be the spirit of our daily life.

CLOSING PRAYER

O my Father! I desire to walk in Your presence this day and be perfect. You have commanded it; and You give the enabling grace. I desire to be perfect with the Lord my God. I desire to serve You with a perfect heart. I desire to be perfect, as the Father is perfect.

These are Your own words, O my God! I resolve to accept and obey them in childlike simplicity and trust.

I thank You for the unspeakable gift, Your beloved Son, who was Himself perfected through suffering and obedience in His sacrifice on the cross, and by that sacrifice has perfected us also. I thank You that through Him You now perfect me in every good thing, Yourself working in me that which is pleasing in Your sight. You will show Yourself strong to them that are of a perfect heart.

I thank You, O my Father, for the blessed expectation Your Word holds out of being perfected in love here on earth; for the blessed witness of the beloved disciple to its truth in him and around him; for the power and light of the Holy Spirit that sheds abroad Your love in our hearts, and makes it all a reality and a consciousness. The Lord will perfect that which concerns me. To Him be the glory. Amen.

INDEX

Christian women 182
Christian world xii, 94
Christ in us 109
Christ Jesus 160
Chronicles 263
Church of Christ 35
co-laborers vii
Colossians 69, 282
commandments 245
communicate 316
communication 190
Communicator 32
condemnation 77
confession 100
confidence 84
confound 128
conscience 298
consciousness 200
contractor 226
Corinth 202
Corinthians 73
Cornelius 72
counsel 70
Creator 32, 36
culture 79
Cyprus 151
Cyrene 151

D

danger 57, 107
darkness 130
dark world 133
David 45
dead 102
death 57
deep meaning 98
deliverance 50
Deliverer 77
dependence 129
desires 65

despondency 77
destiny 118
Deuteronomy 88
diligence 145, 166
Divine energy 139
Divine glory 144
Divine indwelling 320
Divine life 145
Divine Love 320
Divine things 320
Divine truth 131
dominion 312
doxology 312
Dr. Candlish 2
Dr. Chalmers 2
Dutch Reformed Church 1, 2,
    8, 10
Dutch Reformed Church 17

E

educationist 137
Edwards, Jonathan 2
effectual prayer 99
Emma 11, 16
encourage 58
enemies 82
energy 128
England 8
English 4
enthusiasm 310
Epaphras 285
Ephesians 104
Ephesus 222
Epistles 104
Europe 10
evangelization 136
Everlasting 118
Everlasting God 86
Exeter Hall 27
Expectation 101

Pure Gold Classics

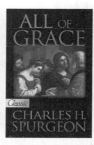

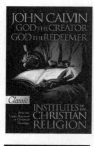
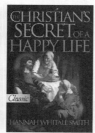

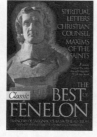
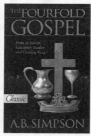

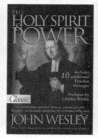
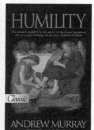

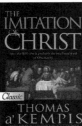

THE IMITATION of CHRIST
Classic
THOMAS a' KEMPIS

IN HIS STEPS
Classic
CHARLES M. SHELDON

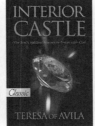

INTERIOR CASTLE
Classic
TERESA of AVILA

THE KNEELING CHRISTIAN
Classic
AN UNKNOWN CHRISTIAN

MADAME JEANNE GUYON
Classic
EXPERIENCING UNION WITH GOD

MORNING BY MORNING
Classic
CHARLES H. SPURGEON

THE OVERCOMING LIFE
Classic
D.L. MOODY

THE PILGRIM'S PROGRESS IN MODERN ENGLISH
Classic
JOHN BUNYAN

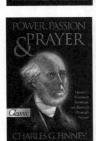

POWER, PASSION & PRAYER
Classic
CHARLES G. FINNEY

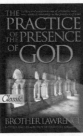

THE PRACTICE OF THE PRESENCE OF GOD
Classic
BROTHER LAWRENCE

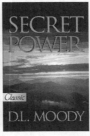

SECRET POWER
Classic
D.L. MOODY

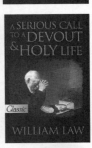

A SERIOUS CALL TO A DEVOUT & HOLY LIFE
Classic
WILLIAM LAW

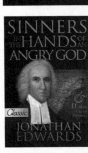

SINNERS IN THE HANDS OF AN ANGRY GOD
Classic
JONATHAN EDWARDS

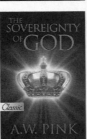

THE SOVEREIGNTY OF GOD
Classic
A.W. PINK

TABLE TALK
MARTIN LUTHER
Classic

INCLUDES AUDIO EXCERPTS CD
R. A. TORREY
Classic
THE HOLY SPIRIT WHO HE IS AND WHAT HE DOES

Includes Audio CD in Tozer's Own Voice
TOZER
Classic
FELLOWSHIP OF THE BURNING HEART

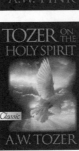

TOZER ON THE HOLY SPIRIT
Classic
A.W. TOZER

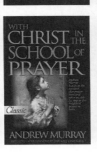

WITH CHRIST IN THE SCHOOL OF PRAYER
Classic
ANDREW MURRAY

WILLIAM WILBERFORCE
Classic
GREATEST WORKS

Pure Gold Classics

CHRISTIAN CLASSICS

A classic is a work of enduring excellence; a Christian classic is a work of enduring excellence that is filled with divine wisdom, biblical revelation, and insights that are relevant to living a godly life. Such works are both spiritual and practical. Our Pure Gold Classics contain some of the finest examples of Christian writing that have ever been published, including the works of John Foxe, Charles Spurgeon, D.L. Moody, Martin Luther, John Calvin, Saint John of the Cross, E.M. Bounds, John Wesley, Andrew Murray, Hannah Whitall Smith, and many others.

The timeline on the following pages will help you to understand the context of the times in which these extraordinary books were written and the historical events that must have served to influence these great writers to create works that will always stand the test of time. Inspired by God, many of these authors did their work in difficult times and during periods of history that were not sympathetic to their message. Some even had to endure great persecution, misunderstanding, imprisonment, and martyrdom as a direct result of their writing.

The entries that are printed in green type will give you a good overview of Christian history from the birth of Jesus to modern times.

The entries in red pertain to writers of Christian classics from Saint Augustine, who wrote his *Confessions* and *City of God*, to Charles Sheldon, twentieth-century author of *In His Steps*.

Entries in black provide a clear perspective on the development of secular history from the early days of Buddhism (first century) through the Civil Rights Movement.

Finally, the blue entries highlight secular writers and artists, including Chaucer, Michelangelo, and others.

Our color timeline will provide you with a fresh perspective of history, both secular and Christian, and the classics, both secular and Christian. This perspective will help you to understand each author better and to see the world through his or her eyes.

14-1770 George Whitefield, alvinist evangelist known powerful preaching d revivals in England d America. Friend of John esley.

20-1760 "The Great vakening" in America. umerous revivals result widespread Church wth.

41 Handel's *Messiah* mposed.

56-1763 Seven Years r in Europe, Britain feats France.

59-1833 William lberforce, British olitionist and author of *Practical View of ristianity*.

75-1783 American volutionary War.

79 Olney Hymns blished, John Newton's *nazing Grace*.

89 French Revolution gins.

92-1875 Charles ney, American angelist. Leads Second eat Awakening in 1824.

05-1898 George eller, English evangelist ounder of orphanages; hor, *Answers to Prayer*.

13-1855 Soren rkegaard, Danish losopher & theologian; hor, *Fear and mbling*.

16-1900 J.C. Ryle, hor of *Practical Religion d Holiness*.

1820-1915 "Fanny" Crosby, though blind, pens over 8,000 hymns.

1828-1917 Andrew Murray, author of *Humility, Abide in Christ, With Christ in the School of Prayer,* and *Absolute Surrender*.

1828 Noah Webster publishes a dictionary of the English Language.

1829 Salvation Army founded by William and Catherine Booth.

1832-1911 Hannah Whitall Smith, author of *The Christian's Secret to a Happy Life* and *God of All Comfort*.

1834-1892 Charles H. Spurgeon, author of *Morning by Morning* and *The Treasury of David*.

1835-1913 E.M. Bounds, author of *The Classic Collection on Prayer*.

1836-1895 A.J. Gordon, New England Spirit-filled pastor; author, *The Ministry of the Spirit*.

1837-1899 Dwight L. Moody, evangelist and founder of Moody Bible Institute in Chicago. Author of *Secret Power* and *The Way to God*.

1843-1919 A.B. Simpson, founder of Christian and Missionary Alliance, author of *The Fourfold Gospel*.

1844 Samuel Frank Morse invents the telegraph.

1847-1929 F.B. Meyer, English Baptist pastor & evangelist; author, *Secret of Guidance*.

1857-1858 Third Great Awakening in America; Prayer Meeting Revival.

1851-1897 Henry Drummond, author of *The Greatest Thing in the World … Love*.

1856-1928 R.A. Torrey, American evangelist, pastor and author.

1857-1946 Charles Sheldon, author of *In His Steps*.

1859 Theory of evolution; Charles Darwin's *Origin of Species*.

1861-1865 American Civil War.

1862-1935 Billy Sunday, American baseball player who became one of the most influential evangelists in the 20th century. *Collected Sermons*.

1867 Alexander Graham Bell invents the telephone.

1869-1948 Mahatma Gandhi makes his life's work India's peaceful independence from Britain.

1881-1936 J. Gresham Machen, "Old School" Presbyterian leader, writes *Christianity and Liberalism*; forms the new Orthodox Presbyterian Church in 1936.

1886-1952 A. W. Pink, evangelist & biblical scholar; author, *The Sovereignty of God*.

1897-1963 A.W. Tozer, author of *Fellowship of the Burning Heart*.

1898-1900 Boxer Rebellion in China deposes western influence, particularly Christian missionaries.

c. 1900-1930 *The Kneeling Christian* (Written by The Unknown Christian.)

1901 American Standard Version of Bible published.

1906 Azusa Street Revival, Los Angeles, instrumental in rise of modern Pentecostal Movement.

1906-1945 Dietrich Bonhoeffer spreads Christian faith to Germans in opposition to WWII Nazism.

1914-1918 World War I.

1917 Bolshevik Revolution in Russia.

1925 Scopes Monkey Trial pits Bible against theory of evolution.

1929 US Stock Market crashes, 12 years of Great Depression.

1939-1945 World War II. Holocaust in eastern Europe under Hitler.

1947 Dead Sea Scrolls found in caves in Judean desert.

1948 State of Israel reestablished.

1949 Communist revolution in China; religion suppressed.

1952 RSV Bible first published.

1960s Civil Rights movement in the United States.